A Guide for Grassroots Leaders

ORGANIZING

"Si Kahn is people-oriented, and we haven't been hearing much from that type of individual lately. His new book on community organizing should be read by anyone threatened by the Reagan Administration's budget cuts."

—Graciela Oliveraz, Former Director
Community Service Administration

"In Organizing Kahn gives us many of the tools that we will need to empower ourselves, to move from being victims to having the power to control our own lives together."

—Mark Rosenman, President
Beacon College

"Women will find here invaluable material on developing leadership skills, and a wealth of stimulating ideas and detailed information, all of which we can and must use if we are to achieve the power to change our lives."

—Jane Gould, Director
Women's Center, Barnard College

"Leadership development is the key to building a cadre of Third World activists for the '80s. This book provides many helpful insights for minority organizers and organizations."

—Hulbert James, Director
Center for Third World Organizing

"A great volume of knowledge and resources that's about real economic and political empowerment of poor and minority people. And the timing is perfect."

—Carrie Graves, Deputy Director
North Carolina Traning and Resource Center
for Social Change

"Si Kahn puts common sense into community words and helps us to understand that we can all be organizers as long as we have the commitment and concern."

—Barbara Bode, President
The Children's Foundation

"Despite efforts to keep us separate and alienated from each other, despite efforts encouraging us to accept the power structure as it is, people across the United States continue to meet and attempt to organize to change their lives. Finally, there is a manual—a "cook book," as the author says—that speaks to those people and that gives vital information on how to get and keep the power."

—Sandie Kills Pretty Enemy, President
Research and Educational Environment
Foundation

A Guide for Grassroots Leaders

ORGANIZING

Si Kahn

McGRAW-HILL BOOK COMPANY
New York St. Louis San Francisco Auckland Bogotá
Guatemala Hamburg Johannesburg Lisbon London
Madrid Mexico Montreal New Delhi Panama
Paris San Juan São Paulo Singapore
Sydney Tokyo Toronto

1 2 3 4 5 6 7 8 9 0 F G F G 8 7 6 5 4 3 2 1

First McGraw-Hill Edition, 1982

LIBRARY OF CONGRESS CATALOGING IN PUBLICATION DATA

Kahn, Si.
Organizing, a guide for grass roots leaders.
Includes index.
1. Leadership. 2. Community development.
I. Title.
HM141.K29   303.3'4   81-8380
ISBN 0-07-033215-0   AACR2
ISBN 0-07-033199-5 (pbk.)

Book design by Roberta Rezk.

For my partner, Elizabeth Kamarck Minnich, who helps me
see the world in so many ways. For her clear vision,
for her friendship and for her love, this book is dedicated
to her.

Acknowledgments

WRITING THIS BOOK has been like an organizing campaign. In the course of putting it together, I've worked with dozens of organizations and hundreds of individuals. All of them contributed to the book. Without the ideas, experiences, successes, and failures that came from working with these people and groups, this book would have been far more difficult to write.

Several organizations deserve special thanks. Much of my training work during the past two years was done as Consulting Trainer to the Midwest Academy (600 West Fullerton Avenue, Chicago, Illinois 60614), which provides training, technical assistance, and written resource materials to grassroots leaders, organizers, organizations, and coalitions. Their insights and experience have been of major importance to me in developing the ideas in this book.

Initial support for writing *Organizing* came from The Youth Project, Inc. (1555 Connecticut Avenue N.W., Washington, D.C. 20036), which provides technical assistance in fundraising and other areas to grass roots organizing. Several of the training sessions through which materials for the book were developed were conducted cooperatively with the staff of their Appalachian Field Office. The Youth Project also helped me establish the Grassroots Leadership Project, which provides leadership training and organizing assistance to grassroots organizations in Appalachia and the South.

Many of the ideas on the uses of culture in organizing were developed in the course of cooperative work with the Citizen Heritage Center (2001 University Avenue SE, Minneapolis, Minnesota 55414). Citizen Heritage provides training, consulting, and resource materials on history and culture to people's organizations.

My five years of work with the Amalgamated Clothing and Textile Workers Union (ACTWU) on the J. P. Stevens Campaign were an invaluable source of experience, inspiration, and insight. I'd like to thank both the ACTWU staff and the J. P. Stevens workers themselves, especially the union leaders in Roanoke Rapids, North Carolina, who shared so much with me.

Some of the work which is now part of this book was originally commissioned by the Art Wexler Memorial Foundation as a living memorial to Art Wexler. Their support is gratefully acknowledged. I hope that this book will be used in ways that help carry forward the spirit of his life.

I've tried to remember all the individuals who so generously gave time and ideas to this project, and I hope that none of them has been left out.

Michael Ansara
Ira Arlook
Arnold Aronson
Bernie Aronson
Rob Bauman
Dave Beckwith
Frank Blechman
Barbara Bode
Jan Bone
Heather Booth
Harry Boyte

Betsy Brinson
Meg Campbell
Michael Cane
Vince Carroll
Ellen Cassedy
Kim Clerc
Gerry Conroy
Lenny Conway
Bob Creamer
Mary Daskais
Rochelle Davis

Gary Delgado
David Dotson
Sara Evans
Harry Fagan
Secky Fascione
Kim Fellner
Joan Flanagan
Ellen Fleischman
Tom Gaudette
Carrie Graves
Lupe Guajardo
Janet Gutkind
Marilyn Haga
Mike Haga
Bob Hall
Paula Hammett
Mary Harrington
Dan Hendrickson
Miles Horton
Chip Hughes
Joanne Jankovic
Rabbi Benjamin Kahn
Jenette Kahn
Jackie Kendall
Judy Kincaid
Charles Koppelman
William Peter Kosmas
Mary Lassen
Diane MacEachern
Peggy Matthews
Steve Max
Margaret Messick
Nick Mills
Bill Mitchell
David Mitchell

Phil Moore
John Musick
Doyle Neimann
Karen Nussbaum
Maureen O'Connell
Karen Paget
Ralph Paige
Mary Preniski
Miles Rapoport
Wade Rathke
Pat Raymond
Ken Reardon
Lynn Rhenisch
Ellen Ryan
Denise Scheer
Les Schmidt
Ellen Schumer
Jim Sessions
Chuck Shuford
Pat Speer
Greg Speeter
Don Stillman
Cathy Sullivan
Marge Tabankin
Karen Thomas
Shel Trapp
Baldemar Velasquez
Claudia Vlisides
Darlene Weaver
Paul Wellstone
Jennie West
Dorothy Wexler
Fritz Wiecking
Jeff Zinsmeyer
Dave Zwick

My children, Simon, Jesse, and Gabriel, have been wonderful companions, and have given me support and inspiration. Our work together to build a family has been my most challenging and rewarding organizing campaign.

Special thanks are due to the "production team": Wendy Anderson, who transcribed and edited hours of tapes; Cindy Currell and Jim Overton, who pitched in with scissors and staplers to help make final deadlines; Ellen LaBarbera, who did a superb and caring job of editing the final manuscript; and the staff at McGraw-Hill—Tom Dembofsky, Joanne Dolinar, and Herb Dreyer—who have worked so hard to help pull this project together.

Bertha Gober, Holly Near, and Bernice Johnson Reagon generously allowed me to use their wonderful songs in this book. Holly Near's records can be ordered from Redwood Records (Box 996, Ukiah, California 95482). Both Redwood and Flying Fish (1304 West Schubert, Chicago, Illinois 60614) produce and distribute records by "Sweet Honey in the Rock," an extraordinary singing group founded and led by Bernice Johnson Reagon. Flying Fish also produces my own records *Home* and *Doing My Job,* which include the songs "People like You" and "Gonna Go to Work on Monday."

Finally, I'd like to thank Josh Dunson of Real People's Music (4113 North Greenview, Chicago, Illinois 60613), who represents me for concerts and speaking engagements, for his help and support.

Si Kahn
May, 1981

Contents

1. Organizing

ORGANIZING IS PEOPLE working together to get things done. Let's say you're fed up with the high prices and poor quality that you get at your neighborhood supermarket. Now, you could try to do something about it by yourself. You could go to the manager and say, "If you don't straighten up, I'm not going to shop here anymore." You could write letters to the newspaper complaining about the food. You could write to the president of the chain. But they're not going to pay much attention to you. If you're just one person they don't really care whether you shop at the store or not.

On the other hand, let's say that you and thirty of your friends stand in front of the store passing out leaflets about the high prices and poor quality. Next, seventy-five of you sign an ad in the newspaper asking people not to buy at the store until it changes its policies. Then a petition signed by several hundred people in the neighborhood is presented by a dozen of you to the president of the company. They're going to listen and act. They may not care about the amount of money that *you* spend in one week. But multiply that by three or four hundred and you have a lot of cash. That income, that volume, is important to the store, where you as an individual aren't. The power of a lot of people working together is enough to make changes where one person can do very little.

Let's take another example. Say you're a senior citizen living in a large city. You're angry because poor public transportation where you live makes it hard to get to places you need to go. You can do a lot of things on your own. You can write letters to the editor. You can make calls to the radio and television stations. You can telephone every politician in the city. You can write angry letters to the mayor. You can go to city council meetings to stand up and complain. But as long as it's just you, it's not likely that much is going to get done. The people who would have to make the changes you're seeking are always going to ask themselves one question: "What's going to happen if I don't do it?" If you're the only one making waves, the answer is "Probably not very much."

On the other hand, suppose you and three hundred other senior citizens do all of these things *together*—carry petitions to the newspaper, appear as a group at the radio and television stations demanding to be heard, show up all at once at city council meetings, go together to the mayor's house. Then it's not just awkward and embarrassing. It's a real sign of the power that you have to deliver. Regardless of age, three hundred people are three hundred voters. Any politician knows that three hundred voters can make a big difference in an election. That's why they'll listen to a group, and that's why they'll often give in to the group's demands.

The fact that you're right usually has very little to do with whether or not you win. People with power and privilege rarely give it away because it would be "right" to do so. The question is, are you powerful? If you have power, then you can get something done.

Does organizing really work?

The best way to answer that question is to look around you and see who is organized and who isn't. Generally, the people who have the power are the ones who are best organized. Where does your money go? A lot of it goes to health care. Doctors can charge such high rates because they are so well organized that they have almost a total monopoly on health care in this country. If you rent, a lot of your money goes to the landlord. Landlords have organized to pass laws that protect them and not you. Part of your budget goes for food, for the high profits of chain stores that have organized to keep out competition, to keep food quality down and prices—and profits—up. Lately, more and more of your money is going to utilities, which have organized to raise your fuel prices and their profits to outrageous levels. The fact that our tax dollars help those who already have the most money more than they help us reflects the fact that those people are well organized and we aren't.

In the United States today power is concentrated in the hands of a small number of well-organized individuals and corporations. These corporations and the individuals involved in them have extraordinary power to make decisions that affect all of our lives. Corporations have again and again shown an ability to work together to fix prices regardless of the suffering and hardship that it has caused people and even the country itself. In recent years the prices of gasoline and fuel oil have jumped to three and four times their earlier levels. The oil corporations, which also control so many of our natural resources such as coal and hydro-electric power, have increased their profits up to 800 percent in one year.

This is real power. It is a kind of power working families have never really known. How many working families have ever been able to increase their income four times in one year? How many working families have never been threatened with unemployment or layoffs? How many working families have been able to escape the payment of taxes altogether? How many working families have been able to break the law and avoid punishment?

This is exactly what is going on in our country today. This small group of corporations and individuals is steadily and systematically chipping away at the freedoms that all of us have. The rights that we are guaranteed under the Constitution and the Bill of Rights are being taken away by the actions of the corporations, because without economic freedom there can be no political freedom.

We see our lack of power as individuals and families in many areas of life. We see it in the prices we pay for the necessities of life: for food, for clothing, for utilities, for housing, for medical care. In many cases the prices for these items are so high compared with what most people make that they're not even available. It's becoming almost impossible for a working family to even own a house. In rural areas the price of land has gotten so high that it's impossible for anyone other than a corporation to think of owning and operating a farm.

How does the opposition exercise power?

The opposition controls us and our lives in a number of different ways. Power is exercised through control of resources. Ownership of factories and businesses gives power over people's jobs and job security. Ownership of natural resources—coal, timber, land, water, oil, uranium—gives power to set prices, to ensure higher profits, to control supply and demand, to make the necessities of life scarce.

The power of these investments is reinforced by control of the political process. This in turn depends on the power of money, of cold cash. Again and again we see the ability of the opposition to influence elections at all levels of government—national, state, county, city, local—through the tremendous amounts of money that are spent. The politicians are elected through the use of these enormous campaign contributions, but they then owe a responsibility to their backers—at least on the particular issues that the backers are interested in. As a result, many of the laws that are passed favor the self-interests of wealthy individuals and of the corporations rather than protecting the ordinary people and families that make up the majority of this country. For example, unions are the only real power that working people have to balance their own rights against those of the people they work for. But the laws governing relationships between union workers and their employers have been rewritten again and again over the years to favor management so that the rights of workers to organize have been severely undercut.

In some cases power is exercised by individuals. There are definitely individuals who own so many different things and who play such a strong role in politics that they have tremendous power. But even the power of these individuals depends on being organized together. The power that the average employer has, for example, comes not only from control over jobs and the profits that are made on those jobs, but also from the power that is exercised nationally by groups like the United States Chamber of Commerce, the National Association of Manufacturers, and the Business Roundtable. These groups work together to create legislation that is favorable to businesses and employers. They pressure the different agencies of government into carrying out existing laws in a way that favors those who have rather than those who have not. It's no accident that the laws in this country tend to favor corporations, wealthy individuals, factory owners, landlords, and investors.

The corporations argue that the rest of us have all the rights we need to make it in the system if we really try. A person who is unemployed has the right to go anywhere and apply for a job. They claim that if a person can work for long enough and accumulate enough money, she can even start her own factory. Someone who cannot afford housing has the right to offer the landlord less rent whether or not in fact that landlord will accept less. We all have the right to "prove" ourselves, to seek additional education or training, to improve our skills to make us more employable or desirable. If we are without work and without money we have the right to go to the government agencies set up to help us: to the administrators of Social Security, welfare, public housing, Medicare, Medicaid, food stamps. If we're turned down by these agencies and programs, we have the right to appeal their decisions through administrative and judicial procedures—even to the Supreme Court of the United States.

In theory, as far as those who have power are concerned, no one should be complaining. But, in fact, as anybody who has ever tried to use them will tell you, these rights exist in theory but not in fact. In fact, if you're out of work, you're out of luck. In fact, if you're evicted, you're on the street. In fact, if you're old, there's no place for you. In fact, if you're poor, you're probably going to stay poor. In fact, if you're discriminated against, you're just going to have a hard time. Despite supposed guarantees for the rights of the individual, a single person has almost no power whatsoever when it's necessary to confront the organized power that controls our lives in so many different ways.

Can organizing work for ordinary people?

It's evident that organizing works for people who have wealth and power to begin with. But there is also a whole history in this country of organizing by ordinary people that has been tremendously successful. If you look at the history of our country, you'll find that most progress was made because people *organized* to make it. The American Revolution, for example, didn't just happen. It was *organized*. The people who organized it held meetings, planned strategy, developed leadership, set up systems of communication, defined issues, took direct action, used public relations, raised funds, built coalitions—just as we do in community organizing today.

Most of the rights and benefits we have now weren't just given to us. People organized to get them. Many of the things we now take for granted had to be fought for. Today most of us who work have pension plans, paid vacations, paid holidays, sick leave, and overtime benefits. We didn't get these benefits because the companies suddenly decided to give them to us. We have them because millions of people in the thirties and at other times organized unions to force their companies to give them these benefits, which were then adopted by the society as a whole. The fact that women have the vote or that black people have some of their civil rights protected came about not because of the good-heartedness of the government, but because these groups organized to demand those rights. Even public schools and public education came about because people in this country organized to insist that their children, as well as the children of the rich, had a right to education.

What are the benefits of organizing?

Organizing has both short- and long-range benefits. In the short run it's an effective tool for getting things done: for improving schools, for lowering taxes, for establishing rights on the job, for improving transportation and health care, for protecting and defending neighborhoods and communities. Many of the everyday problems that we face as individuals can be dealt with by organizing.

But organizing has other benefits that may in the long run be even more important. Through organizing, people learn something new about themselves. They find dignity in place of mistreatment. They find self-respect instead of a lack of self-confidence. They begin to use more fully the skills and abilities that they possess: to work with other people, to influence, to speak up, to fight back.

Through organizing, people begin to rediscover themselves. They find out who they are, where they came from, their background, their history, their roots, their culture. They rediscover the things in their family, their gender, their ethnic or language group, their race that give them strength. They rediscover their own history of struggle and resistance.

All of us are partly what we think we are, and we think we are what we've been told we are. So when we're told that our group has never made waves, stirred up trouble, or questioned authority, we tend to think that's how we should act as well. When we're told our group has always kept to itself and done things on its own, we tend not to question that.

But the real history of people in this country is not of passively accepting whatever was handed to them but of fighting back. This was true during the American Revolution and it's true today. But most of us have lost this legacy of fighting back. We're told that the American way is for all of us to join together and cooperate for the national good. So we're expected to do our part, to sacrifice, to do without, to be quiet, not to demand but to ask for favors.

Whom does all this benefit? It benefits the people who control the corporations, the government agencies, and the political parties, who therefore control many parts of all of our lives. We ordinary people tighten our belts on energy consumption so that the oil companies can profit. We do without police protection in our neighborhoods while the city uses our tax money to build industrial parks which are given tax-free to profit-making industries. The city builds convention centers while our schools fall apart.

In organizing we begin to rediscover our own needs and demand that they be filled. In doing so we rediscover our strengths, our roots, our heritage. We relearn the skills of cooperation, of collective action, of working together, of supporting each other. In this knowledge and this experience is the beginning of real power for people.

Organizing is for people with problems—or so we think. It *is* good as a tool, a weapon, a means. But it is also an end in itself. As we organize, we reclarify ourselves as individuals because we learn to speak for ourselves in ways that make us heard.

Who can organize?

One of the wonderful things about organizing is that almost anyone can use it. True, there are professional organizers, such as the author of this book, who earn a living helping people organize themselves. Sometimes to listen to us professional organizers you'd think that organizing was a very difficult and mysterious way of doing things. Organizers, like many professionals, sometimes exaggerate the skill needed to do what they do. They talk in a mysterious language: actions, models, constituencies, coalitions, agendas, strategies, tactics. This kind of "shop talk" sometimes makes people believe that there is something very complicated about the organizing process. But, in fact, good organizing is an uncomplicated way of doing things. It depends on the basic skills that most of us have to some degree. While there are not hard-and-fast rules for organizing, there are steps that need to be taken in most situations. These steps can be learned by ordinary people.

Most people don't think of themselves as organizers. In fact, most people don't think of themselves as someone who could ever be an organizer. Organizing is looked on as something difficult, dangerous, romantic. The organizers you see in the movies are usually handsome, strong, tough, young, white, and male.

Luckily, it's not true. If you had to fit the movies' image to be an organizer, most of the fine organizing that's been done since this country was founded would never have taken place. The history of organizing in the United States is a history of people of both sexes and of every age, color, nationality, religion, language or ethnic group. Wonderful organizing that made life better for thousands of people has been done by high school students, paraplegics, people in their seventies and eighties and nineties, mental patients, and all kinds of other ordinary people.

The reason that ordinary people make good organizers is that the skills of organizing are everyday skills. They're the kinds of skills that help us do well in daily life at home, with our families, with our friends, and at work. People who are good at dealing with people make good organizers.

If you are a typical person, you're probably thinking that this is some sort of public relations hype. You're saying to yourself, "I could never be an organizer or a leader." But most people who are leaders today in communities, in factories, in schools, in institutions, started out thinking the same thing. They thought that they could never speak in public. They believed they could never confront their landlord, or boss, or city council representative. They felt that they could never chair a meeting or put together an agenda. They assumed that no one would listen to them, follow them, or take them seriously, and so they were afraid to act at all. It is easy to punish individuals for standing up. We remember that—and we are kept from discovering that groups that stand together are a whole different matter.

These feelings are part of the price we pay for the way we're brought up. They come from a lifetime of working in separation, of being discouraged from coming together to work for a common goal. But the truth is that most people have within themselves a tremendous capacity to work together, to provide leadership, to offer inspiration, to organize others. For most of us these abilities have been beaten down so far that we don't have the confidence even to begin. But throughout history, people who never thought they could become organizers have led important movements for change in their neighborhoods, in their schools, in their workplaces. Every group of people—black people, white people, old people, young people, women, men, factory workers, farmers, taxpayers, consumers—has produced real leadership from individuals who thought they could never be leaders.

Anyone can organize. Anyone can learn the basic principles of organizing. There is no tool more effective. You can "learn how to win friends and influence people," you can "discover your human potential," you can "modify your behavior," you can "become more assertive." But nothing can change your life as much as finding other people who want to move in the same direction you do and learning to work together with them to accomplish the goals that all of you want.

Why do people organize?

People organize for a number of different reasons. Sometimes they are approached by someone who asks them to organize. This person can be a neighbor, a friend, a co-worker, a relative, a representative of a neighborhood or community organization, or a staff organizer for a union. The approach may be very simple. Someone says, "I'm mad. Let's get together and see if we can do something about this."

Sometimes the answer is "No, I'd rather do it myself." Many of us have become suspicious of each other. If someone comes to the door with a petition, we think twice before we sign it, if we sign it at all. If we're asked to a neighborhood or community meeting, we can often think of more reasons not to go than reasons to go. But often the answer is "Yes." It depends a lot on how we're approached, what we're approached about, and what we're asked to do.

Other times, we begin organizing because we've run out of other things to try. We've done everything that we know how to do on our own to solve the problem. We've complained to our friends. We've gotten mad. We've written letters to the editor. We've called up the radio stations. We've complained to the boss. We've threatened. Nothing seems to work.

Finally, we start to ask other people, "Hey, have you been having this problem?" We find out we're not the only ones who are mad and think something should be done. There are people on the block, in the neighborhood, in the plant, in the schoolroom, who feel the same way we do. They're frustrated by the lack of answers. They too want to get something done. That's the start of organizing: recognizing that individual solutions are not working and that therefore the answer has to be working together.

Why don't people organize?

Not everyone who has a problem is going to organize. Some people will keep trying individual solutions, even if they don't seem to be getting results. Other people will just give up and think about something else.

There are a lot of reasons why people resist organizing. For many, it's something new and therefore something to be feared. They have never done it and so they find it hard to think of ever doing it. For others, there is a fear of some of the things that they think they might be asked to do as part of organizing. They're afraid that they'll be asked to take on public responsibility they don't feel equal to. They may be afraid of making speeches in public. They may be afraid that they'll appear ignorant or act like they don't know what they're doing. Lack of self-confidence, coupled with a fear of strange situations, is one major reason why people don't organize.

Another reason is fear of what will happen if they *do* organize. You see this often in union organizing. Workers are afraid that if they join the union they'll get fired, or lose their seniority, or be transferred to a lower-paying or less desirable job or into a dangerous or unhealthy area of the plant. They're afraid that they'll be painted by management as troublemakers, agitators, and singled out for harassment and intimidation.

Sometimes this fear is justified. Harassment and intimidation are used on people who try to organize, not only in union situations but in other kinds of organizing as well. But sometimes this fear is exaggerated by what people have heard about organizing.

Those who have power—corporations, doctors, political establishments, and the like—have tried to keep the secrets of organizing to themselves. Not only are ordinary people not taught to organize, they are actively kept from even thinking about it. Most of us are taught from our earliest days of school that organizing—people getting together to accomplish what they all want—is somehow un-American. We don't learn about the organizing that has been done throughout the history of this country, by people of all ages and races, from every state and part of the country, around all kinds of issues. So we don't learn that organizing is as American as apple pie, and is a basic part of the way this country works. We're taught to associate organizing with "union corruption," with "communism," with "troublemakers," with "hippies."

Nothing could be further from the truth. Organizing is basic to how the American system of democracy and representative government is supposed to work. But because people are not taught about organizing, we see it as something that is not done by "people like us."

Instead, we are told that there are better ways of solving our problems. At work we're told that if we'd only go to the boss one at a time and talk calmly about our problem something would be done. At school we're told that if we're having a problem we should come in and see the teacher, the counselor, or the principal after school and everything will be fine. Ann Landers and Dear Abby tell women to have a private chat with their husbands if there are problems at home. People on welfare are told to talk to their caseworkers in private and confidentially.

Over and over we are encouraged to look for individual solutions. We are taught to act as individuals, not as groups. But the truth is that individual action rarely gets things done. It keeps us separated from each other and prevents us from making the really basic changes that need to be made.

There are other reasons why society encourages us to take individual approaches to solving our problems. Individual problems can be handled without making major readjustments in the system. If one worker in a plant keeps complaining privately to the boss about wages, it is easy enough to make a slight adjustment in that worker's pay or to promote that worker to a supervisory position. If, rather than going to the boss, that worker decides to use her leadership skills to bring other workers together, it may be necessary to give a raise to everyone.

If one individual goes to city hall and complains about the taxes on his house, it may be worth it to the city to keep things quiet by cutting those taxes a little bit. If several hundred taxpayers complain, the only solution may be a general change in the tax structure which would benefit private homeowners rather than private corporations. By encouraging all of us to seek individual solutions, society keeps from having to make major changes in the way it operates, which might be far more expensive in the long run.

Another reason for encouraging individual solutions is that they tend to make people blame themselves for their own problems. Most of us tend to think that we have more problems than other people. We don't recognize how many of our problems are shared by people around us. So we think that if we would just work a little harder, dress a little nicer, or talk a little better those problems would be solved.

The system deliberately encourages this attitude. Workers are told that if they could just bring their production up a little bit there might be a promotion in the works for them. Women are told that if they could just keep the house a little cleaner their husbands might love them more. Minority groups are told that if they could only find the right channels to go through their problems would be dealt with—one at a time.

We tend to see our failure to get a better job, to have more of a voice in our community, to have a better home life, as a personal failure. This undercuts our confidence in ourselves. It makes us believe that we are really not as good as the people who run the country, the factories, the schools. We begin to suspect that maybe they are right when they tell us we should leave things in their hands. Let them make the decisions. Let them give us what they think we should have.

So all of us end up being a little less than we could be. We lack confidence to take matters into our own hands. We become separated and alienated from each other. Confronted with an opposition that works closely together, that makes strategy together, that exercises power together, we become unable to change the things that make life difficult for us.

There is another reason why we are encouraged to act only as individuals in this society. People who have power know only too well what happens when other people get a little taste of it. They know that once people learn that by organizing they are able to change small things, they will start to think about changing larger things. They know that the workers who succeed in cleaning up a dirty canteen in the plant will start trying to do something about wages and seniority as well. They know that people in a neighborhood who by working together force the city to clean up a few vacant lots start talking about how they can get police protection and fairer taxes as well.

Are some people easier to organize than others?

In organizing, as in so many other things, it seems as if the grass is always greener on the other side of the fence. The members of almost every group think that they are the most difficult people to organize. Often, for example, when you're working in a situation that involves both blacks and whites, the whites will say, "You know, black people will stick together. They stand up for each other. They're not afraid to back each other up. If white people would only do that, we could get somewhere." On the other hand, the blacks will say, "You know, the thing about white people is they all hang together. They're not like black people, fighting each other. They know what they want and they'll stand together to get it."

What's fascinating is that almost any group tends to see itself as divided and other groups as unified. Actually, no group is *easy* to organize. But no group is impossible to organize. Every group has special strengths and special problems that need to be made part of an organizing strategy.

In rural areas, for example, people are spread out. Going from door to door to see people is hard. So is bringing people together for meetings. Strategies which might involve a trip to the state capital to lobby are difficult because of the long distance people have to travel. On the other hand, in a rural community there are often more established traditions of cooperation and people helping each other. There are fewer competing events and activities, so that even though people have to go farther to see each other there is more reason to do so.

No matter what group you're working with, there will be some things that will make them easier to organize and other things that will make them harder to organize. What's important is to recognize for each group what the strengths and difficulties are. Don't assume that what worked for one group will work for another. Just as each person is special and needs to be treated as an individual, so each community or neighborhood or group of people has its own special qualities. Understanding these qualities and working with them makes the job of organizing more effective and successful.

It is also true that the same group of people will be easier to organize at some times than at others. People organize when they have a good reason to do so, at least as far as they're concerned. A good time to get people talking about taxes is when the county has just announced a property tax increase. A good time to organize around safety in the neighborhood is when a woman has been assaulted on the street at night. People are often more willing to organize when a specific issue arises—either to defend their standard of living and way of life or because they see some kind of gain they can make at that time.

People also are easier to organize when they see a chance of winning. Most people have all the problems they can handle and some that they can't. They'd like to see solutions to those problems. But their life experiences have shown them that solutions are unlikely. Often we wonder, for example, why people whose houses are falling down won't organize around poor housing conditions. The answer often is that they don't think they can do anything about it. They may be right or they may be wrong about the reality of what can or can't be done. But if they think something can be done they are much more likely to organize than if they think nothing can be done.

Communities, like people, have periods of activity and periods of rest. Just as people are sometimes able to take risks, try new ventures, step outside themselves, so communities sometimes are willing to chance new ways of doing things and take collective risks. At other times communities, like people, may be cautious. Sometimes we end up thinking that a community can't be organized when the real answer is that it can't be organized this week, or this year, or around this particular issue.

Sometimes, for example, when a community has just finished a long but successful organizing campaign, we try to push it right away to start another one. But what is needed is a resting period when people consolidate, celebrate, and rebuild their strength for another long, hard fight. The natural rhythms of communities, like the natural rhythms of individuals, are important and need to be watched carefully in putting together an organizing campaign.

Where do you start?

The best place to start is where you are, with the people you care about, the issues you're angry about, the things you'd like to have changed in your life and the lives of the people you spend time with. Start with the people you work with and live with, the people that are like you, who share your concerns and interests. Organizing doesn't need to be big to be successful. A small group of people can accomplish a tremendous amount.

One of the extraordinary things about organizing is how many people will take part in it once it gets started. Most people want to do something to make their lives better. But most people also think that there is little or nothing they can do. So they sit back waiting for someone to do it for them, waiting for someone to tell them what to do. Often it's the action taken by just one person, sometimes someone who has never done anything like it before, that is the spark to set off a major organizing campaign.

Some years ago when I was living in Fannin County, Georgia, the county commission announced a major increase in property taxes. All of us were mad. We hung around the tractor place complaining. It was all that anybody talked about. But nobody was doing anything. Finally, one of the union members at the copper mine put a three-line ad in the paper. It said, as nearly as I can remember, "I'm mad about my taxes and I want to do something. If you want to do something, too, meet me at the courthouse tonight at 8:00." Three hundred people showed up at the courthouse. That was the beginning of an important movement to change not just taxes but government in that county. Everyone wanted to do something, everyone was angry, but it took the action of one person to change that anger into activity.

Organizing doesn't always work. Not every fight is won. Not every problem is solved. But more often than not, if you take the first step, other people will follow.

How do you get started?

Because the history of organizing has to some extent been written by organizers, it's easy to get the idea that you need to have a professional organizer on call before you even get started. It can be helpful to have someone with previous organizing experience to talk with, to think through issues and ideas with, to help plan strategies and choose tactics. But most of the important social and political movements in this country have been started by ordinary people on their own.

Besides, although most of us haven't organized unions, political campaigns, or neighborhood groups, we do have a lot of organizational experience which we often fail to recognize. Many of us have worked in synagogue and church groups, as members of unions, in parent-teacher-student associations, in CB clubs, in farmers' or veterans' associations, in other types of organizations. Many of the same skills that are used to build these organizations are useful in the kind of organizing that we're talking about here. Think about your own life and the times that you were part of an organization. Go back to the things that you did and the things that you learned. You'll probably find that you have a lot more organizing skills than you ever thought. These skills can be the beginning of a do-it-yourself approach to organizing. The rest of this book is about how to do it yourself, and *why*. There are really no mysteries, no secrets. All of us have or can develop the knowledge and experience to play an important role in changing our world for the better. Each of us will have different skills and abilities, different values and priorities. But all of us, working together, can be leaders in building a society that works for each of us.

2. Leaders

A LEADER IS SOMEONE who helps show us the directions we want to go and who helps us go in those directions. All of us in our own lives have had people who played that role for us: parents, teachers, friends, spouses, children. Leaders give us a sense not only of who they are but of who we are. Good leaders are willing to step outside of themselves into others' lives.

In organizing, when we talk about leaders, we're talking about the kind of people who can play this role not just for one person but for many people. They can give a sense of vision and direction to the group, not just one individual at a time, but all together. Leaders can appeal to the common feelings and hopes that bind a group together. They can give the group back a sense of itself.

Leaders are people that others follow. There is no such thing as a leader without followers. The best leaders inspire people not just to follow the leader, but to follow themselves, to grow in their own abilities, to give direction to their own lives.

Rarely does this happen just by example. Leaders have to do

more than simply *be* leaders. They need to *work* as leaders, to help other people become leaders themselves.

What kinds of people make the best leaders?

When you think of the leaders that you've known or known about, you'll probably find that they were different from each other many ways. Just as all of us respond to different kinds of people, different groups respond to different styles of leadership.

There is no one type of person that makes the best leader. Leaders are women and men, young and old, black, white, Hispanic, and Native American, rural and urban, working and poor. Few of these people grew up expecting to be leaders. Like most of us, they never thought that anyone would seek them out, listen to their advice, come to them for help, work with them, take direction from them. Many of the people who today are well-known grass roots leaders were at one time afraid of speaking to a small group meeting.

This is a side of leaders we don't often see. We see the finished product, not the long and painful process by which people got where they are. When we see that person, we say to ourselves, "I wish I were like that person, but I could never be." But one of the most extraordinary things about the leaders of people's organizations and people's movements is how many of them *are* people like us. Most of them also used to think, "I could never be like that." But most people *can* be like that. Leaders are not born. Leaders are made through experience, work, and training.

It doesn't matter if you've never spoken in public in your life. It doesn't matter if you punch a clock in an office day after day. It doesn't matter if it seems as if half of your life is spent pushing shopping baskets in crowded supermarket lanes. It doesn't matter if you retired five years ago and haven't done much except watch television since. With work and time you can become a leader in your community.

Why do people decide to become leaders?

Most people become leaders because they're angry. Sometimes they themselves don't even recognize that they're angry. They may feel that they're only depressed and discouraged at how hard life can get. But that depression and discouragement comes from the anger that is rooted in powerlessness.

People become leaders because they're tired of being pushed around, tired of seeing others pushed around. They're angry at watching their communities and neighborhoods destroyed for profit. They're angry at watching their earnings eaten up by inflation, their taxes wasted. They're angry at seeing other members of their group pushed around: other women, other blacks, other Hispanics, other senior citizens, other workers, other community members, other gays, other Native Americans.

People decide to become leaders when they get the first taste of that something special organizing gives, the taste of fighting back, the taste of taking back what is rightfully yours.

People also become leaders when they suddenly see leadership as a real possibility for them. They go along thinking, "I could never be like that." One day they realize, "I *could* be like that." This realization is the first step.

This process of moving from what seems impossible to what seems possible is important in motivating people. Most of us want things that we think are within reasonable reach. Part of the process of maturing is learning what things are open to "people like you" and what things are not. You learn early, and often through harsh lessons, how far you're expected to go as a black, a Native American, a woman, a Hispanic, a poor person, a worker. Over time, to protect your own sanity, you stop wanting the things that you can't get.

Most of us, when we're very young, want to be leaders. We want to have people respect us and like us. We want to have people listen to our advice. We want to be able to do things that make a difference to people. But most people who aren't born to wealth and power have that sort of ambition knocked out of them at an early age. It's only when we again begin to see that we too can become leaders, that we start taking the first step.

This is why it's so important for leaders to take as their first responsibility the development of other leaders. The changes that need to be made in this society cannot be made by a handful of people. If we are to have truly representative economic and political democracy in this country, we need to have grassroots leaders everywhere: in each neighborhood, within each constituent group, within each institution, on each block, in each rural community. These leaders will be produced through their contacts with other leaders, because they're inspired by them to say to themselves, "I could be like that, too."

How does a person get to be a leader?

One reason that people are often discouraged from trying to become leaders is that the process doesn't seem clearly defined. In some types of organizing, however, there is a fairly clear step-by-step process through which one becomes a leader. You see this in union organizing, where there is a clearly defined route to follow to become a recognized leader within the union.

Most union leaders first become active in the local union at their plant. In an unorganized plant, a worker will start out by being a member of an organizing committee, working for the union in her department and on her shift. Once a contract has been signed and the union recognized, she would work to become a shop steward, an elected representative inside her own department. A shop steward helps other workers handle their grievances and plays a part in the official decision-making process within the union local. The person might also become an officer of the local if it is newly organized.

In an established local a person usually needs to spend several years as a shop steward learning skills and proving his effectiveness as a leader who can deliver to his constituency. Later he might run for election to a local office such as president, vice-president, secretary, or treasurer.

In many unions local officers will be borrowed from time to time to work on organizing campaigns at other plants. This is a way of both giving them some organizing skills and taking a look at how well they work in those kinds of situations. Someone who proved her or his effectiveness might then be offered a regular union staff position as an organizer. Others might choose to stay inside the plant and to run for other elected positions above the local union level.

In other kinds of organizing there is rarely as clear a route to becoming a leader. But the principles are the same: starting small, beginning close to home, developing skills, proving what you can do, broadening your experiences, developing additional skills, undertaking greater responsibilities.

What personal qualities should a leader have?

(1) *A good leader likes people*. Most of the work of organizing is work with people: talking with them, listening to them, working with them in groups. Most of the time you spend as a leader is spent with people. If you don't really like people, if you don't really enjoy being with them, it shows. But if you really do like people, that shows, too.

(2) *A good leader is a good listener*. You may be surprised that "a good talker" wasn't listed first. But in organizing, listening is more important than talking. In this world, the people who aren't on top don't get listened to very much. Nobody asks their opinions. Nobody wants their advice. But most people have pretty good opinions, at least about the things that affect their own lives. They'd like someone to listen to those opinions.

(3) *A good leader makes friends easily*. If you're going to spend a lot of time working with people, it helps if they like you and think of you as a friend. If you're not open to making new friends easily, it may be difficult for people to work with you.

(4) *A good leader builds trust easily*. Building trust isn't quite the same as having people like you. All of us know people we like but don't quite trust. But in organizing, we need to be more than popular. We need to be trustworthy. When we organize people, we encourage them to take risks in their lives. They need to trust us enough to take those risks.

(5) *A good leader talks well*. You knew that one would be in the list somewhere. But talking well doesn't mean being a public speaker. It just means being comfortable talking about your own ideas. It also means being able to express those ideas in plain enough language so that most people can understand them.

(6) *A good leader helps people believe in themselves*. It's hard for people who are powerless to believe in themselves. Everything in this society teaches them not to have confidence in themselves. But if people are going to change their lives by working together with other people, they need to rebuild that confidence. They need to believe they're as good as anyone else.

(7) *A good leader can let others take the credit*. If you solve other people's problems for them, *you* get the credit. But if you help them solve that problem for themselves, *they* get it. As a leader you have to be big enough to let that happen.

(8) *A good leader works hard*. If you become a leader, sooner or later someone is going to ask you why you do nothing except talk all day. But talking and listening are hard work, especially when you're dealing with the problems of people. Sometimes it's hard to keep going, especially when there's no solution in sight. But you need to be able to do it.

(9) *A good leader doesn't get discouraged too often*. Everyone gets discouraged from time to time. It's impossible not to, when you're working with people who have serious needs that in many cases aren't going to be met. But if you get discouraged too often, you can't work effectively.

(10) *A good leader has a sense of her or his own identity*. In organizing, we're helping people discover who they are. To do this well, we need to know who *we* are. Especially when we work with people from a different background, we want to be sure that

we don't try to pretend we're really like them. When you're working with people who are different from you, there's a distance between you and them that you need to respect. That's hard to do if you don't know who *you* are.

(11) *A good leader asks questions.* Asking questions is one of the best ways to get people to think, speak, and act for themselves. If leaders were only allowed three phrases, they should be "What if . . .?" "What do you think?" and "How do you feel?"

(12) *A good leader is open to new ideas.* In organizing we're always trying to learn from experience. But we also know that just because something worked the last time doesn't mean it will work this time. As a leader, you should be open to any idea the people you work with suggest, even if at first it seems unfamiliar or strange. You never know.

(13) *A good leader is flexible.* You'll find that people and events often change quickly. You need to be able to change with them. If a plan you spent a lot of time putting together depends on a certain situation and that situation changes, you have to be emotionally able to abandon your plan and come up with a new one.

(14) *A good leader is honest.* You shouldn't fool either the people you work with or yourself. You don't want to pretend that things are going well when they aren't. You need to be honest enough to tell people things they may not want to hear.

(15) *A good leader is self-disciplined.* In some situations you may be out there all alone. You need to be able to set goals for yourself and evaluate your progress. Sometimes you have to keep working even though there's no one making sure that you do.

(16) *A good leader is mature.* One of the dangers of organizing is that you may end up working out your personal problems at the expense of other people. If you're in a period of tremendous emotional change yourself, it may not be the best time to be a leader.

(17) *A good leader sets limits.* Just as you don't want to unfairly use the people you work with, you don't want them using you. If you start out doing everything for people, you'll never be

able to help them do things for themselves. You need to be able to say "No."

(18) *A good leader is courageous*. This doesn't mean that you need to be prepared to face physical danger. The courage a leader needs is of a quieter kind: keeping going when it's hard to do, being able to tell people things they don't necessarily want to hear, taking risks, opening yourself to criticism.

(19) *A good leader has vision*. In organizing, we're trying to do more than just fix up a house here or get a job there. We're trying to build a better world through people working together. A good leader has a dream of that better world.

(20) *A good leader has a sense of humor*. As a leader you see a lot of pain and suffering. It's hard not to take that suffering and pain on yourself. But you can't allow it to dominate your life. You have to laugh sometimes, too. Working with people is a serious business. But if we're all seriousness every minute of the day, it tears us apart.

You may have been surprised at this list. Maybe you expected that a leader should know a lot about government, economics, social work, strategy, tactics, federal programs, advocacy, media, public relations, foundations, grants, state agencies, legislation, lobbying. Knowing these things can be helpful. But you can learn them as you need them, or find other people who know about them. If you have most of the qualities listed above, you can be a great leader.

What skills does a leader need?

Leaders also need a wide range of skills. Of course, not every leader needs every skill. In organizing we are concerned with building cooperative teams of leaders, not superpeople who can do everything.

Because the skills of leadership can be defined and can be learned, it's possible to plan ways of becoming a more effective leader. An overall list of the skills which leaders of an organization need to share would include the following:

(1) *Working with people:* Being able to talk to people one-on-one, listen well, help them work through their own ideas, encourage their own leadership potential, motivate them, help them feel better about themselves, and push them toward making realistic commitments.

(2) *Issues:* Being able to define issues in a community, understanding what makes good issues and what makes poor issues, and being able to work with people to define their own needs and priorities.

(3) *Meetings:* Knowing how to hold a successful meeting, set an agenda, chair, deal with some of the problems that can come up in meetings, and encourage participation by all people at a meeting.

(4) *Organizations:* Understanding how organizations work, some of the different ways that organizations can be structured, and decision-making processes within an organization.

(5) *Strategy and tactics:* Knowing how to develop both long-range and short-range strategy, set goals and establish priorities, and choose and use tactics.

(6) *Money:* Understanding how to raise money for an organization both from basic sources of external fund raising and by establishing grass roots fund raising within an organization, planning budgets, and managing the finances of an organization.

(7) *Research:* Learning how to do investigative research, understanding the uses of information in developing strategy and tactics, having a sense of what information is useful and what isn't, and knowing how and where to look for information.

(8) *Communications:* Maintaining a system of communication within the organization, knowing how to use basic tools such as newsletters, leaflets, pamphlets, phone banks, and advertising, and building person-to-person systems for communicating in order to create a real group from a bunch of individuals.

(9) *Media:* Learning how to deal with public means of communication (radio, television, and the press), conduct yourself in an interview, establish working relationships with the media, in-

tegrate the media into strategy, put out a basic press release, and stage press events.

(10) *Training:* Defining the basic needs of individuals and groups, setting up training programs to meet those needs, and training people yourself.

(11) *Culture:* Learning the basic history of people's struggles, understanding some of the historic battles that people have fought in this country from which we have learned many of the lessons that we use today, helping people appreciate their own group's culture, understanding the culture that you yourself come from and how to use it as a way of giving you and other people strength, and developing a vision that is real to you of where your own work fits.

(12) *Institutions:* Developing a sense of what the important institutions are in struggles for change and having an understanding of institutions such as unions, synagogues, and churches, and learning how to work with them as part of coalitions.

(13) *Politics:* Understanding basic techniques of electoral politics and knowing how to develop electoral campaigns on issues and run candidates for public office.

(14) *Public Speaking:* Improving your ability to speak with small and large groups and being able to communicate a sense of values and visions as well as strategy and tactics.

(15) *Staff Supervision:* Helping to supervise a staff, working with other leaders to develop staff policies and procedures, learning how to hire and fire when necessary, and learning how to get the best out of staff members without letting them control your organization.

(16) *Power:* Learning how power works, who has it, how they got it, how they keep it, and how to take it away from them.

How can a person learn leadership skills?

The best way to learn leadership skills is through experience. Start small. Don't try to learn everything at once. Concentrate on learning a few basic skills at a time.

The way to do this is to find an organization and become an active member. Most people's organizations need all the help they can get. Willing volunteers are almost never turned down. Start by trying out the things you think you'd most like to do. Most people do best what they like best. If you think that you'd be especially interested in learning how to work door-to-door, start there. If you think that you'd really enjoy helping to put together fund-raising events, volunteer for that. Over time try to work at a number of different jobs within the organization. Each different thing that you do is a chance to learn new skills and to gain experience. It's also a chance to work with other people and to learn from them.

Don't try, though, to imitate the particular styles of others. You need to learn to work in harmony with your own personality, to be the kind of person that you are, not what someone else is. You can learn from another leader what some of his or her skills are. But your best strengths are going to be those that come from inside you, from the kind of person that you are. Learn to recognize your strengths and build on them.

A lot can be learned from reading. There are books on organizing in general and on the various aspects of organizing: public relations, fund raising, electoral politics, unions. There are books that talk about the histories of organizations. There are books and articles written by people who have been leaders and staff members of organizations. Reading is not a substitute for experience, but in many ways it can help you to better understand your experiences.

Develop a network of people to learn from: other leaders, staff persons, lawyers, researchers, trainers. Ask questions. Everybody likes to talk about what they do and what they know. Having this kind of network also gives you people to fall back on when you're not sure what to do yourself. They may not have the answers, but they can help you figure out the right questions.

Get as much formal training as you can. Many organizations sponsor their own training programs for leadership and staff. There are also excellent programs run by various groups to train people in organizing, fund raising, research, and administrative skills. Again, this training can't substitute for experience. But it can help you to interpret and understand your own experiences and to build specific skills. Don't try to take in all the training you can at one time. It's helpful to work for a while before attending training so that it has more meaning for you.

In all these ways you can become more skillful. But just as being "a good person" isn't enough, being skilled isn't all there is to being a good leader, either.

What makes a good leader?

It is often very difficult to tell who will be a good leader. Because our ideas of leadership so often come from what we see on television and in the newspapers, we tend to adopt the models of leadership offered to us by the corporations and by government. But these may not be the kinds of leaders we want in our organizations.

In a people's organization a leader needs to have a real commitment to democracy, to helping other people develop their own leadership skills, to including people rather than excluding them. Leaders in a people's organization need to be concerned not only with *what* is won but with *how* it is won. The process by which we fight our fights, win our victories, and suffer our defeats has a lot to do with what kind of organization we become in the long run, as well as with what kind of leaders are developed within that organization.

A leader in a people's organization—unlike a leader in business, industry, or government—should not try to establish a power base for himself or herself but should instead attempt to build a broad base of leadership and power which is shared by many people. It is far more important to be able to convince other people inside the organization to take on increased responsibility, try out new skills, and play a role in the organization than to take on all the work yourself. Organized strength comes from working together, not from one person doing it all.

Responsible leaders take seriously the needs and require-ments of their organization. They are able to achieve a balance between what the organization needs from them and the other demands in their lives. They are reliable, but they are also able to avoid the overcommitment of work, time, and emotion which causes burnout. Our leaders are too valuable for us to lose them to overwork and overload.

Good leaders are people who are respected by their friends, their neighbors, their families, and the people they work with. An organization is judged by its leaders. The leaders are who the public sees; to the public, they *are* the organization. So it is important that our leaders be the kind of people that members of the organization are proud to be represented by.

This can be a delicate issue. Sometimes a leader is good *except for* his or her position on a particular issue. Sometimes you hear, for example, that a particular leader is good *except for* his feelings about women. *Except for*'s like this are dangerous. We have to be clear about the principles we have in our organiza-tions. The membership of the organization and the new lead-ership will be educated by the old leadership. Too many *except for*'s in the leadership core will result in an *organization* that is good *except for*. These *except for*'s, because they serve to divide people and because they exclude people, will in the long run undermine and can even destroy an organization.

A leader needs to have a base. By a base we mean a group of people who see that individual as their leader. Too often when we talk about leaders what we really mean are the people who speak well. But often these people speak only for themselves. Unfortu-nately, in some organizing campaigns leaders without followers seem to surface more quickly than anyone else. These people may simply like the publicity. They enjoy being the focus of attention. Sometimes they are actually working with other orga-nizations to take over our organization and destroy it from within.

However inspiring it may be to have leaders who can make flowery speeches, it is far more important that they influence and are able to lead people within the organization. If someone does not have a base, if she or he does not actually influence other members of the organization, then that person is not a real leader. Our leaders need to be judged by what they do, not simply by what they say.

Our leaders should help us remember the values that underlie our work. They can remind us of the history of people in this country who have fought for their rights. They can help us feel a part of that history, part of a growing and increasingly strong movement to change this society to benefit the majority of the people in it.

This kind of inspiring vision is often the base of leadership ability. But it doesn't need to be seen only in impassioned speeches. Leaders can be quiet and gentle. They can listen far more than they talk. If they are able to bring out the best in the people with whom they work, then they are truly leaders.

What makes a bad leader?

There are a number of qualities that we want to avoid if possible in leaders. One is a lack of respect for others. However much we know, other people's opinions and judgments are still valuable. The leader who stops listening to other members, who begins to feel that he or she knows all the answers, is not helping the organization.

It is bad when leaders begin pushing others around. Sometimes leaders pick up this tendency from staff in an organization. Sometimes we pick it up from the models of leadership that we see at work. We are all familiar with the boss who hollers at everybody in the office or in the plant: "Do this, do that, I want to see this floor shining, I want to see this letter typed in five minutes." That's not the way we should be getting things done in our organizations. The fact that you as a leader begin to develop a certain amount of power within an organization doesn't give you the right to treat people the way that management does.

Leaders can also become unreliable. You probably know people who always promise to be in a certain place at a certain time and then never show up. Everyone will make a mistake now and then. Everybody has emergencies. Everyone forgets sometimes. But the so-called leader who consistently fails to show up when there is work to be done, but seems to be always present when it's time to speak in front of the cameras and reporters, is not much of a leader.

Another problem with leaders stems from personal troubles that interfere with their effectiveness. People have a right to their personal lives. But when those personal lives begin to affect the organization, the rights and needs of the organization also must be considered. The leader who habitually drinks too much, who uses drugs openly, who is known in the community for "running around," who is openly sexist or racist, will eventually become a problem to the organization. Remember that the organization will be judged by its leaders and by what they do personally as well as by what the organization does officially. We need to be careful of leaders whose personal lives are unstable to the point that they begin affecting the organization.

We need to be careful of leaders who have close ties of friendship, kinship, or work with the opposition. It's not that easy to separate what you do from who you are. A leader who is close kin to the management of a plant, a leader who lives next door to the supervisor, a leader who spends free time out with the boss, may or may not have the best interest of the organization at hand. But such leaders will always be suspect, at least in the eyes of some members, and they are open to influences that may undercut their commitment.

We also need to be careful of leaders who are unwilling to accept group discipline. Most of us have run into this kind of leader. We may have even been guilty of it at some time ourselves. This kind of leader is always going off and speaking for the organization without first finding out the organization's position. But a position of leadership in an organization is a position of trust. It's not a license to go off saying what you think in the name of the organization. Rather, it's a responsibility to find out what the people in the organization think, to make sure the organization has made its own decision before announcing it in public.

Decisions need to be made organizationally. Once a decision is made, the leaders of the organization need to take the responsibility for carrying it out. Leaders who are unwilling to accept this type of group discipline and who insist on doing things on their own and according to their own judgment will cause difficulties within the organization.

How many leaders does an organization need?

The kind of leadership we read about in the history books can best be described as one-person leadership. In the past this often meant one-*man* leadership. It's like the stories of the knight on horseback who all on his own is going to kill the dragon. A people's organization, on the other hand, needs as many leaders as it can get. Remember that one of the most important roles of an individual leader in a people's organization is to produce other leaders. It also helps to remember the size of the dragon—just how many heads it has.

There are many reasons why a people's organization needs a variety of leaders. We need different leaders because that is one way we appeal to different people. Also, people will judge the possibility of playing a role themselves in the organization by what they see in the leadership.

You see this very clearly in union organizing campaigns. Sometimes the problems of organizing in general can be seen especially clearly in union organizing because organizing unions depends on being able to prove the support of a majority of people in the workplace. In a neighborhood, several dozen residents out of several hundred may be able to force the city to negotiate with them. Inside a plant, however, management cannot legally sit down and negotiate a contract with the workers' union unless it represents over 50 percent of the employees. Union organizing is of necessity majority organizing. So in union organizing you learn fairly quickly that your organizing committee needs to represent all the different kinds of people that work in the plant. For example, suppose you're working to organize a plant which is one-third white, one-third black, and one-third Hispanic, with equal numbers of old and young workers and equal numbers of men and women. If the organizing committee is composed mostly of young black men, you're going to have a hard time attracting the whites, Hispanics, women, and older workers. An effective organizing committee has to represent the cross section of people that the organization seeks to attract as members. So we need a broad leadership group rather than a few individuals, however good these individuals may be.

Sometimes this means that we need to go more slowly than we otherwise would. Let's go back to the union organizing example. What often happens is that some groups in a plant are more anxious to move than others. It might be that the black workers, because of discriminatory practices by management, are much more anxious to organize a union than the white and Hispanic workers. However, since these black workers comprise only one-third of the work force, they will need to attract other workers to the union if they are to be successful in organizing the plant. This means that they need to add white and Hispanic leadership to the organizing committee, plus women and older workers. They will probably have to put off taking public action until this is done.

Sometimes leaders make the mistake of thinking it is better to get something going right away and that we can always add the other groups to the committee later. This is just like the *except for* problem. There is no such thing as an organizing committee which is representative *except for* women, or *except for* blacks, or *except for* older people. The leadership group has to be made up of the same people that in the long run are going to make up the organization.

In most communities this means a broad leadership group. That group should represent all of the different constituencies we are trying to organize: by race, by language, by ethnic group, by gender, by geography, by age. For example, if we are organizing public housing tenants in a city, the leadership needs to include a representative from each of the housing projects, as well as representatives of other groups.

We also need to have a broad leadership group because no matter what we do we will lose some leaders. They may become tired of what they are doing. They may burn out. They may come under pressure from their families to take on less responsibility. They may change jobs to a position which brings them into more contact with the power structure. They may sell out. They may move away. They may die or become too sick to work effectively.

We shouldn't expect that all of our leaders will continue as leaders. Over time much of the leadership of any organization is bound to change. If we haven't done a good job of developing new groups of leadership, who will lead the organization?

We also need a leadership group rather than a few individuals because not all leaders are the same. People have very different skills. Some leaders are good at chairing a meeting. Some leaders are good at sitting quietly in a meeting and making one or two points that are important to reaching a decision. Some leaders operate best in front of a camera, others on the front porch or in the living room of someone's home. Some leaders are visionaries. Others are hardheaded, practical thinkers who are always remembering the small details that make something go right.

We need all of these different kinds of skills. No one person has all of the skills we need in a leadership group. Some of these are conflicting skills and can't be found in the same person. The tension between the practical details and the long-range vision, between the public speaker and the quiet behind-the-scenes negotiator, are real conflicts that an organization must deal with in order to stay healthy.

Large leadership groups also allow us to rotate leadership. One of the problems that you often see in an organization as it grows older is that leadership becomes set in its ways. If someone has been chair of an organization for five years, that organization begins in some ways to resemble that person. Other people are bound to resent that kind of continuing leadership, especially if it doesn't provide room for them to play a role as leaders also.

In addition, when only one or two people are in the leadership of an organization, they are tremendously exposed. They are subjected to pressures by the opposition, to harassment, to intimidation, to attempts to buy them off. The organization becomes so identified with them personally that it is difficult to get the power structure or the press to listen to anybody else. We need to build in very early in the organizing the principle of rotating leadership, so that there always are many people who can be asked to speak for the organization. We want to encourage a leadership group in which the leaders depend on each other rather than having the entire group depend on them.

How can leaders best work together?

One of the best qualities a leader can have is an ability to work cooperatively with other leaders. If you start working with an organization that's already there, you'll probably find yourself part of either an informal or a formal team.

Working as part of a group has many advantages. You feel less isolated. You can benefit from the ideas that others have. You have a chance to watch other people working and to learn from them. You have a sense of solidarity. If nothing else, the chances are fairly good that on a day when you're depressed, at least one other person is feeling good enough to help cheer you up.

But working as part of an organizing team also can include problems. There can be competition among the different people for who is going to do what, for who is going to be the most recognized. Different members of the team may have different ideas about what's necessary to do. Sometimes the problems between leaders can become serious enough to tear an organization apart.

The problem of working together needs to be approached systematically, just like an organizing campaign. It's usually helpful to get together regularly to talk over what's going on, to divide up the work, to criticize each other constructively. Sometimes it's useful to have one person coordinate the work of the team so that there are fewer missed signals and less poor communication. When you're working with a team, take advantage of the chance to spend time with the other team members. Go with them when they're working. Watch how they do things. Everybody has special skills that they've developed. Everyone has his or her own way of handling different situations. Watch how other leaders talk to people, how they present themselves, how they talk about issues. If you borrow a little bit from a lot of people, you can add to your own basic strengths as a leader and organizer.

How can someone work best on her or his own?

Suppose there is no organization to work with. Let's say that you're the one who's going to do something. You're angry about what's going on, and you want to organize around it. But you have no organization, no organizers, no leaders to work with.

In a situation like this, do it yourself. But try as quickly as possible to find other people who, even if they're not any more experienced than you are, are willing to work with you. Some of the ideas in this book can be used to lay out a strategy for your campaign, and for beginning to build an organization.

It would also make sense to try as quickly as possible to make links with a person or organization that has had this kind of experience and that could help you. Organizing can be very hard, lonely work. Even those of us who have been doing it for a long time often get the feeling that we're in way over our heads. Sometimes we are. When you start getting that feeling, it's helpful to have someone else to talk to, someone who has been doing it for a while, if only to have that person tell you that the feeling of being up to your neck in quicksand is normal—as well as to give you some advice on how to get out.

How can a person monitor his or her own work?

One of the most useful skills to a leader is learning to monitor his or her own work. Depending on the organization that you're working with, other people may or may not tell you what you're doing right and wrong. But it's important to be able to set goals for yourself and to measure what you do against those goals. These need to be both personal and organizational goals.

Start with the lists of leadership qualities and skills in this chapter. Every month or so go back to them and ask yourself, "What have I learned about each of these particular qualities or skills? What skills do I have now that I didn't a month ago?" If you find that you're not learning a particular skill, try to find a way to put yourself in a situation where you can learn it.

Set goals. If you've decided to build an organization in your neighborhood, make a schedule for how you expect your work to go. Figure out how many people you want to see, when you want to have your first meeting, how soon you want other leaders to begin taking responsibility inside the organization. Sit down regularly and compare the work that you're doing with the goals that you set for yourself.

If you're falling short, it doesn't necessarily mean that you're doing anything wrong. It's hard to predict exactly how an organizing campaign is going to go. But you will at least have a sense of where you wanted things to go and where they are really going. Keep written records: who you saw, what they said, what issues were important, what meetings were scheduled, who came, what was done, what strategies were adopted, what actions were planned. Over time these kinds of records help you to know if you're working effectively. For example, if your records start to show a steady drop in attendance at meetings, you need to take a look and see what's happening. If you go back through your records and realize that people you saw six months ago haven't been seen since, you need to do something about it.

Keeping records and setting goals helps you to measure the progress of your own work. It's also useful to have someone else helping to monitor your work. Ask another leader, a staff member of the organization, or a friend to help you do that. Involve the other person in setting goals. Every once in a while sit down with him or her to talk through how you're doing. Sometimes someone else can help us to see things that we ourselves can't see as well.

What are some of the dangers to watch for with leaders?

Many things can happen to individual leaders that can be damaging to the work they're doing and to the organization.

Sometimes leaders become too concerned with their own power. They decide that the more power they have, the better off they are. So they start grabbing power and refusing to share it with others. Check yourself to be sure that you are still working *with* other people. Leaders can start thinking they are so important that they hold on to their power at the expense of the organization.

Sometimes leaders get lazy. They feel that they no longer have to do the work they did when they were starting out. They order members, other leaders, and staff of the organization to do things. But part of being a good leader is always continuing to do at least some of the things that you did when you were starting out. A willingness to do all kinds of work helps motivate others to do it, too.

The opposite problem is leaders who overwork themselves. The organization becomes so important to them that they spend every waking hour working for it. They exhaust themselves physically and emotionally. But a leader on the edge of collapse isn't much use to anybody or to an organization. We are building for the long haul, to make this a better world for everyone. This is not going to happen in five years or ten years. We need leaders who can work not just for a year or two but for thirty and forty and fifty years. It's better to work slowly and carefully for a long time, steadily gaining skills and experience, than to burn out quickly.

Leaders sometimes start thinking that they speak for everyone, whether or not they were asked for their opinion. They're always willing to make public pronouncements on any issue regardless of what their organization thinks. But a leader's responsibility is to *represent* people, not to think for them and act for them. It's the organization's responsibility to make decisions and to hold leaders accountable to the organization. It's the leader's responsibility to help that happen.

Sometimes leaders start thinking that their power is personal, that they're listened to because of who they are rather than because of the people that they represent. Such leaders will sometimes start telling staff or other members of the organization what they're supposed to do. But the power of a leader in a people's organization comes through the power and structures of the organization. Decisions have to be made by and through those structures: the boards, the committees, the chapters. Leaders should not speak for the organization. The organization should speak through its leaders.

What are the responsibilities of a leader?

The responsibilities of a leader cannot be separated from the needs of his or her organization. A leader needs to think of the welfare and health of the organization, of its needs and priorities. Decisions have to be made by whatever process the organization has set up to make those decisions: small group meetings, committee meetings, chapter meetings, board meetings. Leaders need to have the patience to wait until those decisions are carried out, as well as the determination to make sure that they get results.

People's organizations need a broad base of power, not a few individuals speaking for them. It is the responsibility of the leaders of an organization to make sure that the base stays broad. It is the responsibility of the membership to see that individual leaders stay accountable to the organization.

How does a leader relate to other leaders?

People's organizations need collective leadership—groups of leaders with different backgrounds, skills, and experiences who can help each other out. What people's organizations don't need is one strong leader who dominates. But building collective leadership is difficult. There are often natural feelings of competitiveness among leaders. There may be competition for elected offices within the organization because of some of the benefits they bring, such as travel or possible staff positions. A responsible leader will take the initiative in trying to build this kind of cooperative relationship, however difficult it may be to achieve.

How does a leader relate to staff?

Some people's organizations hire part-time or full-time staff to do part of the work. This staff is responsible to the leadership and membership of the organization, but that responsibility is on an organizational, not a personal, basis. There is a particular line of authority through which decisions are reached within the organization and communicated to staff. For example, a recommendation may be made by a committee. The committee reports to the board of directors of the organization, which adopts the recommendation as an official position. This decision is communicated to the staff director, who in turn passes it on to the staff.

Clearly leadership is involved in this type of decision-making process. On the other hand, an individual leader doesn't have the right to take an individual staff person aside and say, "Here's what I want you to do," unless that authority has actually been delegated to that leader. Remember that your authority as a leader comes through the organization. You need to respect these lines of authority in order to play your part in keeping the organization strong and healthy.

How much power should a leader have?

We are building organizations of people who as individuals and families are relatively powerless. It would be nice if all powerless people as they began to achieve power through the organization were able to handle it without any problems. But it's natural to expect that certain problems are going to come with new power. When someone who has never had any recognition in her life is suddenly being chased after by television and newspaper reporters, and asked her opinion on every issue under the sun, it sometimes goes to her head. When someone who has never played any such role finds himself on the board of directors of an organization with a staff of 100 people, he may start to think that he as a person is powerful. But the power of grass roots leaders must be power through their organizations, not personal power.

A leader can provide vision. A leader can give a sense of direction. A leader can work to make an organization more responsive and responsible. A leader can inspire members of staff and other leaders. All of these capabilities involve different kinds of power. But that power must be used responsibly. The power of a leader in a people's organization needs to be used to build power for other people. The only power that lasts comes from this kind of careful building.

How much time should a leader put in?

There is no set amount of time that is right or wrong for a leader to work in an organization. What most leaders run into are the realities of the rest of their lives, the fact that they have families, jobs, obligations, and personal needs that make it impossible for them to work full-time for an organization. Over time these kinds of conflicts begin to build up. It will be different in different cases. Some leaders may start feeling pressure from their families to spend more time at home—not an unreasonable request if a leader has been spending sixty, seventy, or eighty hours a week with an organization. At the same time the organization may be making more and more demands on that person, especially if a second level of leadership has not been developed. Leaders who have a problem being able to delegate work and responsibility may find themselves working harder and harder as time goes on. At the same time, they may begin to find themselves resentful of staff, who are paid for the time they put in, whereas leadership is not.

Generally leaders tend to overwork rather than underwork. A typical pattern is for a leader to start putting almost all of his or her free time into the organization. Then, as the other pressures build up—from family, from jobs, from friends, from personal life, from emotional demands—the person cuts back suddenly. It's far better to try to figure out what is an amount of time that can be put into the organization on a long-term regular basis. It's better to have leadership that works ten hours a week for ten years than leadership that works eighty hours a week for two.

How does a person deal with the emotional pressures of being a leader?

Overwork is only one problem that can affect leaders in people's organizations. Even in the best of times, organizing is an emotionally hazardous occupation. People involved in organizing have unusually high levels of emotional pressures: burnout, marital problems, alcoholism, drug abuse, and other symptoms related to overwork and stress. In the worst of times, when the leadership of people's organizations is being harassed, intimidated, followed, interrogated, and physically abused, these pressures can mount uncontrollably.

The long-term survival of leadership is critical to the growth of a people's movement in this country. In the past we've paid too little attention to the skills needed for survival. But these skills are necessary to every individual who has a role as a leader within a people's organization.

There are a number of ways in which you as a leader can deal with the emotional problems and pressures of organizing.

(1) *Try to avoid overwork.* Learn to delegate responsibility rather than taking on whatever comes your way. Set limits on the amount of time you're available to work.

(2) *Set goals that are reasonable and manageable.* Reasonable goals will help you measure your progress. They'll help you avoid the feeling of frustration that comes when everything seems to be happening at once.

(3) *Develop a personal support system.* Try to find several people you can talk to about the emotional pressures that you encounter as well as the political problems that you have to solve.

(4) *Preserve time for yourself.* Make yourself a resolution that no matter how crowded the day or how critical the issue you'll still take time to do something that is important to you. Spend time with your spouse, your friends, or your children. Play a game of tennis or softball. Watch television. Read a book. Do whatever it is that relaxes you. No one, no matter how skilled, no matter how dedicated, no matter how experienced, no matter how visionary, no matter how political, can work sixteen hours a day, day after day, without cracking up. Don't allow yourself to be guilt-tripped into driving yourself crazy. Every person is too valuable to us to lose people to burnout and overwork.

(5) *Take time to celebrate.* Sometimes because the problems we deal with in our organizing are so critical, we tend to become overly serious. People can't survive without humor, without laughter, without enjoyment, without pleasure. Try to build this into your organizing. Victories should be celebrated with the people you work with, by yourself, with the people that you care about.

The kind of world we build is determined in many ways by how we build it. We have to begin working in ways that reflect how we want to work. If the lifestyle of our leadership means they're unable to sustain a long-range struggle, we will have a problem in convincing other people to also want to become leaders.

Leadership in people's organizations should be consistent with family, home, work, religion, community, and other commitments that people have. Leaders need to set an example so that other people feel that they also can take leadership roles.

How does a leader's role change as the organization matures?

There are cycles of leadership, just as there are cycles for organizations and for people. As you grow in experience, as you gain skills, your own visions expand. You look for new challenges, new ways of doing things, different ways of making an impact.

Some leaders find that they are satisfied to stay with an organization for a long period of time. They begin to take an increasingly senior role in decision making. They become important in developing new leadership. They spend more time with questions of policy, strategy, and long-range visions.

Sometimes a leader will choose to step back from the formal decision-making process. It's not unusual for the president or chairperson of an organization to decide to step down after a number of years in office. Such a person might move on to a different role in the organization. This role might be as a staff person or as a senior advisor to the organization. This kind of change in leadership of an organization can often be healthy and constructive, especially if it's prepared for carefully. Leaders tend to set their mark on an organization. But over a period of time, if there are no changes in the leadership, an organization may become less flexible and creative. It makes sense for new leadership to move in. This doesn't mean that the old leadership failed. Transition and change can make for new ideas, bring new people in, inject new blood into the organization.

A changeover in leadership may also be necessary as a way of developing a broader leadership group nationally. We need to have more people who have the experience of playing different roles in a people's organization. Opening up positions in an organization to new leaders helps give them the experience to develop themselves, their skills, their abilities, their visions.

At the same time we also begin to develop a group of leaders who have the potential to play other roles nationally in the growing movement for change in this country. There is a tremendous need for staff persons of people's organizations. Too often the staff in people's organizations are young, relatively inexperienced college graduates who do not come from the same backgrounds as the people they are organizing. They do not have the experience of being organized themselves or of being leaders in a people's organization. As we build a movement for change nationally, we should develop staff persons who have these experiences. We need people who can look back on the day when they said, "I could never be like that." We need people who at one point lacked the self-confidence to speak in public. We need people who took the first steps to build neighborhood organizations and community groups, who learned the skills of leadership by leading, who developed their abilities as organizers by organizing. We need those people who have served as leaders in our organizations, who have spoken not simply for themselves but for their constituencies, who have learned to represent organizations and individuals. The special skills that these people bring make them excellent candidates for staff positions in people's organizations. Increasingly our organizations must look to their own leadership and to the leadership of other people's organizations for their staff.

Where can a leader find other leaders?

One of the most valuable things that a leader can do for an organization is to find and develop other leaders. But where do you find them?

Start with the people already inside the organization for whom you have the most respect, the people who honor their commitments, who deliver what they promise. Think about the people who are always there when you need them, who are always willing to do the work, who don't mind taking risks. Think about the people who seem to get along with people, who have an ability to motivate people.

Sometimes it helps to look for people who have previous organizational experience. If you're building a community organization, some of the people in the group who are union members may already have experience in leadership roles. They may understand some of the things an organization needs to do, which can be helpful in building another organization. Remember, though, that different organizations operate differently. Not all organizations teach people the values of cooperation and working together.

Most people will say, if you ask them, "I don't know anything about organizing." But many people do have experience working inside an organization. They may have this experience as a part of their church or synagogue group. It may come from the union that they belong to. It may come from experiences in student government. It may come from being a member of or even helping to organize a CB club, a motorcycle club, a charitable organization. The same skills that go into building these types of organizations are useful in building a people's organization.

When you find people that you think have leadership potential, encourage them. Let them work along with you. Give them the sense of what you do as a leader. Help them go through the same process that you are going through, learning skills, becoming familiar with the organization, getting to know the people in it. Help them to develop the skills of working with people individually and in small groups, handling communications, dealing with the media, putting together actions, negotiating, planning, developing strategies, and choosing tactics.

In the long run nothing is more valuable than the leaders we develop. Someone who has been a leader in one organization can go on to help many other organizations. There is a tremendous lack of this kind of leadership. If we are really to have changes in this society we need hundreds and thousands of people who know how to play this kind of leadership role.

No one else will do the work of developing leadership for us. The colleges and universities are not about to start turning out people's leaders who will challenge the way things are run now. Members of Congress are not going to resign in order to become the leaders of community organizations. Major corporations are not about to loan us their key people to aid us as our strategists. If we are to have enough people resources to really change this country, we ourselves have to help those people to develop.

Will we ever have enough leaders?

People are always talking about the lack of leadership in our country today. They talk most about it in an election year. Will the presidential candidate be the kind of person who can lead this country? Will the senators and congressional representatives provide the kind of leadership we need so badly? Where are those who have the wisdom and the courage to lead us out of the troubles we're in today? Why don't we have leaders like we used to?

Well, actually the problem is that we do have leaders like we used to. The United States has all the leaders it needs. The problem is that they're on the other side of the fence from most of the people in this country. Do you want to find leaders? Look at the heads of the corporations. Look at the presidents of the oil companies. Look at the officers of the banks and insurance firms. Look at the real estate speculators. Look at the politicians who take either direct bribes or indirect ones in the form of campaign contributions to do favors for the rich and powerful. These people are leading this country, and they are leading it down a path that means disaster for most poor and working people, whose powerlessness is needed for those on top to stay there.

What the United States needs today is not more leaders but

the right kind of leaders. We need more people in leadership who are there to serve the real interests of the American people, not the special interests that already have so much power over all of our lives. We need leaders who are sensitive to building a really democratic society, one that respects people because of race, creed, national origin, and sexual preference and not in spite of them. We need leaders who have the experience of leading that comes out of their neighborhoods, communities, and workplaces.

Today, most of the so-called leaders of our country come not out of popular movements and local organizations but out of law schools. Something like three-quarters of the people in Congress are lawyers—which explains a lot about the kind of laws that get made in this country. We need leaders who have the experience of having been followers, who have been a part of organizing efforts, who know what it is to work in a regular job, who know what it is to be without wealth and power, who know how hard it can be to make ends meet. We need leaders who are responsive to people's needs.

Hopefully we will reach a point in this country where a person doesn't need to be a lawyer to be a leader. Now, this won't happen because the lawyers step aside to make room for poor and working people. But as all of us build power through our neighborhood organizations, our community organizations, and our unions, we can begin to take more of that power. In some areas people have come out of neighborhood and community organizations and been elected to public office. As we improve our organizing and our skills, more and more poor and working people's organizations will be able to elect their members and leaders to political offices.

Leaders are the heart of an organization. Leaders with skill and dedication do wonderful things in building the strength of a people's organization. But organizations also help to develop leaders. In some ways leaders are the most important product of the organizing process.

Leadership is not an easy role. The process of developing the skills, the abilities, and the experiences is a long one. The personal toll that many leaders pay is high. But there is no other thing as necessary to the struggle for change. Leaders create a sense of the possible. The best leaders in their own lives and work project to others a vision of the future for which we are all working.

3. Organizations

ORGANIZING. ORGANIZER. ORGANIZATION. These three words come from the same root word. They show the relationship between organizations, organizers, and organizing. An organizer is a person who does organizing. Organizing means building organizations.

Organizing is a way for people to work together to solve their problems. Let's take a look at some of the other ways in which these problems are often dealt with.

One approach to problems is called *service*. In service work someone is solving the problems of another person. The welfare agency does service work. The caseworkers who visit a welfare recipient are (in theory, at least) supposed to be serving that person. Most government programs designed to aid the poor are service programs. They provide something to a person, sometimes whether that person wants it or not.

Social service is a traditional approach to the problems of the poor which has been used for a long time in this country. It has its roots in the old ideas of charity and helping the poor which you find in the Bible. Around the end of the last century, some people began to examine these ideas of charity and say, "Rather than simply giving money or food to the poor, why don't we find ways of helping them help themselves?" One of the leaders in this movement was Jane Addams, who founded a settlement house in Chicago called Hull House. These ideas led to government programs such as Social Security, unemployment insurance, old-age assistance, Medicare, and Medicaid.

The important thing to remember about service programs is that they involve somebody trying to help someone else. They treat each individual separately. They do not in any way build power for people.

A second approach to solving problems is called *advocacy*. Advocacy is when a person speaks for somebody else or for a group of people. Lawyers are advocates. When a lawyer goes into court and says, "Your honor, my clients are being denied their rights of due process by being evicted without notice," that lawyer is serving as an advocate for those people.

An advocate tries to change the way in which agencies or institutions operate. Sometimes an advocate can even operate without the knowledge of the people he or she is representing. Because people do not usually participate in the process of advocacy, it doesn't change the way in which they relate to each other or to the power structure. Advocacy may make real improvements in people's lives. It may change the operating conditions of agencies or institutions. But it does little to alter the relationship of power between these institutions and the people who deal with them.

A third approach to solving problems is called *mobilizing*. Mobilizing begins to involve people in controlling their own lives. When 100 senior citizens go down to the courthouse to protest cutbacks in emergency fuel assistance, they are mobilizing. In mobilization people may testify, they may march, they may picket, they may write letters to the editor or to the president of the company, they may make phone calls. They may use all of the strategies and tactics that are also used in organizing. The difference is that mobilizing usually concentrates on one short-term issue and doesn't attempt to build a permanent organization. It does give people a sense of their own power and is often a step that leads to organizing.

All of these methods may bring about real changes for people. The first two methods, service and advocacy, because they do not involve people in taking steps to control their own lives, usually cannot bring about lasting change. People do not learn through advocacy and service the skills to change their lives: the methods of working together, making decisions, planning strategies and choosing tactics, taking action, putting pressure on the opposition. They do not learn the way to solve the problem the next time. Service and advocacy may make the immediate situation somewhat better, but they do not even begin to change the long-term relationships of power and control. Mobilizing and organizing do.

Some people feel that it's better not to build organizations, that organizations by their nature tend to become bureaucracies, to become corrupt, to make people think in noncreative and rigid ways. They argue that it's important to involve people in solving their own problems, but that this is best done by mobilizing each time a new issue comes around.

But organizations have many advantages. When you begin building a permanent organization, the people who are a part of it learn to work together as a regular group. If you have to mobilize each time you have a new issue, you may end up with different people each time. An organization has continuity. It has members and leaders who gain experience from issue to issue. An organization has an independent financial base (usually developed after long periods of careful work), whereas in mobilizing you need to pass the hat each time to get the necessary funds. In an organization you can build into today's issue the issues that you will tackle tomorrow, with each strategy adding strength to the next.

When you look at all the problems that most of us have to

face, it seems clear that only powerful permanent organizations will eventually be able to solve them. Certainly the opposition—the corporations, the banks, the political parties—would not consider being anything except permanent organizations. They know the strength that comes with organization. Can you imagine the slumlords in your community only getting together when they had an emergency or crisis? Of course not. They have a continuing organization that works to protect their self-interest, that makes long-range plans, that strategizes. We pay the price for how well they're organized. We need to learn the same lesson and organize ourselves as well.

It's true that sometimes short-term goals can be achieved without an organization. But when you consider the amount of work that goes into mobilizing around even a small issue, it makes sense to take the next step, to build on mobilization, to build on the victory and create an organization that can continue to fight for the real needs of its members over a long period of time.

How does an organization get started?

Organizations are started in different ways. Sometimes people have gotten together and mobilized around a community, neighborhood, or workplace issue. In the course of mobilizing they recognize the strength that they have when they work and act together. Someone asks, "What are we going to do when this is over? Are we just going to go back to the way we were? Or are we going to take a lesson from what we've learned and continue the fight?"

Many organizations are born from this kind of questioning. Good leaders ask these questions when they become involved in a hot issue in their community. Say to the people that you're working with, "Look, we made a good start. Look at how much we've done in just three weeks. Are we going to let this all fall apart? Or are we going to really do something with what we've put together? Are we going to keep this going and start talking about some of the other problems we never before thought we could deal with? Here we've won something we never thought we could win. Look at how much more we could do if we kept going together.''

Organizations are started in other ways as well. Sometimes organizers go out and start organizations. Some very good organizations have been started because organizers who had been working in one area decided to go somewhere else and build an organization. They may have decided there was a good issue that could serve as the first step for that organization. They might have been part of a national network or a statewide coalition which was trying to start a number of local independent organizations. They may simply have wanted to be in that place at that time.

If you've been thinking about the different problems in your community or group, you might consider starting an organization as a way of beginning to deal with them. This is a somewhat different approach from simply saying, ''We have to do something about the lack of garbage service here in the community.'' You would begin by saying to the people you live near or work near, ''You know, this community has a lot of problems. I've been thinking for a while that maybe we ought to all get together and see what we could do about them. The people on the rich side of town have neighborhood organizations. When they want something, their organization goes before the city council and gets it. We ought to consider doing the same thing.''

One reason this is a good approach to take is that if you are going to build an organization, it's helpful to be clear about it from the very first step. If you're mobilizing—trying to get as many people as you can to a city council meeting or to an administrative hearing or to protest in front of a private company— you're not too concerned with what might happen a month or two down the road. But if you're building an organization as well, you need to pay special attention to how you put it together.

Organizations can be very difficult and complicated creations. As an organization gets older, all kinds of problems can begin to appear. Leadership can become tired and burn out. There can be internal fights among the members and leaders, as well as fights between the members, leaders, and staff. Certain personalities can start to dominate the organization. Funds can dry up. The organization can become unclear about its goals and priorities. People may have an image of the organization that prevents them from joining up.

All of these are common problems. But many of them can in some cases be partly prevented by the way in which the organization is built from the start. Careful planning and building can do much to make an organization more effective in the long run.

How can you start an organization?

Let's say that you've made the decision that your group or community needs an organization. You've decided to take the lead in helping put one together. Where do you start? What do you do?

Some people will say that the first thing to do is to call a meeting for the entire community. Get everyone there, announce that an organization is about to be formed, and have people select the name, officers, and bylaws.

There are dangers in this approach. If you start anything, including an organization, before people have had a chance to think through carefully what it means, it may be born in a very different way from what you were thinking of, and may have defects that prevent it from functioning as a healthy organization.

It's much better if you go around and see a number of the people that you think would be key in putting together the organization. Talk to them individually. Get their ideas. Share your ideas with them. Talk about what an organization would mean, what it could do, who could be involved in it. Try to develop some common ideas among these people as to what the organization would be and would do.

This initial group of people can be the organizing committee for the organization. If you're putting together something on your block, you may be able to do all the work yourself. But if you're trying to start something larger—an organization that covers part of a small town or an organization of all the seniors in a medium-sized city—it'll take a lot more than just you to get the job done.

Bring people in from the first step. Let them be included in the thinking, planning, and decision making. If they feel that they were a part of the organization from the start, they'll be more loyal and committed to the organization.

It would make sense for the organizing committee to do some of the preliminary planning for the organization before trying to bring people together in larger groups. The organizing committee does not necessarily make all of the decisions. But it should work on thinking about what the decisions are and how they should be made. One of the responsibilities of a leader is to help other members of the group, including other leaders, make decisions in a healthy, constructive way. You can begin this process with your own organizing committee by asking questions, making definitions, planning, and thinking.

There are many decisions to make about an organization. What size should it be? Who should join it? What structure should it have? Should it incorporate? Should it have elected officials? Should it be nonprofit? Should it have chapters, if it's a large organization? If it's a small organization, should it affiliate with a larger one? Is it going to focus on a single issue or on many issues? Let's look at some of these questions and some of the ways a decision could be reached on each of them.

What size should an organization be?

Someone once asked Abraham Lincoln how long a person's legs should be. Lincoln answered, "Long enough to reach from their waist to the ground."

There is no right size for an organization. An organization

needs to be large enough to get the job done, but small enough so that everyone involved feels a sense of belonging and participation.

Who should the members of an organization be?

Sometimes people feel that an organization should represent everyone in a community or group. That would only be true if everyone in the community or group was on your side. Since this is almost never the case, it's usually best to restrict membership to those persons who are directly affected by the issue or issues that the organization is concerned with, and who share the organization's position. You don't want to have people in the organization who are members of the opposition or who may be targets of your tactics. An organization's members should share beliefs and goals, including common feelings about who the opposition is.

In an extreme case, members of the opposition may even join an organization for the purpose of destroying it from within. For example, a group fighting strip mining had the operator of a strip mine become a member. The strip miner then used his membership rights to create problems for the organization. In one instance he demanded a list of all the members, which he obviously intended to pass out to other strip-mine operators. In this case, a statement limiting membership to people who were against strip mining would have prevented the strip-mine operator from becoming a member and an inside force working against the organization.

Membership should be open to anyone who shares the basic goals and principles of the organization and who is directly affected by the issues. If you want to include people in the organization who are not directly affected, you might consider creating a separate category of nonvoting members so that supporters do not also become a part of the organization's decision-making process.

What is a good structure for a people's organization?

A good structure for a people's organization is one that gives people a sense of belonging and participation, a chance to say what they think, and the opportunity to play a meaningful role in the organization. Like so many things in organizing, this is easier said than done.

This is a different way of looking at how to structure an organization than the way most large organizations such as government agencies and corporations structure themselves. These organizations are not concerned with whether or not most people who belong to or work for them have a sense of participation. They want to be able to make decisions quickly and carry them out. They are concerned with power and how to exercise it as efficiently as possible.

Our organizations are concerned with power, too. But we recognize that our power comes from the people who are our members. An organization which cannot build and keep a membership base will not have power.

One of the ways of thinking about how to structure our organizations is to understand that we want them to be large but feel small. This means breaking them down into working units. A citywide organization, for example, can be organized block by block. Each block club is small enough so that people still have a sense of belonging. When they go to their block club meeting, they see ten, twenty, or thirty people that they know personally. They are important in their block club even though the organization's citywide membership may be in the thousands. This structure is also used in union organizing, where people often meet by shifts, departments, or jobs.

Another way to keep the feeling of smallness is to have chapters. Chapters can deal with local issues. They serve as a training ground for new leaders. Issues that might divide the whole organization could still be worked on if the local chapter members wanted to. It's also important that chapter members feel they have a voice in the decision making that goes on beyond the chapter level. It's helpful to figure out systems of representation that give the members of each chapter a voice at all levels of the organization.

What is a good leadership structure for a people's organization?

In the chapter about leaders we talked about some of the problems that may arise when an individual or small group holds official leadership positions. Such people may begin to dominate the organization. A small leadership group sometimes cuts off newer leadership and makes it more difficult to build depth of leadership within the organization. A small group of leaders also makes a tempting target for the opposition. It's easier to pressure three or four people than thirty or forty.

At the same time, there are real advantages to having a small leadership group. The leaders can be the people with whom members and other leaders identify. They can give real direction to the organization—stimulating creativity, building spirit, and creating a sense of who we are and what we do.

Some organizations will choose to solve the leadership problem by rotating official positions among the leaders of the group. Whatever the long-range solution, in the short run, it's better not to fix leadership until the organization begins to build and mature. In the very early stages of putting together an organization, those people who come forward as leaders are not always the ones who will be best in the long run. People who are the most vocal or the best in public situations often come to the fore in early meetings. If an election is held early, these people will end up with the official leadership positions. If possible, it makes sense to wait until there is a better sense of who is available to fill different leadership positions. Someone not available in the first week may come around at some later time and may be a better person for president or chair than someone who was there at the beginning.

Should an organization incorporate?

Incorporation is really a legal trick thought up by corporate strategists to protect the powerful and the wealthy from the results of their decisions. When an organization incorporates, the entire organization is treated as if it were an individual. It can do the same things legally that any individual can do. However, the individuals who direct the corporation are ordinarily not legally liable for what it does. Say you work at a plant where the board of directors has cut corners on safety. As a result you develop cancer. The corporation may be liable for the damage to your health and life, but the individual members of the board of directors are not.

So incorporation gives the members of the board of any organization, including a people's organization, a certain amount of protection from counterattack. This can be useful, especially when people feel that they're taking risks and are not sure of what the results of those risks might be.

Incorporation also is necessary if an organization is going to try to get what is called "private nonprofit status." This status allows an organization to apply for a tax exemption. Nonprofit status may be important in raising certain kinds of money, such as foundation funds and contributions from wealthy persons.

Be careful when you incorporate. Don't rush into it. Get the advice of a good lawyer who has worked with people's organizations before. When you incorporate you put together articles of incorporation and bylaws that say what the organization is and what it does. The organization needs to be clear not only about what it's doing now but what it might do in the future. A number of people's organizations have been tripped up because their corporation charter only permitted them to work on certain issues. Incorporation can restrict an organization as well as allow a greater freedom of action. It should be done carefully and after considerable planning and thought by the members.

Should a large organization have chapters?

Chapters are useful tools for helping a large organization feel small to the individual members. Chapters have other uses as well. A chapter can be designed to meet the needs of a special part of the organization: a neighborhood, a community, a constituency group. As an organization becomes larger and its membership more diverse, it becomes harder to please everyone. That's when you start hearing old members saying, "You know, in the old days, they really cared what I thought. We did something about the issues I care about. I haven't even cared about the last three issues we've worked on."

A chapter allows a group of people to work on an issue that is of concern to them without necessarily involving the entire organization in that issue. Of course, there need to be some general agreements of principle within the organization about what kinds of issues a chapter can and can't choose to work on. A chapter should not be able to choose an issue which contradicts basic goals or principles of the organization. But within those limits a chapter structure allows local freedom of action that can be very healthy as an organization gets larger.

Should a small organization affiliate with a larger one?

This is the chapter question in reverse. Many organizations start out small but want the power that comes from belonging to something larger.

This is something that happens often with neighborhood organizations. After years of work they may have solved most of the problems that can be handled at the neighborhood level. They need the power to influence decisions at the city, state, or national level which can come from being part of a larger organization.

A decision by a small group to become part of a larger one needs to be made very carefully. Often the large group will want agreements that the small group will have a hard time making. It might mean, for example, giving up some of the decision-making independence of the smaller group, an agreement not to work on certain issues, or a promise to share a certain part of the finances with the larger organization in return for other services.

The decision by a smaller organization to merge, affiliate, or cooperate with a larger one is a complicated strategy decision. It needs to be thought and talked through carefully by the leaders and members of the group. The terms need to be very clear. They need to be spelled out in writing so that all parties understand the advantages and disadvantages of the alliance.

How are decisions made in a people's organization?

Our organizations should have a real commitment to democratic decision making. Most of us have watched the scene in the movies where the boss of the big corporation is meeting with the board. The boss announces exactly what he intends to do and everybody says, "That's fine, J.B.," "That's great, J.B.," "Fantastic idea, J.B." A lot of decisions in the corporate and government worlds are made this way. People who have power hand down orders and expect other people to carry them out.

This is not a good way for a people's organization to operate. It's undemocratic. If we want to build a democratic society, we have to do it by democratic means.

We also have a problem that the government and the corporations don't have. We have to maintain our members. We have to keep them interested in the organization and willing to work for it. The government and the corporations have control over their "members"—the people who work for them: Either they carry out orders or they get fired.

A people's organization can't fire its members. All it can do is fire them up. This means that people have to participate in decision making. Long experience with organizing has shown that people tend to support decisions they feel involved in making. When they feel that they were not consulted, that they did not have a part in the decision-making process, they tend to vote with their feet and walk in the other direction. People's organizations need to develop structures that allow for real representative democracy. In fact, about the only real representative democracy in this country today is that exercised in some of the people's organizations that many of us have helped to build.

How does a people's organization keep going?

There is a lot of romance attached to organizing, organizers, and the organizations that they build. Sometimes we get the idea that because we're involved in fighting for human rights and making life better for people, we don't need to keep the files straight and the books clean. But in reality a people's organization needs to do all of the things that a corporation or government agency does, and needs to do them better. Traditionally Internal Revenue Service audits and similar tactics have been used to discredit and destroy people's organizations. It's wonderful for an organization to be consistently in the streets fighting for justice. But when you suddenly discover that you were so busy fighting in the streets that you forgot to file your quarterly Social Security payments and the Department of Justice sues you for $50,000 in back taxes, it's a different story.

Good business management is important for internal reasons as well. The best organizers in the world tend to become unhappy when they miss their paychecks for three weeks in a row because of a bookkeeping error or because there wasn't good planning for cash flow.

One of the improvements that has come about in our organizations is an understanding that good management, accounting, bookkeeping, and records are necessary to defend our organizations. They can even contribute to increased efficiency. This is a hard struggle. The models and methods for management that we've seen are those used by the people on the other side of the fence. Many of their methods contradict the values that we're trying to build into our organizations and society as a whole. We still haven't found good formulas for making staff truly accountable to leaders, for balancing the need for decision making with the need for staff and membership participation, and for balancing efficiency with cooperativeness. But we have begun to recognize the value of good books, good records, and reasonable administrative procedures. As our organizations become larger and more powerful, these will become even more important. A quick look at all the good organizations that were destroyed because their books weren't in order should be enough to convince us of the need for good management practices.

How does an organization hire, train, supervise, fire, or keep staff?

In the early stages of an organization it is often small enough so that the leaders can do the necessary work on a volunteer basis. But then the organization starts growing. It's no longer a group of friends who get together once a week. All of a sudden you have chapters all over the city, maybe even throughout the state, hundreds of miles apart. The organization is working on many issues at once. There is a need for communication among all the different chapters. There is a need for good public relations. Funds are running short and a way has to be found to raise them. Now it is no longer sufficient to have people working when they can. There is a need for permanent staff for the organization.

Staff can play a very important role in a people's organization. In many cases staff will have experiences from other organizing campaigns and organizations that add to the new organization's total knowledge. Staff will have specialized skills in strategy, tactics, training, media, public relations, communications, finances, fund raising, administration, and other areas. Sometimes because of these skills and experiences the staff members, rather than the leaders, become the decision makers in the organization. It's important to take steps to make sure that the members and leaders retain control of decision making. This is sometimes very hard to do. It is often helpful to set up regular procedures for how the leadership relate to staff. There should be a personnel committee, made up of leaders, which reviews the work of the staff. The staff director of the organization, if there is one, should be directly accountable to the board and should be held accountable by the board.

Some of the problems that arise between staff and leaders can be avoided by the way in which staff members are recruited and trained. One of the issues that is very difficult to decide when an organization is first hiring staff is whether members and leaders of the organization should become those staff persons or whether they should be recruited from the outside.

There are many arguments to be made for recruiting locally from the members and leaders of the organization. They already know the organization, its history, what it stands for, and what it has done. They are loyal to it. They know the community and are recognized and, hopefully, respected in it.

On the other hand, one of the things that sometimes happens when leaders become staff is that leaders who did not get the staff positions start saying, "Look, if *they* are going to get paid for doing this, why should *I* do it for free?" Sometimes other members and leaders are willing to do less work than previously.

There is no clear solution to this problem. Different organizations have tried to resolve the problem in various ways. Several of the labor unions which hire their own members and leaders as staff, have what they call a "back to the bench" rule. This means that after a certain period of time as a paid staff member, a person has to return to a voluntary leadership position. This system is supposed to prevent people from taking too much power and give other people a chance to be paid for their work.

Another solution is to elect the staff people from among the members and leaders. Sometimes, however, this can turn the selection into a popularity contest. The leaders who are the most popular are not necessarily those who would make the best staff persons for the organization.

If staff people are recruited from outside the organization, they need to be carefully recruited, interviewed, and screened by members of the personnel committee and other members and leaders. How do they really feel about poor and working people? Do they have prejudices based on race, gender, age, language or ethnic group, or region of the country that would interfere with their taking leadership and direction from members and leaders? Do they seem to have the maturity necessary to work effectively? Are they willing to accept discipline? Are they willing to undergo the training necessary to make them more effective, or do they feel that they already know it all?

Like so many of the organizational decisions that we face, there are no easy answers to the problems of staff. However, if we develop a good system of accountability, some fairly strict definitions of what we're looking for in our staff, a good recruitment policy, and a long-range training program designed to build skills in both staff and leaders, we will have taken solid steps in the direction of solving some of these problems.

What happens to leadership as an organization expands?

We've already talked a bit about problems that can develop as an organization grows older and larger. Many of these problems have to do with leadership. There is always going to be a certain turnover in the leadership of any organization, but this turnover can have a number of different results. If an organization has failed to develop a second and third line of leadership, then the loss of the older leaders could be a tragedy. The organization can begin to suffer a lack of direction. Newer people who have not been brought into the leadership group in a systematic, well-planned way may be afraid to step into the old shoes for fear of embarrassing themselves. They may feel that they're not capable of doing the job the old leadership did. (A related but somewhat different problem occurs when the old leadership is so badly criticized that nobody else wants to take the risk.)

Gaps can also develop between old leaders and new leaders. Older leaders may decide to hang on to their positions at any cost. They may also feel that the younger leaders don't understand the organization. They'll say things like "You know, they just don't understand it. They weren't with us back when we started. They don't understand what this organization means to us."

These splits can become particularly serious when they extend to the membership. Different leaders or groups of leaders may begin competing with each other for power, especially if there is money or influence at stake. They then begin lining up different members to back them in their positions.

Obviously fights like this can be destructive to an organization. One of the things to watch for when this begins happening is the possibility that some outside force is stirring it up. Sometimes members of our organizations, including even the leaders, have agendas of their own. They may be personal agendas. They may be agendas that are imposed on them by members of our opposition or by other organizations which have an interest in somehow changing what we're trying to do.

All of these situations are difficult to deal with—whether it's older leaders who refuse to make room for newer leaders, a conflict between different leadership factions, leaders competing with each other for power, or other splits that develop in the group. These fights can spill over to the members and staff and can involve everybody within the organization. Even the best planning can't always prevent internal fights.

If such fights do occur, then as a leader you simply have to do your best to try to hold the organization together. That's easier said than done. But sometimes if one leader or a small group of leaders is willing to stand up and make an assertive case that the organization and its needs have to come first, that will help pull things together.

There are other steps that you can take. Sometimes it helps to bring in a few people from the outside, consultants or other friendly persons who can help the organization begin to understand what's going on and find new ways to deal with the problems. Sometimes an organization gets stale in the way in which it looks at itself. It can no longer see what's happening inside. At times like this an outside point of view can be helpful.

Internal splits sometimes develop as a result of frustration. Sometimes an organization has lost several fights in a row and everyone is feeling generally frustrated. We start fighting our friends because our enemies are too tough. Sometimes the organization has simply lost its sense of vision and isn't sure where to go next. The solution to the fighting that results from these tensions may be to find an aggressive new campaign, to expand the membership, to take on a new target, to focus on a new issue. If energies can be channeled in this kind of direction, it may be possible to divert them from the infighting.

It's worth saying again, because it is so important: As a leader, your most important responsibility is developing other leaders. You must stand strong for the need to constantly develop new leaders among the members, to keep the leadership group open so that new people can join it, and to develop training programs to improve the skills of all the leaders in the organization.

What are some of the other problems of maturing organizations?

Organizations rarely remain static. They either grow or they shrink. If an organization, even after a few successful campaigns, fails to develop new campaigns and issues, its membership may begin to fall off. Its leadership may become tired. If the issues have all been similar, it may be difficult to attract people who are interested in other kinds of issues.

The obvious answer to this problem is to move the organization into other issues. But there are problems in moving from a single-issue organization to a multi-issue organization. The old leadership may resist the change. They may see it as abandoning what they feel is the original purpose of the organization. To avoid this problem, it is important from the beginning stages of building an organization to talk about long-range strategy—not just what we're going to do next week, but what we're going to do next year. This will help make moving from one issue to many issues much simpler.

Organizations may also have problems as they expand geographically. Moving into a new area may bring in new leaders who conflict with the old leaders. New chapters may create problems of distance. Particularly in rural areas, developing a new chapter may mean adding responsibilities as much as several hundred miles away from the nearest existing chapter. The new chapter may be several hundred miles from the state capital. If the organization is involved in pressure tactics at the capital, these kinds of distances can put a strain on everyone.

The organization needs to take distance into account as it develops its expansion plans. Labor unions have generally found that if you organize a shop that you cannot provide service to, you will probably lose it after several years. It's not worth organizing something that you can't realistically expect to maintain. If a chapter is simply too far from the main base of the organization to maintain contact, then it may not be the right time to organize that chapter.

At the same time there are things that can be done to maintain a high level of contact within an organization even as it expands. An organization may add regional meetings to chapter and statewide meetings. Other kinds of events can be planned—conventions, caucuses, workshops on issues, training sessions—that bring people into contact with each other. Board meetings may become less frequent but longer.

For example, the Brown Lung Association first organized in

very widely separated towns in North and South Carolina. The chapters were separated by as much as nine hours of driving time. When the board met, even at the most central location, some board members were traveling nearly five hours in each direction. Since board meetings only lasted for four hours, this meant that the people spent more time traveling than they did at the actual board meeting. This resulted in a great deal of frustration for the board members. It also meant that business was rushed, that new business could rarely be taken care of, and that people on the board had no time to make friends with each other. The board eventually decided to meet less frequently, only four times a year, but to make the meetings two- or three-day events. This allowed more time for discussion, for reflection, to deal with new business, and to become a social group where people could get to know each other, see old friends, talk, sing, tell stories, exchange news, and build up a sense of solidarity and spirit.

How is spirit built into an organization?

Sometimes we talk about our organizations as if they were machines. There are so many things to think about, so many things to keep in mind, that even talking about our organizations can become mechanical. But organizations are living, breathing things. They are made up of people like us who have hopes and dreams, fears and visions.

All of our discussion about issues, about tactics and strategies, about planning and decision making should not ignore some basic facts about our organizations. Issues are important. Victories are important. But what most of our members get from the organization goes far beyond the victories and issues. Our organizations provide a sense of soul and spirit to people who have been cut off from their roots, to people who have been denied their heritages, to people who have had their self-confidence destroyed.

Our organizations give people back their hopes and dreams.

As our members meet other people in the organization, as they realize that there are other people who feel and think as they do, they become excited. They develop a sense of loyalty to each other and to the group, a sense of belonging. Some of us call this feeling solidarity: the fact that everybody is solidly together, that we share hopes, dreams, spirit, values, visions.

An organization should have a conscious strategy to build its own solidarity. Our organizations should be dedicated to celebration as well as struggle. When a victory is won, we should celebrate—let our hair down, let loose, dance, kick up our heels, slap each other on the back, hug each other, whatever makes us feel good. Victories are hard to come by. We need to celebrate them as well as we can. They need to become part of our organization's history and culture.

Sometimes we need to celebrate just to celebrate. Just because an organization is trying to change society for the better, doesn't mean that it can't also have bowling parties, bingo games, socials, picnics, potluck suppers, and bluegrass festivals. People can have fun together, enjoy each other's company, learn to know each other better. We need to encourage the members of our organization to talk to each other and to learn from each other's histories.

This is especially true for the leaders of an organization. Many of the leaders of an organization are there because of events that occurred in their past. Something happened to give them a basic commitment to the struggle for dignity and human rights. Sometimes these are things that they have never talked about before. In the process of sharing our stories with other leaders, we begin to establish a shared history that can make all of us proud. We are what we are because of who we used to be, who our parents were, who our grandparents were, what the other members of our race or sex or ethnic group did in the past. Most groups in this country have a proud history of struggle, of fighting back, of standing up for their rights. We need to rediscover that history/ herstory. We need to tell it to our other members through stories, magazines, books, videotapes, and films. We need to have feasts and festivals, celebrations and carnivals to pass on our culture in its full range and depth.

We can participate in the process of creating that culture. So many of the songs that we now sing as history were written by organizations and by leaders in the middle of bitter struggle. Today we sing "Which Side Are You On?" a song that is almost forty years old. Sometimes we forget that it was written by someone who was very much a leader in the struggles of the 1930s, Florence Reece, who provided spirit and soul to many of the battles of mining families in the eastern Kentucky coal fields. We should encourage our members to make songs, to write poetry, to tell stories. We should preserve what they do and pass it on.

People act out of a deep sense of who they are and where they come from. For most of us in this country, that past, that history, has been cut off. Too often today, we are what we see on television. In building our organizations we are also rebuilding a past that has been taken away from us. Our history renewed gives us and will continue to give us the strength and vision to keep building our organizations into the future.

4. Constituencies

ORGANIZING BEGINS with what people have in common. Union organizing deals with the people who *work* in the same place. Neighborhood organizing—sometimes called community organizing—is concerned with the people who *live* in the same place. What is often called "constituency organizing" involves people who have characteristics in common other than where they live or work: gender, race, ethnic background, language, disability, sexual preference, religion. "Issue organizing" brings together people who are concerned with a particular issue: taxes, schools, rape, war, day care, housing, health care.

Trying to divide organizing into these different types, however, can be more confusing than helpful. There is really no common agreement on what some of the dividing lines are. What one person calls "constituency organizing" another might call "community organizing." What's most important is to recognize that all organizing begins with what people share, the things that make them groups rather than simply individuals.

What do we mean by community?

The word *community,* for example, seems to be one that everyone knows and understands. But actually it is used in different ways and means different things to different people and groups. Webster's dictionary says that a community is "a body of people living in the same place under the same conditions." According to that definition, almost anything can be a community. You sometimes hear national politicians referring to the people of the United States as a community. In a technical sense this is true, since all of us live in the same place, under at least some of the same conditions. In general, the smaller an area gets, the more a community has in common. People living in a medium-sized city tend to live under more of the same conditions than people living in a large state.

When people in government, such as community planners and developers, talk about community development, they often mean the development of an entire city. This idea is misleading. You can't develop an entire city. What's good for some people is not good for others. If something is done for one group, another group loses out. There are conflicts within groups. The poverty of one group may be caused by the profits of another.

The internal divisions in any group—the fact that groups of people have different self-interests, loyalties, and problems (some of which may be caused by other groups)—make defining a community for the purpose of organizing difficult. It's not enough that people live "in the same place under the same conditions." They also need to have the same perceptions of those conditions and a common interest in changing them. This common interest may put them in conflict with other members of the same geographical community. It would be impossible to build one organization that could really represent the interests of all of the people in Pittsburgh, Pennsylvania: the steel workers, the street youth, the players for the Steelers and Pirates, the owners of the steel companies, the church members, the union workers, the unemployed, the senior citizens, the women, the blacks, the other minority groups, the bankers, the brokers.

This is one of the classic problems of organizing. Almost every group that needs power is in one way or another a minority. Yet we are in a situation in which many of the levers of power require being able to produce a majority of people. In the long run most of us would like to see in this country a democratic and representative government that is really controlled by the people. Under certain circumstances it may be possible to do this through our present system of elected representatives. But how do you build a majority movement out of a group of minorities, many of whom conflict with, don't get along with, or don't share interests with each other?

A working definition of *community* for organizing purposes, then, has to be different from the dictionary definition. Our definition comes from the idea of a "community of interests." People have certain interests in common that can provide the basis for bringing them together within an organization.

What is neighborhood organizing?

This community of interests may be based on where people live. People who live near each other do have certain interests in common, regardless of other conflicts. In a city, the people who live in a neighborhood will share certain problems: unrepaired streets, poor fire protection, unresponsive police, under-funded neighborhood schools (if there still are any), heavy traffic, pollution from nearby industrial facilities, lack of recreation for children. These problems affect all the people in that immediate area and can be the basis for building a neighborhood organization. An organization built around one of these issues can also go on to deal with other issues. Although we've used the example of a city neighborhood, this same analysis is true whenever people live in the same place: along a valley creek in a rural area, in a village on a reservation, in a public-housing high-rise for seniors.

In some cases it's easy to decide what the "natural" community or neighborhood is. If we're talking about organizing in a high-rise for seniors, people either live in that high-rise or they don't. In a mountain valley, where there is only one entrance and one exit, it's clear who lives there and who doesn't. But in much other organizing it's very difficult to set the boundaries.

Sometimes neighborhoods are separated by natural or artificial barriers: a large highway, a railroad track, a busy street, an industrial site, a river, a power line right-of-way. Over time these barriers tend to direct the flow of people's lives.

The development of artificial boundaries over the years in our cities has refocused neighborhoods so that the lines are drawn very differently now than they were fifty years ago. Let's say a group of houses which once connected to the rest of the city is now bounded on the west by an interstate highway, on the east by a shopping center, on the north by railroad tracks, and on the south by an industrial park. Over the years the people in those houses will tend to develop certain feelings and problems in common. People will tend not to cross those barriers in the course of their daily lives. They'll direct most of their energies to things happening within that area.

The preceding example is one where the neighborhood is defined by its outside limits, by the barriers that prevent it from expanding beyond them. Neighborhoods also develop because they are focused on a center. Many of the neighborhoods in our cities grew up this way. The center may have been a factory that was built fifty years ago. At that time the company may have even built housing for the workers. People who worked in the factory lived in the surrounding area. Changes in employment patterns and transportation may have resulted in the factory workers moving farther from the plant. Many people in the neighborhood may now leave it to work. But the neighborhood will still have many things in common based on its common history.

A similar process goes on in many areas with regard to churches and synagogues. In many cities, neighborhoods comprised those people who lived together in a parish, who went to church or synagogue together, who saw each other at church or synagogue activities. In this kind of situation the natural divisions for neighborhood organizing may also follow parish lines.

All the different ways that urban areas are divided will influence the development of common interests that help define a neighborhood. School districts are a good example. The families whose children go to the same school tend not only to live together but also to have issues related to that school in common. Where people are in the same areas, the drawing of voting district lines also influences people's common interests. All of the different ways in which a community is divided for purposes of politics or administration will have an influence on how that community defines its own boundaries.

How do you organize across neighborhood lines?

Different neighborhoods may have developed in response to different conditions: natural barriers, artificial barriers, or central institutions such as a church, factory, or school. Nevertheless, most urban neighborhoods have many of the same problems. There is a fairly standard list of problems shared by most neighborhoods in cities of any size today.

Most of these common problems also target a common opposition. The solutions to most of the problems of neighborhoods are in the hands of city government and its allies: the banks, the insurance companies, the real estate developers and speculators. As a result, there is usually the potential to build broader organizations which cross neighborhood lines. An example might be a citywide organization made up of all of the neighborhood organizations. The neighborhood organizations combine their power to focus on the need for citywide solutions that affect everyone.

This is one of the great strengths of neighborhood-based organizing, especially when these neighborhoods are also brought together in a broader, more powerful organization. People have the advantages of belonging to a small, local, geographically-based organization where they work with their friends and neighbors, where events happen locally, where they can see the concrete results close to home. They also have the advantage of being a part of something larger and more powerful which can solve problems that demand more than the pressure one neighborhood can bring to bear.

So far, so good. Most of us can follow fairly clearly the idea of developing an organization along these lines. Neighborhoods are organized. Their organizations solve problems that are specific to each neighborhood, which can be solved with a small amount of pressure and organizing. They then come together in a larger organization which pressures at a higher level for those things the neighborhoods have in common.

There are some immediate problems. One has to do with the fact that there are usually only so many resources to go around and the opposition can play one neighborhood off against another. They can say to an organization which represents fifteen neighborhood groups and is demanding recreational facilities, "We're prepared to build four recreational centers in different parts of the city. That means four of you will get centers and eleven will not. Who should get them?" This approach can be used to split neighborhood groups from each other. It gets them fighting each other and weakens the over-all power of the organization.

Some people would interpret this as being a disadvantage to using neighborhoods as a base for organizing. But this problem occurs any time an organization becomes larger, whether it becomes larger by incorporating more neighborhoods or by bringing in other types of groups and their organizations.

There is a deeper problem as organizations grow and as we make decisions about how an organization will be structured and put together. It comes from the fact—a fairly simple fact, but one often overlooked in organizing—that people are never members of only one group. Ordinarily there are several different groups that a person feels part of, identifies with, and participates in.

One of these groups is the neighborhood. A second is the racial or ethnic group to which people belong. These ethnic or racial groups will have a common identity, common issues, and often a common culture and common concerns that may conflict with or go beyond the direct interests of the neighborhoods where people live.

For example, black people in most cities live in a number of different neighborhoods. Some of these neighborhoods will be primarily black, while others may be racially mixed with whites, Hispanics, and other groups. There will be neighborhood issues that these people are concerned with because of living in the neighborhood. But there will also be issues that they will see as specifically black issues: black appointments to city government, employment of black workers at all levels of government and industry, discrimination in hiring and promotion. These will be issues with which most black people will identify regardless of what neighborhood they live in.

These issues may conflict with the priorities of neighborhood organizations in the same city. A common demand of neighborhood organizations, for example, is to upgrade and improve neighborhood schools and to strengthen the concept of the neighborhood school. Black citizens may feel that this approach results in primarily white school districts receiving a higher percentage of resources and in perpetuating segregated schools. They might advocate a citywide busing program to balance all schools racially, thereby ensuring that educational resources would be fairly divided. These two positions are in conflict. To bring neighborhood organizations which advocate neighborhood schools together in the same organization with a citywide black organization which is in favor of citywide busing is a very difficult and delicate task. It involves balancing the common interests not only of neighborhoods but of other groups or *constituencies* as well.

What is a constituency?

In organizing, we call a group a *constituency* when its members have certain things in common. For example, the *constituents* of a state legislator are the people in his or her legislative district, who at least in theory are all represented by the same person. They also have in common that they live in the same area. The employees in a factory, who all work together, are a constituency.

In addition to living or working together, a constituency may have other things in common. These common threads may be problems and issues. They may be a common history, or common values. Let's take a look at some of the constituencies that are often involved in organizing.

What are some important constituencies?

Some constituencies are linked by racial or ethnic origins. Polish-Americans are a constituency, with some of their own special concerns and issues. Blacks are a constituency. Hispanics are a constituency; in some areas Mexicans may be one constituency and Puerto Ricans another. They may share some issues in common because of their common language. But others may be different because of differing national origins.

Constituencies can be based on other similarities and issues as well. Women are a constituency. There are issues on which most women agree: the end of discrimination against women in hiring and promotion, stopping sexual harassment on the job and elsewhere, combatting spouse abuse. On other issues which affect them as a constituency, women are divided. There are strong factions supporting and opposing ratification of the Equal Rights Amendment (ERA). There are also strong forces on both sides of the "right to choose" abortion issue. The fact that all women have some things in common does not mean that they agree on all issues. This is typical of constituency groups. Despite their common ties and bonds, and their agreement on some issues, constituencies may be on opposite sides on other issues.

Another key constituency is seniors. Seniors generally will have certain issues that they focus on: Social Security reform, housing, access to services, health care delivery, and transportation. In addition to their concerns as seniors, seniors may also have other concerns because of other constituencies that they belong to. They may be active, for example, in Hispanic political organizing and share concerns as Hispanics. They may also be active in their own neighborhood organization which is dealing specifically with neighborhood issues that are not exclusive to either Hispanics or seniors.

Sometimes all of these different lines and divisions are difficult to understand. The important thing to remember is that no person is a member of only one constituency. A person may be equally a member of many constituencies. That person may be active in organizations which are put together to meet the needs of each of these constituencies.

In some cases, the self-interests of these organizations may be in conflict with each other. For example, a black woman may be a member of a union which has been instrumental in improving wages and fringe benefits where she works but which has generally opposed affirmative action programs which would benefit black workers and women workers. She may be active in women's groups which support the "right to choose" and ERA although she is also a member of a parish council which opposes both.

How do organizations represent constituencies?

Constituencies are a critical part of our decision-making in organizing. Often constituencies will have developed organizations to represent their point of view and deal with the issues that are of concern to them. Women's organizations, black organizations, Hispanic organizations, the organizations of other minority groups, and seniors' organizations are all examples of constituency group organizations. In a sense even neighborhood organizations are constituency groups. It's simply that the constituents they represent are linked by where they live as well as by other characteristics.

An institution such as a synagogue or church, which has a broad membership base and a well-defined institutional self-interest, is an important factor in developing organizational approaches to people's problems. Like all organizations and institutions, churches and synagogues will have some issues on which they can line up with other groups in the neighborhood and some on which they cannot.

Unions represent another type of important constituency organization. Unions are the only major institutions in this country which are owned by working people. Many of the economic and social benefits that poor and working people have today can be directly traced to the work of the unions over the last fifty years, including free public education, Social Security, workers' compensation, unemployment benefits, and civil rights legislation. The unions' endorsement of the Equal Rights Amendment, even though many individual members of the unions personally opposed it, has been critical in supporting that legislation. As with other organizations, the positions taken by a union may not reflect the thinking of each of its members and may conflict with the positions taken by some of its allies.

Constituency-based organizations, then, are different from neighborhood-based organizations only in not always being rooted in a particular place. Neighborhood organizations are made up of the people who *live* in a particular area. Labor unions are made up of people who *work* in a particular place. But all types of organizations are bound together not simply by where people live or work, but by the issues and values that they have in common. One of the key long-range challenges in organizing is to be able to bring different constituencies and their organizations together so that they work with, rather than against, each other.

5. Issues

PROBLEMS. If you're like everybody else, you've got all the problems you can handle. Most of us make barely enough money to get by. Our taxes are too high. Our schools aren't good enough. The basic services we pay for through our taxes—police and fire protection, roads, garbage collection, social service, sewage—are rarely as good as they could be. In some areas these services aren't even available. Transportation is bad. Health services are poor and so expensive that most of us can barely afford them. Jobs and decent housing are hard to come by.

If you sit down with your friends, your neighbors, your family, the people you work with, and try to make up a list of the problems that some or all of you share, it's going to be a long list. These are hard times for everyone: individuals, families, neighborhoods, communities. We all share a long list of problems that we would like to do something about.

What's the difference between a problem and an issue?

Problems are different from issues. Problems are the things that an outside observer looking at a community would say are wrong with it. But not everybody in the community would agree. People need to feel strongly about a problem for it to be an issue. It must be something that enough people feel strongly about to be willing to work to change.

So issues are problems that people feel strongly about and want to do something about. But in order to be a good issue, a problem must have a solution that can be achieved by people working together. The sad fact is that there are all kinds of problems that are serious, that affect people's lives, and that people feel strongly about that they really can't do much to change right at this time.

An example is jobs. In almost every community large numbers of people who want to work can't find jobs. If you listen to what people talk about, you're almost sure to come up with jobs as a problem that needs to be solved. Unfortunately, there is usually only so much that people organizing locally can do to create jobs. They may be able to improve conditions on the job through union or occupational safety and health organizing. Cooperatives and community-owned businesses can create some jobs. But to actually create new jobs would involve influencing national policies that right now are beyond the scope of power that most of us have. Jobs in this situation would be an example of an issue that would not be a good one to choose in an organizing campaign, because of the probable lack of success in trying to deal with it.

What are the most likely issues to organize around?

There is no standard list of issues that make for effective organizing. Two communities may have the same problem. But in one community people may feel strongly about this problem and in another they may not care much about it. People in the first community may have a reasonable solution to the problem. In the second community, because of different resources or political situations, the problem would be far more difficult to solve.

In choosing issues, look at all the conditions that affect people individually and together. The issues in the following list are going to be common to many communities, but they are by no means the only issues that will come up. You should be especially sensitive to local issues, including ones that no one has run into before as far as you know. Because these issues will be particular to a community, it's hard to predict what they're going to be. But they may be the issues that people care the most about.

This list isn't complete, but it does give an idea of some of the problems people have organized around in recent years:

Housing	High rents
Crime	Polluted water
Spouse abuse	Recreation
Roads	Jobs
Underemployment	Transportation
Job discrimination	Sexual harassment
Housing discrimination	Credit
Police brutality	Job health and safety
Handicapped access	Toxic wastes
Strip mining	Red-lining
Job training	Health care
Family planning	Rats
Fire protection	Schools
Taxes	Access to services
Legal protection	Political representation
Consumer protection	Child abuse
Treaty rights	Utility rates
Bilingual education	Welfare rights
Tenants' rights	Right to organize
Day care	Drug abuse

If you think back through American history, you'll probably come up with other issues that people have won through organizing: no taxation without representation, an end to slavery and lynching, women's suffrage, laws against child labor, free public education, the right to collective bargaining, the eight-hour workday. You can look back at one of our country's basic historical documents, such as the Bill of Rights, and see what the issues of the 1780s were:

Freedom of religion
Freedom of the press
Right to keep and bear arms
Protection against unreasonable
   search and seizure
Right to trial by jury
Protection from cruel and
   unusual punishment

Right of free assembly
Freedom of speech
Right to petition the government
No peacetime quartering of
   soldiers in the home
Right to a speedy trial
Protection from excessive bail
Right to due process of law

How do you find out what issues people care the most about?

We talk a lot about choosing issues. But issues often choose us. This is especially true the first time that a neighborhood, community, or workplace organizes. Often what happens is that people learn about a new development that is going to affect their lives. The local utility company announces an increase in its rates. A developer announces plans to build a new shopping center right next to a residential district. The county commission announces that a neighborhood school is going to be closed. The city announces that it's going to make a two-lane road through the neighborhood into a four-lane highway. Several senior citizens are assaulted while walking to the grocery store. A woman is raped on the way home from work at night.

Such occurrences will often move people into action quickly. Sometimes we call them defensive issues, because people are defending their way of life and standard of living. Many organizations that now deal with a whole range of issues were formed around one issue.

When people feel very strongly about something that is happening to them, it rarely makes sense to sit down and look at all the other issues they could deal with. People want to do something about the situation. They want action, not talk. Hopefully the issue is a winnable one. But even if the issue cannot be won in the short run, sometimes it is important for people to stand up and say exactly what they think. People want to fight for their visions, for the things they care about. There are times when people don't care whether or not an issue is a good one, whether or not they can win. They want to stand up and fight for what they believe in.

As organizations grow, the question of choosing issues becomes more strategic. This is also the case with organizations that become larger and begin working in communities and neighborhoods other than the ones that they started in. Then it becomes really necessary to find out what people are thinking about problems, what issues they have, and what directions the organization can move in.

How do you find this out? By listening. By encouraging people to talk about their lives, their hopes, their dreams, their problems, the way things used to be, the way things could be. Most people are wonderful talkers, given the chance. Leaders should be wonderful listeners. Listening is a skill you can practice on your own or in workshops and training sessions.

Some of this work can be done individually as you visit with people in their homes, on the job, in stores, in neighborhood or workplace hangouts. Try to get people talking about what they'd like to see happen. Most people spend a lot of time thinking about how things could be different. They just don't have the experience of talking about such things in public. Often they'll try to put that responsibility on you. They'll ask, "What do *you* think we should do? What do *you* think the next step should be?" But if you're a leader, it's important that you take on the responsibility for helping people learn how to do this type of thinking for themselves. Turn the question back to them. Ask them, "What have *you* been thinking? Where do *you* think we should go? What have *you* looked at? What are *you* talking about? What are your friends talking about?"

Sometimes an organization will decide to send its leaders and staff door-to-door to find out what other people are thinking. When you are knocking on doors, a prepared survey form can help you to organize your thoughts. On the other hand, sometimes people respond to a printed survey form without thinking too deeply about it. If you're using a checklist, ask people for specific examples. If you ask them, "Do you think schools are a problem?" and they say, "Yes," ask them *how* schools are a problem. What things have happened? What examples do they know of? Who else have they heard talking about it? Go beyond the general to the specific so that you can pin down the actual changes people would like to see.

One of the best ways to find out what people care about is to do it in small groups. When you can get a good discussion going inside a small group, people begin to reinforce each other. As strong feelings are expressed by one person, other people begin to feel strongly as well. Most of us are embarrassed to feel or talk too strongly about anything. We were taught at an early age that we are supposed to be reasonable in our demands and in our expectations. Sometimes it's necessary to get people together in a group so that by reinforcing each others' feelings they can begin to recognize how angry they all are and how much change they would all like to see.

As a leader you'll want to help this kind of discussion get going and give it some shape and direction. That doesn't mean that you want the group to accept your own ideas. You're trying to help other people come up with their ideas.

Here is one suggestion for a way to get a discussion going. Let's say that you have a group of eight or ten neighbors meeting at your house to talk about problems in the neighborhood. Start out by asking everybody to write down on a piece of paper the things that they think are problems in the neighborhood. Give people enough time so that they can think about this carefully and write down as many things as they want to. Remember that in many groups not everyone writes easily or at all. So tell people that they can either think of or write down the list.

When everyone is finished, say, "OK, let's go around the room and everyone name one item from her list. I'll write everything on a piece of newsprint as we go around. We'll see how many times we can get around the circle before we run out of ideas." Go around the circle, one person at a time. Try not to let anyone give more than one idea. Keep going until all the ideas from each person's list are exhausted.

The advantage of this method is that it lets everybody participate. Everyone gets a chance to say at least one of his or her ideas. In most groups it will be possible to go around the circle several times. This method also keeps any one individual from dominating the discussion. If you just ask one person to say what he thinks, he might come up with eight or ten ideas. This could prevent other people from having their ideas recognized. Even if people aren't the first to name a particular idea, when it goes up on the piece of newsprint they'll recognize it as theirs. This gives them a sense of identity with the idea, even if they didn't get to say it themselves.

When you finish you should have an overview of the problems in the community and some sense of how people feel about them. Now you come to the hard part: deciding which of these issues to work on.

What makes a good issue?

As we discussed earlier, a good issue is a problem that people feel strongly enough about to work to change. But there are other things that make an issue a good one for an organization to take on.

(1) *A good issue is winnable*. If it's absolutely impossible to do anything about the problem, it doesn't make sense to work on it. One of the best ways to decide whether an issue might be winnable is to think through what your organization's strategy for dealing with the issue might be. That way everyone begins to get a sense of what it would take to win: how many people, how much work, how much time, how much money, what allies, what

tactics. Sometimes an issue that seems extremely difficult is actually much simpler once you get a look at the strategy. On the other hand, sometimes an apparently simple issue is in fact much more difficult than it appears at first glance.

Be careful not to underestimate what people are willing to do when they feel strongly about an issue. Sometimes we feel that if an issue can't be won quickly, it shouldn't be taken on at all. But again and again we find examples of groups and communities that took on seemingly impossible issues and fought for years before finally winning.

In 1965, for example, farming families in Allegheny County, North Carolina, and Grayson and Carroll counties, Virginia, were faced with a proposed power dam project on the New River which would have flooded out their homes and farms. At that time it looked as if the Appalachian Power Company, which wanted to build the dam, was going to get its way. People fought back for almost ten years. They were at the point of defeat several different times. But they stuck together and eventually were able to defeat the dam project once and for all. Many outsiders said it was an impossible fight. But because people were fighting for their homes and for their lives as they had lived them, it was worth it to them to make the fight. And in fact it turned out to be a winning issue after all.

We always need to be careful not to sell people too short and assume that they don't have the courage, the stamina, or the will to fight through a seemingly impossible situation. People have a history of being able to rise to the occasion when they need to.

(2) *A good issue builds the organization.* Organizing builds organizations. Any group of people has so many problems that it doesn't make sense to organize to deal with just one of those problems and then let things drop. We want to organize for the long haul, so that the skills people learn working together on one issue can be applied to other issues as well. In building a strategy we should be looking at ways to build the organization, both for the issue that we're dealing with today and for other issues that we want to deal with tomorrow.

What do we mean when we say that an issue builds the organization? We mean that it involves people in the actual work of winning on the issue—large numbers of people, not just one or two lawyers or advocates. It gives them a sense of participation, the experience of standing up and fighting back. It builds spirit. People feel good about what they're doing.

(3) *A good issue unites people.* The people you're working with need to agree on what the problem is and what should be done about it. If half the people you work with are on one side of the issue and the other half are on the other side, you (and they) are going to have problems. Let's say a major company announces a plan to build a new chemical plant in your community. The plant is clearly going to pollute the area. Many people in the county are going to be against the plant because of the destruction of the environment and what that means to their way of life. Other people are going to feel that the plant means jobs and that jobs are simply something that they have to have if they're going to survive. If your organization tries to take a stand on this issue with half of its members in favor of the plant and half of them against it, the organization may destroy itself in the process of trying to deal with the issue.

As a leader you need to work very hard to help people think through these decisions. It's here that the importance of helping people think through carefully how they really feel about an issue is so evident. People need to be in touch with their real feelings about difficult and complicated issues. Otherwise they may agree in public out of a desire to go along, politeness, or concern for the organization. In private they may find themselves unable to support the issue. This in turn can divide them from the organization.

(4) *A good issue affects a lot of people.* Even in a small community, people have different problems. They will probably feel strongly about the problems they have. But if only one or two people have a particular problem, it's not a good one to organize around.

(5) *A good issue involves people.* When we talk about organizing, we're talking about involving people in solving their own

problems. This means that the way the problem is solved has to be one in which people can participate. If the solution to the problem is to turn it over to a sympathetic lawyer, the problem may be solved. But the people affected by the problem won't have a sense of victory. They won't learn to work and fight together so that they can solve other problems as well.

(6) *A good issue is strongly felt.* Sometimes you run into a problem in a community that can be solved fairly easily, but people just don't seem to care much about it. Be careful if you seem to be running into this situation. It may be that you're paying too much attention to your own values and not enough to theirs. If you try to organize people to deal with an issue they don't particularly care about, you'll probably end up deciding they can't be organized. The truth is probably that they just don't want to be organized around that particular issue.

(7) *A good issue is simple.* A good issue can be stated in one simple sentence. It should be clear that there is a right side and a wrong side to the issue, and that we're on the right side. An issue so complicated that several pages are required to explain it is hard to organize around.

Who should decide on issues?

One of the things that should be clear from what we've just talked about is that the process of deciding on issues should involve as many people as possible. The more people who are involved, the more carefully they decide, the more likely that they'll have a real commitment to the issue.

As a leader it's not your responsibility to choose issues, but to help people go through the choosing process carefully and well. Everyone would rather be asked what he or she thinks than told what to do. This is as true in an organizing campaign as anywhere else. Think about yourself. Suppose one of your neighbors came up to you and said, "We've been meeting over the last three weeks. We've decided that we're going to oppose the new hospital the city plans to build in our neighborhood. We want you to come down to our office and help us mail protest letters to the mayor." The chances are that even if you agree with that position, you're not going to be very enthusiastic about going down and doing the work. Why? Because you weren't asked to be a part of making the decision. You wouldn't feel a part of the decision. You'd feel excluded. You'd feel as if some other people got together in a back room and decided what you should think and what you should do.

On the other hand, if a neighbor comes to you and says, "You know, there's been a lot of talk in the community about this new hospital that's being planned. Some of us are going to get together tonight and talk about what we ought to do. We'd really like to have you there to help us out." You're more likely to go and say what you think. Once you've said what you think, you have a certain personal interest in the issue and are more likely to volunteer to take on work. Even if you don't go to the meeting, you're more likely to feel part of the issue *because you were at least asked to come.*

It's a bit like the process of building a house. If the foundation is built carefully, is square and true, it's easier to make the house the way it should be. If you don't take your time putting the foundation together, the house is going to tilt or shake. It's the same way in organizing. Each step leads into the next. Each level is built on the one before. As a leader, the more you can involve people at each level in making the decisions that affect their own lives, the more you can give them a sense that they're important to the decision-making process, the more they're likely to be involved later.

How important are winnable issues?

If you're trying to organize people, you need to build up their confidence in their ability to change things. One of the reasons people don't have this confidence is because they don't have the experience of working together successfully to accomplish change. Now, if the first time people get together and try to do something they lose, they may say to themselves, "Well, that didn't get us anywhere. There's no point in trying anything else." It's better if the first few issues a group works on are easily winnable, so that by winning they can build up their self-confidence enough to go on to more difficult issues.

One winnable issue often used in neighborhood organizing is getting a stop sign at a crowded intersection. Being against stop signs is like being against apple pie. If citizens are angrily demanding a stop sign, almost any city administration, no matter how unresponsive otherwise, is going to put up that stop sign. It doesn't cost much. It's easier than running the political risk of not putting up the sign and then having some child run over at that corner. So if people demand the stop sign, they'll probably get it.

Now, this sounds like a perfectly reasonable way to start a group. But there are some problems to this method of beginning to organize. What happens when you run out of easy wins?

This question reminds me of how I tried to get my children to like fishing. I've always been crazy about fishing. Naturally enough, I wanted my kids to like it. But when they were young I was afraid they wouldn't have the patience to appreciate it. I thought it would make sense to start them out easy. So I took them to a pay-as-you-catch trout pond down the road from where we lived. (For those of you who live in cities, these are commercial ponds that are heavily stocked with fish that bite every time you throw a hook in.) Sure enough, every time the kids threw a hook in they caught a fish. And they sure loved fishing.

After a few trips to the pay-as-you-catch pond I decided they were ready for *real* fishing. So the next time we went down to the lake. About five minutes went by and they started complaining, "Where are all the fish? What's wrong with this lake? How come we're not catching anything?" They wanted to go back to the *good* pond. But there I had to pay for every fish they caught. They had become so used to catching fish without any work, that they weren't able to fish for long enough in an open lake to catch anything at all.

Obviously it's best to focus on winnable issues that can be won in a reasonable amount of time. But the problem is that it's often impossible to know if and when an issue can be won. You as a leader of the group may think that there is no way a particular issue can be won. But the history of organizing shows that this is often much harder to predict than we would like to think. Often what looks like a fairly easy fight turns into a knock-down-drag-out. And sometimes what looks like an impossible victory is in fact within reach.

Sometimes, too, the more easily an issue can be won, the less central it probably is to people's lives. This isn't always true, but often the things that are given up willingly by the opposition are not the things people care the most about. Sometimes we underestimate how hard people are willing to fight for the things they do care about. There are groups that have taken on issues that were difficult from the start and have stuck it out and fought year after year. Sometimes we can draw on people's hidden resources in exactly the degree to which we appeal to the things that they want the most.

It's your job as a leader to encourage people to dream, to think about their deepest hopes, the things they want the most, what they want for their children and grandchildren, what they want for themselves. That doesn't mean that you don't fight for stop signs. But it's important not to limit what people might be willing to do by choosing issues that are too easy, when they want to take on the hard ones.

How do you define an issue?

Sometimes an organization can make a long fight on an issue and not be sure whether it won or lost. Suppose your group demands a traffic light at a busy intersection. Six weeks later the city comes by and puts up a four-way stop sign. Did you win or did you lose? You didn't get the traffic light. But you got stop signs.

What happened was a compromise. Compromises are common in political problem solving. Of course you can always call a meeting and explain that the stop signs are really a victory. But that's hard to do if people have already decided that a win means a traffic signal. It's much more effective to define what a victory would be at the time you decide on an issue and plan your strategy. The group should consider all the possible ways of solving the problem. Remember that just because you feel that a particular solution is the right one doesn't mean that the opposition will agree with you. They may also want to show their independence and prove that they don't do whatever groups tell them to do by solving the problem in a different way from what the organization demanded.

It's better if everyone in the group understands what can happen from the beginning. People should feel, "Look, we're going to try to get a traffic signal. But it's likely that the city is going to try to do something a little less than what we're asking. So we may actually get a four-way stop sign or a two-way stop. But that's a step and we're going to see it as a victory." If people know what to expect and have had a chance to talk about and think through their expectations, they're less likely to feel, "We didn't get anything," when in fact they got a lot.

Often at the time an issue is chosen no one bothers to think of all the different ways that the problem could be solved, and which of these would be acceptable and which wouldn't. As a leader, you should help people to explore the full range of possible solutions to a problem. Talk about what a partial victory might be and what a complete victory would be. This approach also allows a group to develop a series of steps toward a long-range strategy which can be victories in themselves. For example, the group might set up a series of steps toward getting the traffic signal:

(1) Getting a petition with 100 names on it to present to the city council.

(2) Being placed on the agenda at the city council meeting.

(3) Getting fifty people to the council meeting to support the presentation of the petition.

(4) A favorable vote by the council to do something at the intersection.

When reached, each of these goals can be celebrated as a victory. By breaking the strategy down into steps, we let people see their progress as they work on the issue rather than only at the end when it's a win or a loss. People can feel good about the fact that even though they don't yet have a traffic signal, they did get 100 signatures on a petition. They can be proud of themselves because they packed the city council chamber, whether or not the council agrees to take a vote that particular night. As a leader you can help people define these steps and goals as a way of keeping them involved in the campaign as it goes along.

Should an organization deal with more than one issue at a time?

It would be nice if organizations worked as well in real life as they do on paper. On paper what we say we do in organizing campaigns is to focus on an issue, win that one or lose it, and then go on to the next one. In real life, what usually happens is that right in the middle of one campaign, something else happens. People become even more fired up about that than they are about the first issue. Now the organization faces a tough decision. Do we also concentrate on the second issue? If we do, will we lose our ability to deal with the first? Will we spread our resources too thin? If we don't deal with the second issue, will we lose our members because they feel that we're no longer serving their needs?

These are complicated questions and not easily answered. An organization does have to respond to the needs of its members as they see them. On the other hand, there are real limits to what any organization can do. Taking on an issue when there aren't sufficient resources to do the job well can be destructive to the organization.

Some of the same questions that you ask in choosing an issue are helpful here: How strongly do people feel about the second issue? Is it an issue that has to be fought right at the moment? Could the fight be postponed for a while? What's going on with the first issue? How much of the organization's resources is it taking right at the moment? Does the organization have the resources to handle two campaigns at once?

It's important for an organization, just as it is for a person, to finish what it begins. On the other hand, organizations, like people, do change their minds. Sometimes what seemed like a top priority a year ago no longer seems as important today. This may reflect changing conditions in the community. It may come from the members' growing sense of their own power and self-reliance. As a leader you need to keep asking, *"What if?"* What if we take on the second issue? What if that offends the people who think the first issue is all-important? What if the opposition succeeds in dividing us because we have two issues to deal with?

Generally, if the organization has the people willing and able to do the work necessary for two issues, it makes sense to add the second issue. Adding another issue broadens the potential membership base of the organization. People will see the organization's willingness to expand into new issues as evidence of the importance of the organization. Organizations, again like people, tend to be judged by what they do, not by what they say about themselves. Maybe we describe ourselves as a broad-based neighborhood organization trying to deal with the many needs of the community. But if all our energies have gone into stopping an interstate highway through the neighborhood, then we'll be known as "the people who are fighting the interstate." People who want to fight the highway will either join or support us. Others who don't care about the highway or who favor it will stay away. If we now expand to take on the issue of good schools in the community, we're saying something about ourselves as well. We're saying that we really are here to deal with broad community needs, not with just one issue.

The question of one issue versus many issues is an old one in organizing. We talk in organizing about single-issue and multi-issue organizations. Single-issue organizations, as you would expect, focus on one issue and, at least in theory, exist only to resolve that one issue. We mentioned earlier the fight against the dam on the New River. The people in that area built an organization to stop the dam. But when the dam was stopped once and for all, that organization disbanded and people went back to their regular lives.

Now, some people would say that there's nothing wrong with this way of doing things. They'd say that if an issue is important enough to fight about, all energy should be focused on that issue and that once it is won there is no longer a need for the organization to continue. But there's another side to the argument. It's almost impossible to find a poor or working-class community that has only one problem. Can you imagine a neighborhood where the houses are all owned by slumlords and are falling apart but where the local school is first-rate? Have you ever seen a rural community where there are simply no jobs for people to work at but where everybody lives in a nice house? Could you ever find a community that had been red-lined by the banks and the insurance companies but where police and fire protection were excellent? Of course not. The problems of being poor and powerless tend to lump together. People who live in falling-down housing also tend to have to send their children to falling-down schools. People who lack jobs also tend to lack good health. People without representation also tend to lack protection.

So in many ways when we go to the trouble of putting together an organization that only deals with one problem we're wasting energy and losing potential. It's almost like building a house and then not living in it. If we're going to go to the time, trouble, pain, and heartache to build an organization that can solve one of the problems we have, why should we let it fall apart without trying to deal with the other problems?

But if we're going to do this, we need to begin at the beginning. The members of our organization need to expect that we will go on as an organization to deal with other issues besides the one that originally brought us together. One of the responsibilities of leadership is to keep reminding people that today's campaign is not the only campaign. We fight these battles not only to win but also to build our strength so that we can take on other battles.

The process of conducting a campaign around today's issue should feed into planning strategy for tomorrow's issue. We should always be thinking and saying, "What can we do as part of this campaign to make the next one easier? What issues do we want to take on after we resolve this one? How does this affect our strategy? What should we do today to make tomorrow easier?"

As organizations grow in membership strength and leadership abilities, they become more capable of taking on two or three campaigns at the same time. As a leader you want to encourage people to keep their vision open-ended. Don't let people say, "I'll be glad when this is over because then we won't have to meet anymore." Help them to feel, "If we win this one, we're going to have the strength to go on to the next one."

How can issues be taken away by the opposition?

Sometimes we can get into a situation in our organization where the opposition gives us what we want before we get the chance to organize around it. This may seem strange at first. But if you look at it from the point of view of the people who have power, it makes a lot of sense. Sometimes it seems as if the people in power have more respect for the organizing of poor and working people than some of us do. They believe what we say. They know that once people get a taste of their own power it's hard to turn them back. They know that once people learn how much can be accomplished through organizing, it's hard to get them back to the old individual ways of doing things. So sometimes when those in power sense trouble, they'll immediately give in on a few easy issues as a way of trying to calm people down. They'll try to move quickly so that they can get the credit rather than letting the credit go to the people who are organizing and their organization.

This situation occurs often in union organizing. As soon as the company hears that its workers are starting an organizing campaign, they begin to make minor improvements. The bathrooms are cleaned. The canteens are painted. The lunch break increases from twenty to thirty minutes. Wages are raised a nickel or a dime an hour. The purpose behind these changes is to make people think they're better off than before, and to take issues away from the union's organizing campaign.

The company knows that the union is going to try to win on small issues to demonstrate what it can do. So it tries to solve the problems in the workplace before the union can get a foothold. The company understands from years of experience that it's cheaper to put out a little hush money now than pay the costs that will arise if workers gain the right to have a voice in their working conditions.

In the same way, when we start organizing the community, sometimes the established institutions will make some minor changes, both to try to buy people off and to take issues away from the organization. As much as possible, we want to be in a position to take credit for those victories. People should see them as the result of their organizing, not the good-heartedness of the people in power.

For this reason it often makes sense for an organization to lay out some of its goals very early in the game. One of the things that you can do as a leader in this situation is to tell people what to expect. Say to them, "You may not think we're going to get very far, but watch. We're going to ask for conditions to be changed at the school. But don't be surprised if other things start to change as well. But it's not going to be because the people down at city hall had a change of heart. It's going to be because they're scared of us, of what we can do through our organizing."

You can also be specific about some of the things that might happen. If the organization comes up very early with a list of its long-range demands, then it's in a position to claim credit if some of these changes come about. It's important to be clear that you don't expect everything to happen at once. But it's helpful for an organization that wants to stay around for a long time and wants to be a real force in the community to say clearly what its vision of the future is. We need to say what we want in terms of home, schools, safety on the streets, the quality of people's lives, the sense of community. Even though we fight on specific issues, our organizations stand for much more. They stand for people working together, respecting each other, achieving dignity and self-respect, speaking out, establishing a feeling of community and solidarity. In the short run we may be focusing on a utility rate increase or making the streets safe at night. But in the long run we're talking about much more basic changes. These changes can only come if not only our neighborhood, community, workplace, school, or group is organized but if thousands and thousands of groups like ours organize around the United States with the same goals in mind.

Any organization, no matter how small, can be part of this movement. Just as people join together in a neighborhood, organizations across the country can join together. Through our collective strength we can begin to make some of the changes that will make life better for all of us.

This is one of the most basic responsibilities of grass roots leaders: to help people think through and be able to talk about their vision of the future, to understand that although we may be talking about stop signs today, we are talking about the dignity of people and creating a society in which that dignity can flourish for tomorrow.

6. Members

WE LIVE IN A SOCIETY where people have been reduced to numbers. Our lives have become series of computer printouts. People feel isolated, unvalued, uprooted. People's organizations try to give people back the sense of belonging, of being part of something larger than themselves, of being valued for who they are individually. We want our members to feel that they are more than simply a vote, a number, an occupational code in an office or factory.

By personalizing our organizing, we build organizations that can do this. Personal contacts are at the heart of any organizing drive and of any people's organization. No skill is more necessary to leaders in our organizations than to be able to work effectively with people.

In organizing we move from the individual to the group. But we need to start with the individual. People need to make up their minds individually that they want to be members of the organization, that they want to commit themselves to beginning to change their surroundings. A factory with two thousand workers is still organized one worker at a time. A neighborhood with a thousand families needs to be organized one family at a time.

The opposition relies on sophisticated media to get its message across. We are bombarded by advertising: television ads, radio ads, newspaper ads, direct mailings to our homes, surveys to find out what we want to buy, phone calls urging us to subscribe, sales brochures placed under the doors of our houses and the windshield wipers of our cars. In organizing we use some of these same techniques. But we should remember that the opposition can usually do a better job of exploiting advertising than we can, because of its sources of money and technical help. Thus, when we get into a fight with a corporation or a city or county government, we are at a disadvantage if we try to fight through an advertising battle.

The best answers to the opposition's advertising tactics are the personal relationships that we have built up within our organizations. Person-to-person contacts build organizations where people feel equally valued. When someone takes the trouble to visit you and talk with you about her or his organization, it means something, especially when you know that person is not being paid to hustle you.

We are not trying to push people to buy a particular product. Our organizations are not hair sprays, underarm deodorants, or nasal decongestants. They are not packages that people buy over or under the counter. We want more than money from people. We want their time, their work, their commitment, their loyalty, their participation, and their enthusiasm. We want them to find meaningful roles as members of our organizations. Only when people have work to do that means something to them will they continue to be members.

Paid advertising doesn't tell us what individuals think or feel. Person-to-person contacts can. The information that we bring back as we work with people individually helps us to do a better job of building an organization that makes room for people with different backgrounds, experiences, abilities, skills, interests, and commitments.

How do you recruit members?

The first step in recruiting members is to decide who is going to be contacted. This is a strategic decision that needs to be made by the organization. If an organization has not yet been formed, you and the other people that you're working with need to make the decisions.

Sometimes it's easy to figure out who needs to be contacted. If you're organizing in a nursing home, you want to talk to the other people in that home. If you're organizing in a neighborhood, you want to start with the people who live near you, that you know best.

Start small and close to home. Let's say you're organizing in your neighborhood around the issue of overflowing sewers. It's helpful to start by making a sketch of the neighborhood on newsprint or wrapping paper. Show the streets, the houses, and the names of the people who live in those houses. Figure out what area is directly affected by the problem. Make a list of the people who live in that area. These are the people you want to contact.

Start with people you know well rather than with people you haven't met yet. It takes a while to build up confidence in your ability to talk with people, not just as a friend, but as a leader and organizer. If you start with people with whom you already have a comfortable relationship, it's sometimes easier.

One of the secrets of successful person-to-person contact is good planning. Start by figuring out where and when you want to see each of the people on your list. If you're going to visit people in their homes, some times are better than others. You don't want to walk in the door five minutes after someone gets home after a long day on the job, or just as the family is sitting down for dinner.

You might want to see people in places other than their homes. Some homes get so busy with the television set going, records playing, phones ringing, people walking in and out, that it's almost impossible to hold a good conversation. In a case like that you might want to meet somewhere else to talk: at work, in a neighborhood park, in a restaurant, after church or synagogue, in a local bar, at your home, or at the organization's office.

It makes a difference whether you're talking to someone you already know or to people you haven't met yet. Once you've gone outside your immediate circle of acquaintances, it often works best to see people at home. The exception is when the people you're organizing gather in another place naturally.

Lists of where people gather vary from group to group and from neighborhood to neighborhood. You need to make up your own list of places to find and meet people depending on where you're working and with whom. A typical list might include the following:

At their house	At the barbershop
At your house	At the beauty parlor
At church or synagogue	At a ball game
At school	On the street
In the hospital	In a restaurant
At the supermarket	At the bus stop
At work	At your organization's office
On a trip	At the courthouse
On the phone	At the shopping center
At the union hall	At the bowling alley

Try to find a setting where both you and the person you're meeting with will be comfortable. You want a place where you can talk with reasonable freedom from interruption. In some situations it is also important to find a place where you're free from being watched. You want to establish a setting where people feel free to talk to you, where you can create an atmosphere that encourages them to become part of the organization.

How do you set people at ease?

We can do the most effective job of setting people at ease in our person-to-person contacts with them if we are at ease ourselves.

People are very quick to pick up our own feelings about ourselves and what we're doing. If you go to talk to somebody feeling unconfident and unsure of what you have to say, it's likely that the conversation won't go very well.

You can develop ease and confidence through practice, experience, and planning. It may sound foolish, but it really helps to practice what you're going to do and say when you get to someone's door. You can practice by talking to yourself in a mirror. You can ask a friend or another member of the organization to listen to you practice. You may find it useful to talk into a tape recorder and then play it back to hear how you sound.

Don't try to imitate the way other people act or talk. Each of us is an individual with very different ways of doing things. Successful leaders rely on the strengths of their own personalities, the things that *they* do best. Think about the ways you're most comfortable talking with people: the kinds of settings, the kinds of situations, the kinds of conversations. Try to build these ways of doing things into your ways of approaching people to become members.

You'll also find it helpful to make yourself familiar with the issues you'll be talking about before you start recruiting members. People are going to ask all kinds of questions. You're not going to have the answers to all of them. But you should be comfortable in your own mind that you have answers to the most common questions people are going to raise. You want to know a little bit about the issues and how other people feel about them. You want to be able to say something about the organization, how it got formed, what it does, what its history is, how people become members. You may want to be able to explain a little bit about how organizing works, why it is that people getting together can solve a problem that so far no one has been able to do anything about. Your own comfortableness with the things you're talking about will come through and will help set the person you're talking with at ease.

What do you actually say to people?

Let's assume for the moment that you're going to be talking with people you haven't met yet. When you first get to someone's house you want to establish as quickly as possible who you are, what organization you're representing, and what you're there for. Say, "Hi, I'm Si Kahn. I live over on Tremont Street, and I'm a member of the Tremont Improvement Committee. I've been talking to people in the neighborhood about the problems we've been having with the sewers overflowing. Do you mind if I come in and talk with you for a minute?"

Whether or not you should invite yourself in depends on how long you expect to be talking. If all you want is a signature on a petition, you might not want to be engaged in a long conversation. You might decide to stand on the porch and make your presentation. But when you want to recruit someone to become a member of the organization, it's hard to do if you're talking through a screen door.

Explain why you're there. People are naturally suspicious when somebody shows up on their doorstep. They might think you're selling encyclopedias or checking up on them for the welfare department. Generally speaking, when a stranger shows up at the door of a poor or working person, it's bad news. So explain as quickly as you can why you're there. Say, "We've been talking to everybody on this street about this problem." (This way people don't feel they're being singled out.) Or say, "Ms. Smith, three doors down, suggested that I talk to you." (If you're using this approach, you should be sure that you have Ms. Smith's permission to use her name.)

Try to ask questions rather than just giving a set speech. When you ask questions you give the other person a chance to join the conversation. You encourage that person to take a step herself, rather than just be a passive listener. Say, for example, "We've been talking to people on the street about the problems with the sewers. How bad does it get down here?" Or say,

"We're recruiting members for our neighborhood organization, the Tremont Improvement Committee. Have you heard about us?" If the person says, "I haven't heard about you at all," you might mention some active members of the organization that the person might know or some things the organization has accomplished.

You should take time in the conversation to make personal comments as well. After all, you're not selling encyclopedias. You're talking about the concept of solidarity, people working together and building an organization together. If the other person feels that what you're trying to do is make your sales pitch as quickly as possible and leave, he's going to be less open to it. So it doesn't hurt to get a conversation started with him about something he cares about. Sometimes you can look around the room and pick up clues to what someone's interests are: a photograph of him at work, the fact that *Monday Night Football* is on, a dog that keeps wandering through the living room, a tennis racket hanging on the wall. If you can find something you both have in common, it's a good starting point for a conversation and a relationship.

Listen. Most people are natural talkers, given the chance. What's hard to find is a natural listener. Since most of us are natural talkers, it's hard to develop the skill of listening. But like so many other leadership skills, it's something you can practice and get better at. Ask the kinds of questions that get people started. Then sit back and listen to what they have to say. If you spend half an hour listening to someone who ordinarily feels that no one ever listens to her, she's going to think that you're a special person and that the organization you're working with is something special, too.

As you spend more time contacting people and recruiting members, you'll develop your own list of techniques that work for you. It's helpful to exchange these ideas with other leaders and staff. Try out some of their ideas and see if you can make use of them.

Here, as an example, is a list of ideas to help in listening and talking to people. The list was put together by eight members of a public housing organization in Charlotte, North Carolina.

(1) Introduce yourself.
(2) Ask if you can come in.
(3) Talk about something you know they're interested in.
(4) Find something in the home to talk about.
(5) Talk to parents and kids together.
(6) Meet them on their level.
(7) Know the subject.
(8) Know yourself.
(9) Know when to listen and when to talk.
(10) Talk about one thing at a time.
(11) Let them talk—hear what they have to say.
(12) Learn their feelings.
(13) Look at them as you talk.
(14) Explain things clearly.
(15) Try to get them involved.
(16) Let them know they're important to you and the community.
(17) Let them come up with ideas.
(18) Ask questions.
(19) Watch their facial expressions.
(20) Give them praise.
(21) Don't argue.
(22) Don't try to force them to think your way.
(23) Don't curse.
(24) Listen more than you talk.
(25) Answer questions as you discuss a subject.
(26) *Never* cut them off.
(27) Don't insult them.
(28) Don't gossip about or put down other tenants.
(29) Don't make promises you can't keep.
(30) If you don't know the answer, get back to them.

(31) *Or* have them call you.

(32) Use the phone to follow up.

(33) Pick your time.

(34) Keep your cool.

(35) Know your limits.

(36) Stay assertive.

(37) Be yourself.

(38) Know how to delegate responsibility.

(39) Make arrangements for the next visit.

(40) Give them a reason for meeting.

What information do you want?

In talking with people you're also looking for information. If you're working on a particular issue, you want to know how they feel about it. This is an important way of testing your strategy. Let's suppose your organization has decided to focus on sewers as an issue. But as you talk to people you find that everybody is angry about something else entirely. You might need to rethink whether sewers is the right issue to be working on.

You also want a sense of what other things people are angry about. As you talk with people, ask them, "What do you think would make this a better neighborhood? What do you think would make life better for seniors in this city?" You may find some issues that you weren't really aware of or that you hadn't given enough importance to.

You also want to get a sense of what people's skills and abilities are. You want to know what they might be willing and able to do as members of the organization. As you talk about what *you* are doing, if someone seems to show particular interest at some point, make a note of it. That person might also be able to do some of those things.

It's helpful to get information on other people you should be talking with. Just ask directly, "Who else do you know that I should talk to?" Even if you're trying to talk to everyone in the neighborhood, having that personal link makes the contact easier. It's helpful if you can go five doors away and say, "I was just at Mr. Bagley's house and he said I should come see you." You may even be able to get Mr. Bagley to go with you to see his friends in the neighborhood.

What commitments do you want?

Even in a first contact, we want to begin the process of moving people into action. We do this by asking people to make some kind of specific commitment. Usually it's something small: We ask them to sign a petition, to come to a block meeting, to agree to become a member of the organization. But we want to make it clear from the start that our organization is about action, not just sitting by and waiting to see what will happen. We want it clear to people that we want *them* to become members of our organization, to join with us and work with us.

Not everyone you ask to make a commitment will make one. Other people will make a commitment but won't follow through. This often happens. You should expect that at least half of the people who promised to come to the meeting won't show up. But half of them *will* come and many of those will come back again. By involving people in the organization from the start, we are beginning the process of developing new leaders and strengthening the organization.

You may need to pressure people a little to get a commitment. You want to avoid pushing too hard. But a more common problem is not pushing hard enough. We don't just want people to know about us and what we're doing. If we want people to make a commitment, we need to make it very clear that there is a place and a job for them in the organization. They need to know that we want them to join with us and work with us.

One of the secrets to getting and keeping active members is finding things for them to do. Sometimes we get so used to doing things ourselves that we don't consider whether someone else could do them. It's useful to sit down with other leaders, members, and staff and make up a list of things that other people could be asked to do.

When the leaders and staff of Save Our Cumberland Mountains (SOCM), a community organization in eastern Tennessee, put together a list of things for members to do, they came up with over seventy-five ideas. Here are some of them:

(1) Get signatures on petitions.
(2) Sign petitions.
(3) Talk to neighbors.
(4) Make phone calls.
(5) Stop by the office.
(6) Work on issues.
(7) Pay dues.
(8) Write letters to legislators.
(9) Write letters to the editor.
(10) Stay in touch with less-active members.
(11) Clip county newspapers.
(12) Knock on doors in new communities with staff.
(13) Join committees.
(14) Do courthouse research.
(15) Call old members.
(16) Talk to the press.
(17) Speak at community meetings.
(18) Help arrange local meetings.
(19) Write articles for the newsletter.
(20) Staple, fold, and mail the newsletter.
(21) Do other work in the office.
(22) Collect dues.
(23) Take pictures.
(24) Organize grassroots fund raising.

What commitments should you make?

When you talk with people, one of the questions they often ask is "What are *you* going to do for *me*?" People sometimes put this very directly and boldly. You've got to expect that people are going to say, "OK. Suppose I join the organization. What do I get?" You need a good answer to this question. But be sure that your answer doesn't overcommit either the organization or you personally to do things that you can't deliver.

People's organizations can rarely promise anything. We can't promise that every issue will be solved, or that every fight will be won. We can't guarantee people lower taxes, better police protection, more parks, better schools. But we *can* talk about what the organization has been able to do in the past. We can talk about our accomplishments, the concrete gains that people have been able to win for themselves through organizing. We can say to people, "Look, I can't promise you what we'll be able to do about the sewers. But six months ago we took on the issue of streetlights. Maybe you remember that. Now there are three new lights on the street."

Another way of answering this question is to talk about what the organization has meant to you. Remember that it's not just the concrete specific benefits that keep people active in an organization. It's what the organization does for their feelings about themselves. You don't want to wear your heart on your sleeve, but at the same time it's helpful to be able to talk about what the organization means to you—the things that you've learned, the different feelings that you have about yourself, the changes in your goals. We want people to know from the beginning that our organization is not just about sewers and streetlights. It's also about people's dignity, their self-respect, their feelings for each other. It's about building a society we could all be proud to live in.

How much time should you spend with each person?

Sometimes there's so much to talk about that you could spend three or four hours with each person you see. That would be a mistake. People have busy lives. Most of them, between work, family, and other responsibilities, have very little extra time. We want people to know from the beginning that they can play a meaningful role as members in our organization without having to spend all their spare time working for it.

There is no set rule for how long is too long. You need enough time to talk a little bit about the organization, about yourself, about the issue, and about the commitment you want from the person. You also need enough time to develop a sense of the person, to give her a chance to talk, to ask her some questions. Probably this should take between ten and thirty minutes.

There will be cases where you'll want to spend either less or more time. Some people will be so resistant or hostile that it just won't make sense to try to break through that hostility, especially if it ends up making you angry or upset. In the early stages of organizing, we want to build a base of people who feel strongly as we do. Try to spend your time with these people rather than arguing with those who are totally opposed to what you're doing. If you go to see someone about sewers and he wants to attack your organization as communistic and un-American, you're probably just as well off finding someone else to talk to.

You're also going to find people who act as if they've been waiting all their lives for someone like you to come to their door. Sometimes in the first few minutes you get the instinct that this is someone who can be a leader in the organization. In that case you would want more time to get to know the person better, to check out your hunch, and to interest him or her in the organization.

Watch for signs that you are wearing out your welcome. If people start to fidget, light too many cigarettes, go to the bathroom, remember phone calls that they have to make, or move around the room, they're trying to tell you it's time to go. As you spend more time working with people you'll become more attuned to these signals.

Leaving shouldn't be too difficult. You can explain that you have a lot of other people to see before you get back to your family or before you go to work. Thank people for the time you've taken and let them know where they can reach you. Then move on to the next door.

There is another reason for not staying too long, besides wearing out your welcome and alienating potential members. In our organizing we don't want to raise expectations we can't continue to meet. We know from experience that as an organization grows it becomes harder and harder to spend time with members and other leaders. If you spend several hours with someone on your first visit, that may be the last time you have that much time to spend with that person. If you don't see people again for weeks or months, or as you see them for only brief periods of time, they decide that you no longer like them as much as you used to or that they're no longer as important to you and the organization. It's much better to see people for a short period of time at first so that their expectations of how much time you're going to spend with them are not raised too high.

How do you follow up on a recruiting contact?

It's important that your contacts be followed up, either by you or by someone else. This doesn't mean that you have to go back to see people the next week. But you should figure out ways of maintaining regular communication with them. One way is to involve them in the organization's activities. You can say to someone, "We need to talk some more about this. If you come to the meeting next week, we could take a few minutes and go over it again." This at least puts part of the responsibility on the other person.

Telephones are useful for maintaining communication once it's been established. Generally a phone call is not the best way to make the first contact in an organizing campaign. That's almost always done better person-to-person and face-to-face. But once you've established a relationship with a person, calling her or him is a good way of keeping in touch.

You want to follow up carefully on the commitments that you

asked individuals to make. If someone said that she would come to the meeting on Wednesday night, you might call her on Wednesday afternoon to remind her of the meeting and to tell her that you're hoping to see her there. If someone seemed interested in a particular issue, you might call him to tell him about some new information you've just obtained.

Regular contact with members is one of the secrets of building strong organizations. You should also encourage other leaders to work with people you know, especially if these people show leadership potential. Call the new member and say, "Listen, one of my friends from the organization is over visiting me. I'd really like you to meet her. Would it be all right if she came over this evening?"

Another way of following up on a contact is to send a brief note or piece of information. You probably wouldn't want to do this if the contact was with your next-door neighbor. But in most other cases you could say to the person during the initial conversation, "I don't have any information about the organization on me right now. Let me drop something in the mail to you when I get home." Enclose a brief handwritten note, something like "It was good meeting you. Hope to see you at the meeting on Friday."

If people have made other commitments, you should call to see whether they've been able to carry them out. If someone said he would get you the names of several people who might help out on the issue, wait two or three days and then call to see if he's been able to do it. This not only reminds the person of what he said he'd do, it shows him that you were serious in asking him to do it. There is nothing more discouraging than to be asked to do something and then have the person who asked you forget the request.

How often should you see people?

If there were more time, and if there were more leaders, it would be good to see people every week. We know that nothing can bind members together and to an organization like personal contact. Unfortunately, in most situations it just isn't possible to see people individually on a weekly basis. One of the reasons for holding small group meetings and other organizational events is to give people a chance to spend time with the leadership of an organization, without the leadership having to go out and see the people one at a time. So as soon as possible we want to encourage people to come to see us rather than our having to go and see them. If the organization has an office, encourage people to come and spend time there. Call them when you're getting out a mailing or folding leaflets. Ask them to come put in a few minutes of their time. Invite them to small group meetings and committee meetings.

On the other hand, if you've done this a number of times and someone still hasn't shown up, it may be best to look for someone else. A person who keeps saying, "I'll be there," but never comes is not someone who should become a leader in our organization.

What records should you keep?

All of us find that in a very short period of time we begin accumulating more information than we can possibly remember. When you're dealing with 17 issues, 136 people, 4 committees, a board, and 7 other leaders, it's sometimes hard to keep everything straight.

As you meet people, make very basic records of those contacts. They don't need to be complicated. But it helps to keep a file with the names, addresses, and phone numbers of the people you've seen, a brief note of what some of the issues are that interest each of them, and a comment on what each is interested in doing for the organization. Each time you see a person and talk with him or her, write down the date. That way you can go back through your contact cards and make sure that you're not ignoring somebody you should have followed up on. Don't write anything down on a card that you wouldn't want the person to see.

Especially in a hard-fought campaign, written materials have a way of disappearing and showing up in the wrong hands.

What can go wrong?

A number of things can go wrong in contacts. Almost everyone who has gone door-to-door in an organizing campaign has had some bad experiences. They can be tremendously discouraging, especially at the end of a long day. It's hard to keep your spirits up when doors are slammed in your face or when people don't seem interested in an issue you care about.

Sometimes we make mistakes. One mistake is pushing too hard. This can happen when you care deeply about an issue and about the organization. Naturally, you want other people to feel the same way. When people don't share your enthusiasm immediately, you may want to start pushing harder and arguing with them. This is a mistake. If a person feels pushed around, it becomes very difficult to involve that person in the organization later.

Sometimes we make the opposite mistake, which is not pushing hard enough. We go to someone's home. We sit and talk with him for an hour and have a wonderful time. But we leave without his having any real idea of who we are and why we were there.

It's important to keep in mind that you're not just visiting people. You're organizing. You're recruiting people to become members of an organization, to work on an issue. If the person you talked to doesn't have any sense of why you were there, the contact was a failure.

You also can run into problems if you give out incorrect information. All of us find it embarrassing to admit that we don't know something. So when we get a question that seems difficult but important, we'll simply try to answer it as best we can. Unfortunately, if we don't really know the answer, the one we come up with may be wrong. It's much better to say, "I don't know, but I'll find out," than to make up an answer on the spot. Of course, make sure that you do find out the answer and get back to the person with it.

Another problem that sometimes comes up is when you over-commit yourself or the organization. It's an easy thing to do. We say things like "Don't worry, I can always get you a ride there." Or "That's OK, I'll come back tomorrow and we'll talk about it again." Or "I'm sure we can get your daughter out of jail." Or "There's no danger, you couldn't possibly be thrown out of your house." In organizing there are no guarantees. We don't always accomplish what we set out to do. We can't promise that people won't in different ways suffer because of their participation. We have to be careful not to promise people anything that we can't deliver.

Sometimes we try too hard to convince people who are really against us. When we find someone who has leadership skills but who attacks the organization, it's easy to think, "If I could just change this person's mind, imagine how many other people might change their minds, too." But it's usually a mistake to waste time arguing with people. It's better to put our energy into helping the people who are with us to develop their leadership skills.

Sometimes we try hard to convince a person to join because we want as many people in the organization as we can get. Of course we want lots of members. But they have to be the right kind of members. We want people who work well with others, who are open to criticism, who are willing to change their minds. If we run into someone who is angry and critical about us and our organization it can be a real mistake to encourage that person to become a member. It's hard enough to build a successful people's organization without having people fighting us from the inside. If your best instincts say, "This person means trouble," let the person go.

What makes a good recruiting contact?

With a little practice most of our contacts can be good ones. In a good contact both we and the person we talked with come away with a sense of accomplishment. Each of us feels as if something has happened. A relationship has been started or moved forward a step. The person we've talked with is reasonably clear about certain basic things: who we are, why we came to see her, what the issue is, what the organization is and how she can become a member. She feels good about us and about our organization. She's made a commitment, a first step—something small, but a starting point.

Person-to-person contact work can be difficult. Sometimes it seems like more fun to be sitting in an office thinking up grand strategies and tactics. But few things are as basic to building a strong democratic organization as membership recruitment.

First contacts can only happen once. The initial impressions we make in many cases determine whether people will join us, whether they will be willing to work with us, whether they become members of the organization, whether they move on to become leaders in the organization. By continuing to do contact work in new communities and with new constituencies, we strengthen our organizations, build their membership, and broaden their base. We help people get started on the road that we as leaders started on the first time someone came to us and said, "Join with us."

7. Meetings

MEETINGS ARE a basic organizing tool. They serve a variety of purposes and come in different shapes and sizes. There are small meetings in people's homes, sometimes called "house meetings." House meetings are useful to deal with local issues which affect the block or neighborhood. They can be used to help people meet and become more comfortable with each other and to begin involving them in the organization.

Most organizations will have a variety of committees to carry out specific tasks. Many of these committees will meet regularly. The exact committees will vary from organization to organization. But a typical organization will have a finance committee, a personnel committee, a membership committee, and a communications or public relations committee. Organizations may also have committees to coordinate special events or to perform special functions. A committee may be put together only for the purpose of coordinating a specific campaign or action.

Organizations will also have some larger meetings. Most organizations have a board that meets regularly. Organizations will also want from time to time to bring together large numbers of people for other reasons. Some organizations have an annual meeting or convention to which they try to attract as many of their members as possible. Mass meetings may be used during a campaign to build spirit, to inform large numbers of people of what's happening, and to let the opposition know how much strength the organization can pull together.

Regardless of their size, all meetings share several purposes: to give people a sense of participation, to build solidarity, to develop strategies and choose tactics, and to make decisions.

When should you start holding meetings?

Meetings should begin early in the organizing campaign. Remember that organizing is a process of bringing people together. As a leader, one of your responsibilities is to encourage other members of the organization to get to know each other, to learn each other's strengths and weaknesses, and to find ways in which they can work together cooperatively. Meetings help this happen.

What would happen if you tried to have an organizing campaign without meetings? You could work with people individually, visiting with them at their homes, at work, or on the street. You could give them information on what was going on, and ask for their opinions about what should happen next. The danger in this approach is that you, the leader, end up doing all the work and sorting out all the information. While people should look to you for leadership, they should not look to you for every bit of information on what's happening in the organization. If you go too long without a meeting, people will come to depend on you for all their information and will only relate to the organization through you, rather than through each other. If later on you start having meetings and asking people to depend on each other and take responsibility, you may find that they resent it. People will say, "You used to come see us all the time. Now you want us to go out and do the work." It's much better to make it clear in the beginning that people will have to work together as a group to get things done, rather than depending on you as an individual.

What's a good size for a meeting?

The best size for a meeting depends on its purpose. A meeting should be as small as possible while still including those people who have a direct interest in what's going to happen.

There are times when we will want to have the largest possible meeting. Suppose the organization is opposing construction of a hazardous wastes dump near your neighborhood. You decide to call a meeting where people can express their opinions to the media. You want to have as many people attend as possible to show the strength of the organization and of the organized opposition. In this case, we are using the meeting to attract media attention, to increase the spirit of our members, and to give a warning to those opposing us. (The tactical use of mass meetings is discussed in the chapters on strategy and tactics.)

In this chapter, when we talk about meetings, we're talking about *small group meetings*. These are meetings of under fifty people and often much smaller, which are called for the purpose of decision making and information. They include block meetings, neighborhood meetings, committee meetings, board meetings, strategy and planning meetings, and training sessions.

How do you get people to come to a meeting?

Almost everyone who has been a leader in an organization has had the experience of holding a meeting that no one showed up for. There are few experiences quite as lonely as sitting in a room full of empty chairs wondering where everyone is. There is no perfect formula for getting people to come to a meeting every time. But there are a number of ideas that have proved helpful.

Meetings should be held at a convenient place where people feel comfortable. One of the reasons that house meetings are such

a good technique is because they can be held right in the neighborhood where people live. If people just have to walk down the
block or over to another unit in the housing project for the meeting, they don't have to worry so much about transportation. It's
easier to arrange for child care or to bring the children with them.
If transportation is necessary, ask at the beginning of the meeting
who needs a ride home. Try to find someone driving in their
direction who can take them. People can concentrate on the
meeting better if they don't have to worry about getting home
afterward.

Meetings that are held near where people live or work also
have a different feeling from when people have to travel to get to
them. They feel more like neighbors and friends just getting
together.

If the organization covers a large area and has a permanent
office, it sometimes seems easier to ask people to the office for
meetings. But if this involves a good deal of travel, it may result
in fewer people coming rather than more. An office also means
interruptions: people walking in, phones ringing, other members
and leaders of the organization or staff people coming by to see
what's happening. A meeting should be held in a place where
there's little likelihood of interruption. It's not easy to get a good
feeling going in a meeting. Once you get that feeling going, it's a
shame to lose it because of ringing phones.

Meetings should be held in places that are comfortable for the
people attending. If you're organizing senior citizens, try to avoid
a meeting place that involves climbing three flights of stairs. Be
conscious of access for people who are in wheelchairs. If most of
the people you're working with have small children, it's helpful to
hold the meeting in a place large enough so that the children can
come as well. Lack of day care is a major reason why people fail
to come to meetings.

If house meetings are being held, it's a good idea to have them
in a different home each time. This gives everyone the chance to
be the host. It gives each person a certain importance in the
neighborhood and the organization. It also means that no one

person is going to have the burden of a meeting in her or his home week after week. You'll sometimes find that certain people, despite the burden, will ask that the committee meet regularly at their home because of the status that this gives them. But you should think carefully before accepting this kind of offer, since it does put a certain amount of power into the hands of the person in whose home the meetings are being held. It's much better to give each member of the small group a chance to host a house meeting.

The physical setting should be comfortable. When possible it's better to have a room that's about the same size as the group that's meeting. If eight people are meeting in a corner of an auditorium that seats 200, they feel lonely and isolated. If you're meeting in a small room with comfortable chairs and soft lighting, it's easier for people to establish good communication with each other.

Don't forget the props that are needed in a strategy session and discussion. Bring an easel with newsprint and felt-tip markers and masking tape so that completed sheets of paper can be put on the wall. Remember tablets, pencils, and pens so that people can take notes. Sometimes you might want sign-up sheets and name tags. An extension cord and three-prong adapter can solve many emergencies. You might want to make up a "meeting survival kit" with these items to keep in the trunk of your car.

In choosing a meeting place, try to be conscious of how the people you're working with may feel about it. The neighborhood bar may be a comfortable place to meet, but some people in the community may not want to be seen there. A meeting room in a motel can be a problem if the motel has a reputation as a place where people go if they are running around. Better meeting places are those buildings where people feel comfortable going and being seen: a school, church, synagogue, neighborhood club, community center, union hall.

In some cities and towns the business institutions have meeting places that they make available to local groups. Banks and chambers of commerce usually have meeting rooms that are available to the public. But be careful about deciding to use these. They are often decorated and laid out to convey a sense of that institution's power. People may feel that they are being watched—which may be true.

If you're working in an area that is mixed racially or ethnically, in choosing meeting places you need to be conscious of whether they are regarded as turf for one or the other of the groups. In a multiracial organization, for example, try not to meet only in all-black or all-white churches. Choose, when possible, those meeting places that would be seen as neutral or mutual. Alternate meeting places to avoid being identified as any one group's organization.

When should meetings be held?

In scheduling meetings you need to be conscious of the living patterns among the people you're working with. In a factory town where almost everyone works first shift, a meeting at two in the afternoon would not be a good idea. On the other hand, if you're working with a group of senior citizens in an area where many of them are reluctant to go out at night, two o'clock might be the ideal time. In some southern mill towns, where mills run three shifts six days a week, Sunday may be the only time available for meetings that bring everyone in the mill together.

The group that is meeting should make the decision about when meetings are held. In a discussion of the matter, you can help by asking questions to try to figure out the patterns of people's lives: when they go to church, what evenings have regularly scheduled events, what times are best for them to get out, when child care is available, when transportation is the easiest. For a first meeting, you can ask people these questions individually and come to some decision yourself as to what the best time and place would be. However, don't feel that because the first meeting was on Wednesday at three o'clock, all other meetings should be at the same time. Leave that decision up to the group.

Who should call a meeting?

Once an organization is established it usually sets up rules for how and by whom meetings can be called. Most meetings will be scheduled for a regular time and place. The organization will also need to have clear rules for calling special meetings to make sure that these are called in a way that is useful and does not set people against each other.

In an organization where no meetings have been held yet, there's no reason why you can't be the person to call one. Do your best to figure out when and where the meeting should be held. Give people enough advance notice so that they can make plans. If enough people say that they can't attend a meeting at a particular time and place, be willing to change when and where the meeting will be held.

Don't expect to recruit people to a meeting, especially a first meeting, without personal contact. Letters, posters, leaflets, or flyers rarely have the impact of a personal visit or a phone call. If you're working toward a first meeting, the success of that meeting is important enough for you to put a lot of time into it. Go see people individually if you want to have them at the meeting. If you can't see them at home or at work, at least try to make personal contact with them by telephone. Follow up shortly before the meeting. Check with them to make sure that they have transportation and child care. Try to arrange to provide these if people haven't been able to work it out themselves. In some cases you might want to pick people up yourself. It's important enough to get people to a meeting to make it worthwhile putting some time into it.

What should happen at a meeting?

A successful meeting accomplishes several things. First, it communicates information. People go away from the meeting feeling that they know more than they did before they came—about the organization, the issues, and each other.

Second, a successful meeting should result in some decision being made. Meetings which are all talk and no action are frustrating to everyone who participates in them. A good meeting ends with at least one decision made.

Third, a successful meeting results in some agreement on division of labor and acceptance of responsibility. Everyone should leave a meeting with something specific to do and with a good feeling about doing it.

Fourth, meetings should build a sense of spirit among the people attending. They should come away feeling that they had a good time, that they had a chance to participate, that they were listened to, that their opinions were respected, that their ideas were considered carefully.

Finally, a good meeting should help build the organization. People should go away feeling a little closer to the organization, with a greater sense of what the organization does and more loyalty toward it.

How do you prepare for a meeting?

Careful planning is a key to successful meetings. The first planning decision to make is whether to have a meeting at all. You then need to decide who should come, where the meeting should be held, and at what time.

It's important to spend time not only getting people to the meeting but preparing them for what's going to happen there. If people come to a meeting with very different ideas about what's going to happen, all kinds of different things *will* happen. It will be very difficult to get people to work on a common agenda. People will go away feeling frustrated and as if they wasted their time. Someone who has spent several hours feeling that she or he would be better off someplace else *will* be someplace else the next time there's a meeting.

Successful preparation for a meeting involves thinking through carefully what needs to happen at the meeting and then working through these ideas with the people who will be coming before they get to the meeting. Make a list for yourself of what you think the meeting's goals are. There should be some general goals like getting people to know each other and making sure that everyone has a chance to participate. But what is the purpose of the meeting? The meeting should not be held just to plan the next meeting. Some decision needs to be made. What is that decision? Responsibilities need to be divided up among the members. What are those responsibilities? This isn't to say that you decide in advance what the decision of the meeting will be or what jobs members are going to take. But you do need to come up with a rough outline of what the discussion should cover. Having this clear in your own mind will also allow you to move the discussion along more effectively. In this way you can help make sure the meeting accomplishes what it sets out to.

Should an agenda be used?

The word *agenda* comes from a Latin word that means "the things that need to be done." A good agenda is simply an outline of the things that should be done at a meeting. Agendas don't need to be complicated or formal. A short list of the main points that need to be covered is usually better than a long, complicated agenda. This can be copied and given to each member individually, written on a blackboard in the room, or lettered on newsprint and taped to the wall.

One of the advantages of an agenda is that it gives the chair a tool for keeping the meeting moving along smoothly. When the agenda is posted on the wall where everybody can see it, if the discussion starts to wander, the chair can say, "This is a good discussion. But we still need to figure out how we're going to respond to the city council's resolution. Does anyone have any ideas about how we can do that?" If *Response to City Council's Resolution* is written in big letters on the wall, the chair can point to it and redirect the discussion without offending people.

Who should chair?

Nothing makes good meetings happen more than a good chair-person. The chair can set the tone for a meeting. The chair can make sure that everyone participates and no one dominates. The chair is responsible for seeing that the meeting accomplishes something, that decisions are made and work assigned.

The chair should be someone who has the skills necessary to do this. It should be someone good at encouraging people who are shy or quiet to talk. It should be someone who is able to gently but firmly keep any one person from dominating the meeting. The chair should be someone who is neither too quiet nor too domi-nating. The most outspoken member of the group is not neces-sarily the best choice for chair.

If you're the one who has called the meeting, thought through the agenda, gone to see people to get them to come, and talked over what should happen, you're also the logical choice to be the chair, at least at the first meeting. In small group meetings it's a good idea for different people to act as chair at different times. This allows each of them to begin developing the skill of chairing. It also means that authority is rotated. If the same person chairs the meeting each time, only that one person will develop skills and power as chair. We want many members of the organization to share those skills and power.

If someone is going to act as chair for the first time, you or a staff person should help prepare her before the meeting. You should go over the agenda with her and make sure she understands the issues that are going to be discussed. Let her practice what she's going to say and how she's going to say it. If possible, hold a small training session for the members who are going to chair the next few meetings so that they get a chance to practice in a small group.

It may be that neither you nor anyone else in the group feels able to act as chair. You may be tempted to ask a staff person to chair the first meeting. But chairing is a skill you need to learn sooner or later. The first meeting is as good a time as any. It's much better to have a leader chairing the group's first meeting than a staff person. People get their first impression of how the organization operates at the first meeting. If they see staff instead of leadership chairing, they might decide that's the way it's supposed to be.

How do you make people comfortable?

Part of making people comfortable at a meeting involves what happens before the meeting. If people come with a clear sense of why they're there and what they're expected to do, they'll feel more comfortable than if they're walking into an unknown situation.

There is also a lot you can do at the meeting to create a sense of comfort. You and other leaders should greet people as they come in the door. Ask them how they are. Take a few minutes to talk to them about the meeting. Thank them for coming. See if they have any questions you can answer.

It's helpful to have refreshments to serve. When people are nervous they often like to have something else to do with their hands and mouths. A cup of coffee or cola can make it easier for someone to deal with a stressful situation.

Introduce people to each other if they haven't already met. In the introduction try to point out some of the things that they have in common so that they have the beginnings of a conversation. Don't just walk away and leave them staring at each other.

Arrange the room in a way that seems open and not intimidating. Soft chairs rather than hard ones, circles rather than rows, soft lighting rather than bright, glaring bulbs help create a friendly atmosphere.

Start on time. If it's clear that some people are about to come through the door at any moment, however, it might be worth waiting a few minutes to avoid the disruption.

If you're chairing the meeting, you have a chance to set the tone from your opening remarks. Welcome people. Thank them for coming. If you know all of them well enough, you can sometimes make the introductions. Tell some of the nice things about them that other people would be interested in knowing. Everyone feels flattered when they're recognized, especially when the nice things said about them are actually true.

Lay out as clearly as you can what the purpose of the meeting is. Use the agenda so people have something they can follow. Announce how long the meeting is going to be and what time you're going to try to break up. Don't be too serious. Jokes, good humor, and stories set a tone that makes for better discussion. Remember that people will be looking to you for a sense of how they should act. If you act stiff and formal, they'll act stiff and formal, too.

How do you get people to participate?

The tone that you set as chair at the beginning of the meeting will have a lot to do with whether or not people participate. For example, if you talk for twenty minutes, you're in effect saying that you intend to run and dominate the meeting. People will pick up the cue and will either play a quieter role or decide to confront you in an aggressive manner. Keep your opening remarks short and to the point and move quickly into group discussions.

It's better to structure group discussions than to simply to let them happen. If you merely raise a question and throw it open to anyone, what often happens is that the most vocal member of the group takes the floor and talks for twenty minutes, even if you as the chair only talked for five. At least until a group gets used to working together, it's sometimes better for the chair to say, "We need to sit down and figure out the steps to take if we're going to have the demonstration at the courthouse on Wednesday. Now what I'd like to do is ask everyone to make up a list of the steps they think are necessary. That way we get everyone's best thinking. Then I'm going to go around the room and ask each of you to name something from your list. Then we can come up with a group list that we can all talk over together."

By getting everyone to come up with a few of their own ideas you're giving them a chance to participate right from the start. The combined list will represent the best thinking of everyone in the group. Everyone will at least have some of their ideas on the group list. Going around the circle and calling on everyone in turn encourages people to participate.

Of course you can't do this for every point that comes up in a discussion. That becomes awkward and artificial. This is a technique to use at the start of a meeting. Later on in the meeting you could use your option as chair to call on some of the people who haven't been participating. Just say, "Mr. Smith, do you have any thoughts about how we could do this?" or "Mr. Smith, how do you feel about the idea of using leaflets?" Don't push people too hard if they seem reluctant to participate. Pressure to participate can be as discouraging to people as not participating at all.

Should parliamentary procedure be used?

Although parliamentary procedure is often described as a tool for making meetings more orderly, it's really a tool for using power to manipulate group situations. It's a technique that people's organizations need to understand and be able to use—but not in their own small group meetings. In many confrontation situations, especially those involving different levels of government, parliamentary procedure will be one of the tactics used. But for small group meetings within our own organization, parliamentary procedure usually is confusing and can hurt discussion more than it helps. To the extent that it's useful in people's organizations, it should probably be reserved for official board meetings and conventions where it's necessary for legal reasons to record who actually made and seconded the motions. But for encouraging good discussions in small groups, parliamentary procedure is the wrong tool.

Should you keep minutes?

Formal minutes, the kind that tell who said what, who spoke next, who made and who seconded motions, are usually not necessary in small group meetings. They may also intimidate people who want to be able to speak freely and who are concerned about what happens to the minutes after the meeting. Remember that your opposition is always going to be interested in what goes on in your meetings. They can often find ways of obtaining the different kinds of papers that people's organizations produce. As a general rule, it's safer not to put anything down on paper that you wouldn't want your opposition reading. But it does make sense to keep some kind of written record of the decisions reached at a meeting so that people are clear on what got decided and who was responsible for what. This doesn't need to be in the form of minutes. It can simply be a sheet of paper listing different people's names and what they agreed to do.

How long should meetings be?

The shorter meetings are, the better. For most people, an hour is a pretty good slice out of their day. That doesn't even count the time getting to the meeting and getting back. Unless there are complicated or unusually difficult decisions to be made, a meeting should be planned so that it can be over in an hour. If that is the normal length for a meeting within the organization and a particular meeting is expected to last longer, people need to know in advance so they can make plans.

Setting a definite short length for a meeting also helps to get people there. It's useful to be able to say to people, "We're going to meet at one o'clock and adjourn at two." This gives them an idea of what to expect. If the meetings begin on time and end on time, people are more likely to come back. Someone who comes to a "one-hour meeting" set for one o'clock which doesn't start until a quarter of two and then lasts until four o'clock, has spent three hours of her or his time and is less likely to return.

Setting a definite length for meetings in advance also makes it easier to move the necessary business of each meeting along without putting unnecessary pressure on any one individual. The chair can say, "Listen, I've noticed that we've only got twenty minutes left. We still need to figure out who's going to do what for tomorrow. Could we spend some time on that now? If there's time left over we can continue this discussion. Or if some of you want to stay after the meeting is adjourned we could go on with it." This is easier than having to ask people directly to sit down and be quiet.

Should meetings be open or closed?

One of the things that makes meetings effective is everyone having a shared sense of what needs to be done. They should also share some background and assumptions about what is happening in the organization. One of the problems organizations often have is that the same meeting will be attended by committee members who have a specific job to do and by new people who have heard about the organization and have just dropped by to find out what's going on. In this situation any number of things can happen, none of them very good. The committee members may get down to work on various specific items, leaving the newcomers feeling left out and isolated. The committee may decide to take a good bit of time to explain to the visitors what the organization is about and its history. In that case, the necessary business doesn't get done. After several meetings like this, committee members start complaining, "All we ever do is go over the same ground again and again. Why don't we do something different?" The committee may be ready to go about its business only to be interrupted by people who don't understand what's going on.

It's better to limit meetings to people who have a direct interest in what's going to happen at them. It does make sense to have orientation meetings for new people in order to bring them up to date on the history and background of the organization. If a person hasn't been to a meeting, one of your responsibilities as a leader is to give him or her this background individually or together with any other new people who will be coming. But simply to open meetings to anyone who happens to be around at that particular time is a mistake. This doesn't mean that you evict somebody who wanders in the door. But you should be reasonably careful in setting up meetings to make sure that they won't be interrupted by people who don't have a direct interest in what needs to be done.

What if people just talk and won't come to a decision?

This is one of the most common things that happens in meetings. People begin telling favorite stories. They talk about things that have happened in their lives. They start having such a good time that they don't want to get down to the business at hand.

This situation puts the chair in an awkward position. There are several things you might try. We've already talked about using the agenda or the time limit to speed discussion along. Another possibility is to break the meeting down into small groups with specific assignments. This can be a useful technique in large meetings where several people have started talking and everyone else wants a chance to talk as well. If nothing else, smaller groups mean that several people can talk at once in different places. When people in a small group are given the responsibility of discussing a situation for half an hour and coming up with three possible solutions, they're more likely to get down to work.

One of the things that you can do in preparing for a meeting is to make plans for these kinds of situations. Work out jointly with several other leaders the strategy to use. Sometimes this is called having a "floor team." Sit down before the meeting with a couple of other leaders in the group and ask them to back you up in a situation like this. One of the problems with being the chair is that if you have to play too heavy a hand, people begin to resist and resent you. So it's helpful if suggestions come from other people as well. For example, part of the planning might be an agreement that if people continue to resist getting down to decision making, one of the members of the floor team will take the floor and say, "Well, I have to go in half an hour and I'd like to get down to brass tacks. How about if we break up into small groups and see if we can get this thing tied up?"

What else can go wrong in a meeting?

Thinking about some of the things that can go wrong in a meeting is useful in understanding how to help a meeting go right. Here is a list made up by a group of public housing residents of things you can do to disrupt a meeting:

Interrupt.
Talk loudly to your neighbor.
Walk around.
Change the subject.
Make jokes.
Fill in silences.
Bang on the table.
Shout.
Clap.
Cough.
Whisper.
Blow your nose.
Walk out, then walk back in.
Talk about personal problems.
Call people names.
Make personal attacks.
Gossip.
Pass notes.
Clear your throat.
Go to the front and face the audience.
Stand behind the person speaking.
Hold up signs.
Call for prayer.
Fall asleep.

Think about some of the meetings you have attended that just didn't seem to go well. Didn't many of these things happen? The next time you're at a meeting where you don't need to participate and can just watch, notice how things like those listed above can accidentally or deliberately break up a meeting. As a leader, you may have to deal with some of these situations. While it's never easy, it helps to plan in advance how you might handle them. (It's also helpful to remember these ideas for the times when we *want* to disrupt a meeting of the opposition.)

What are the roles of leaders in a meeting?

As a leader, you play a key role in making good meetings happen. You will be doing this sometimes individually and sometimes working together with a team of other leaders.

Part of your work lies in planning the meeting, making sure that it is held at a good time and place, figuring out what needs to happen, preparing an agenda that reflects this, making provisions for transportation and child care, creating a setting that is comfortable and puts people at ease, and working with people individually before the meeting to prepare them for it. Good meetings don't just happen. They're made to happen.

Some of your work comes during the meeting. One of the roles a leader plays is as the chair. But there are other roles as well. You might be part of a floor team that backs up the chair. You might also work toward some specific goals inside the meeting.

It's important that the meeting be understandable to everyone there. You should watch people's faces to see whether or not they seem to understand what's happening. If you get the sense that people are confused, try to clear it up. Don't say, "I don't think Ed understands." Say, "Could we go over that one more time?" or "I'd like to hear that discussion again. I'm not sure on some points." As a leader it's easier for you to ask for clarification than it is for someone who is really unclear.

Try to make sure that other people participate. If another member whispers a suggestion in your ear, whisper back, "That's a good point. You should bring it up." If the person says, "No, *you* bring it up," say, "No, *you* do it." Or you might take the floor and say, "Sarah just made a good suggestion to me and I was going to ask her if she could tell the group about it." (Of course, you should ask Sarah first if it's all right to do this.) In this way you function as a bridge to help other people become part of the group.

Make sure that no one person or small group of people dominates the meeting, including yourself. Small group meetings are a good place to practice democracy. But democracy isn't a process that happens naturally or easily. It has to be worked at. Try to work consciously to limit the role you play in the meeting and to encourage other people who are less self-confident.

How do decisions actually get made in small group meetings?

It's wonderful when at the end of a meeting it's clear to everyone what needs to happen next. Everyone agrees on the issue, the strategy, the tactics, the next steps, the division of responsibility. Each member feels that he or she got a chance to talk, that his or her ideas were listened to and respected. Everyone understands everyone else and feels good about the decisions that were reached. We call this kind of agreement *consensus*. As a decision-making technique, consensus means that we keep talking and working until everyone in the meeting is in agreement. Consensus is a popular technique for decision making in small groups, and one that some people believe in almost exclusively.

The problem is that in organizing it's not always clear what the right answer or even the best answer is, even to the most skilled and experienced leaders and staff people. Consensus assumes that there is a right answer, and that if we talk for long enough everyone will discover and agree to it. This assumption can make for very long meetings.

Consensus sounds like a very democratic process—after all, in the end, everyone is supposed to agree. But in many situations it can put great pressure on the one or two people who continue to disagree with the majority. Say there are ten women in a committee meeting planning the next action against their boss, who has been sexually harassing them. Nine of them want to pass out flyers the next day at work telling about the issue and naming the man responsible. One woman feels strongly that this is the wrong thing to do. Consensus would require her to change her mind to agree with the majority. All the pressure is on her. She is the one blocking group agreement. Just because of her, the meeting has to go on and on. If it weren't for her, the committee decision would be unanimous and everyone could leave.

This isn't democracy. Democratic decision making means that the opinion of the majority rules, but that the opinions of the minority are respected. It's better in this situation to take a vote and let the woman who disagrees with the rest go on record with what she believes. There's nothing wrong with taking action even though everyone in the group doesn't agree on it, so long as each person has had a fair chance to be heard. No matter how good the chairing may be, we can't always reach agreement at a meeting. While taking a vote may sometimes seem like the majority imposing its will on the minority, it's sometimes the only way to preserve the minority's right to its opinions. For this reason, once an issue has been carefully talked through by all people present, voting rather than trying to reach consensus is often a more democratic decision-making method for a small group.

Should staff attend meetings?

Most of us have had the experience of being at a meeting of a people's organization where the staff outnumbered the people. At some meetings staff people even do most of the talking and decision making. This can be downright embarrassing in an organization that's supposed to help people speak for and represent themselves. Staff domination of meetings undercuts the self-sufficiency that we're trying to build among members and leaders of the organization.

If an organization has staff, it may be useful for at least those staff members with specific parts to play to attend some meetings. But they should not have a dominating or controlling role. A staff person should not chair the meeting; staff should be responsible to the chair. Staff people should not initiate their own participation in the discussions unless asked by a member or the chair to add what they think.

It's useful to have staff at meetings because of the amount of time they put into the organization. They have information and knowledge that other people present may not have. They may also, because of their own training and experience, have special insights and skills which can be useful in reaching decisions. But the leaders should make those decisions themselves. This situation can be difficult to achieve. Many staff organizers come from backgrounds in which they are used to speaking out openly and saying whatever they feel. Especially if such staff members are relatively inexperienced, they may have difficulty controlling their comments. But they need to do so.

As a leader you may need to work with staff members individually and in groups to help them learn to play a background role in meetings. Because staff are often college educated and used to speaking publicly, they can intimidate other members of the group who are just beginning to build up their own self-confidence. Staff can have an important role in meetings, but it needs to be under the direction of the group.

There will also be times when groups want to meet without staff. As the group grows in maturity and ability it should increasingly be able to take on responsibility for its own decision making without the need for staff assistance. One of your goals as a leader should be not to involve staff more in the decision-making process but to involve them less. One way of doing this may be for the chair and other leaders to sit down with the staff before the meeting and plan out their role in it, with the mutual goal of increasing the role which leaders and members of the group play.

How do you evaluate what happened at a meeting?

One of the best ways of making meetings better is to take a look after each meeting at what went right, what went wrong, and why. Take a few minutes at the end of the meeting to talk about the meeting itself. The chair can ask, "How do all of you feel about this meeting? Did we meet the goals we set for ourselves? Did we finish our agenda? Did we talk about the things we needed to talk about? Did we make the decisions we needed to make?'' Ask also, "How do you *feel* about the meeting? Was it a good discussion? Did you feel a part of it? Did anybody feel left out?'' Of course you can't always count on the people who felt left out to say they did. But sometimes people will, and that can spark a good discussion about group participation.

You should also follow up on the meeting with people individually after it breaks up. In the days after the meeting, ask people as you talk to them, "What did you think of the meeting on Wednesday? Are you satisfied with the way it went? What suggestions do you have for the next one? What could we do to make our meetings better?''

If we build into our organizing a spirit of self-criticism, it becomes easier to make changes as we need them. Because there are not fixed rules for meetings, some of the things that make a meeting good are simply those things that the group wants. These things can only be discovered by asking the group.

How do you follow up on a meeting?

In addition to finding out how people felt about the meeting, you also want to follow up to see what new ideas they had afterward and how the actions agreed on at the meeting are proceeding. You may want to go see some people individually, especially if you have a sense that they may not follow up on what they agreed to do. You might offer to help some of them if you think that the problem is a lack of skill or experience.

This can be a delicate role. It's sometimes helpful to clarify it in the meeting. If you're the chair you can say, "It's important that we get these things done. So I'll probably be calling each of you three or four days from now to see how it's going and to make sure that no one bit off more than she or he could chew. That way we can get help for people who need it.'' As the chair, you might also ask one of the other leaders to take on the responsibility for following up.

How often should meetings be held?

Most organizations have too many meetings. Usually as time goes by these meetings become smaller and smaller. This in turn is discouraging to the people who do attend and makes it harder to get the necessary work done.

One of the ways to deal with this situation is to have fewer meetings. Once a month is probably often enough for most groups to meet. A regular meeting time helps people remember the meeting and helps them plan it into their overall schedule. If special circumstances require special meetings, it's easy enough to call one.

Don't be afraid to cancel a meeting if there is really no need to hold one. It's better to go ahead and say, "There doesn't seem to be any real need to meet this month. Why don't we all take a break. We've worked hard." This shouldn't be just your opinion, of course. You need to talk to other leaders and members first. Some type of social event in place of the canceled meeting can help build people's spirits and get them ready to meet again.

What are the most important things to remember about meetings?

Here's a checklist of the twenty things that are most important for you as a leader to remember about meetings. Use this checklist when you're planning a meeting to make sure you haven't forgotten anything.

(1) *Plan the meeting in advance.* A good meeting doesn't just happen. It's carefully planned beforehand. Before you hold the meeting, think about what results you want from it.

(2) *Talk with people before the meeting.* Just as you as the organizer need to prepare for the meeting, so do the people who

will be coming. They also need a chance to think about what they'd like the meeting to accomplish, and about some of the issues that will be discussed.

(3) *Prepare an agenda*. Having a written agenda makes it easier to stick to the subject. An agenda doesn't have to be fancy. You can write it on a blackboard or on a sheet of newsprint. At the start of the meeting, go over the agenda with the people present and make sure there's agreement on what the meeting should cover.

(4) *Keep the agenda short*. Don't try to cover everything in one meeting—especially not in a first meeting. Two or three items are usually plenty to talk about.

(5) *Keep the meeting short*. How many meetings have you attended that went on and on and on and on? An hour—or two, at the most—is sufficient for any meeting.

(6) *Start on time*. If people know you'll wait for them even if they're late, they'll be late. You can't always make sure people will come on time, but making a habit of starting the meeting at the announced time helps.

(7) *End on time*. If the meeting is supposed to end in an hour, go for an hour and stop. You may not always get all the necessary business done. But over time people will get in the habit of working a little more quickly than if they think the meeting will keep going for as long as people are willing to talk.

(8) *Have a good chair*. Of course, that's sometimes easier said than done. You don't want a chair who does all the talking, who lets the meeting get out of hand, who wanders away from the agenda, or who lets other people dominate.

(9) *Let everyone talk*. What people hear at a meeting is sometimes less important than what they themselves say. If they all have a chance to participate, they'll probably feel good about the meeting. All of us like to have our ideas listened to.

(10) *Keep meetings small*. Large meetings prevent most people from participating. In a small meeting everyone can play a part. It's also easier to get work done in a small meeting.

(11) *Provide child care*. If you don't make arrangements for child care, a lot of people won't be able to come. Let children come to the meetings. People can take turns watching them if necessary. Besides, often the children turn out to be one of the organization's best resources.

(12) *Use a convenient place*. Find a meeting place that people are comfortable in and that's easy to get to: someone's home, a synagogue, a church, a school, a neighborhood restaurant with a private room. If the meeting place is a little out of the way, make sure people have transportation. Don't hold meetings where people have to walk up five flights of stairs or you'll lose a lot of participants.

(13) *Keep it loose and friendly*. A meeting doesn't need to be stiff and formal. Have fun. Make jokes. Tell stories (but not real long ones). Let people enjoy themselves.

(14) *Have refreshments*. But don't necessarily provide them yourself. That's something members of the group can take turns doing. Be careful about serving alcoholic beverages—there are places where that offends a lot of people.

(15) *Ask questions*. That's a good way to keep the discussion moving, and to make sure everyone participates. If someone hasn't been joining in, ask the person what he or she thinks.

(16) *Reach a decision*. Don't have a meeting just to talk. A good meeting ends with a decision to *do* something. This means more than just agreeing to have another meeting.

(17) *Divide responsibility*. Everyone should go away from the meeting with something to do.

(18) *Write it down*. As ideas are talked about, write them down on a blackboard or newsprint. That makes the discussion easier to follow. It also gives you a record of what went on at the meeting.

(19) *Follow up*. If people agreed at the last meeting to do certain things, find out if they did them. When people carry out the responsibilities they take on, they should be praised and appreciated.

(20) *Celebrate*. If things are going well, if the group is starting to win some victories, reward yourselves. Take a few minutes at the end of the meeting to relax and socialize. Sing. Talk about how everyone feels. Celebrate.

How do meetings build organization and action?

Sometimes it seems as if meetings exist only for the purpose of calling further meetings. People feel talked to death. "Meet, meet, meet, meet, meet. When are we going to *do* something?"

If all the group is doing is meeting and no action ever comes out of it, something is wrong. But meetings are one of the basic tools by which we build toward action in an organization. We use meetings not just to make the decisions that lead to action. Meetings help us make sure that those decisions are understood and shared by the people who will have to carry them out.

We use meetings for political education, to help the members of our organization build a sense of the dynamics of organizing and of power. We use them to build togetherness, to create the sense of group spirit and of working together for a common cause.

Meetings help overcome fear. In meetings people get to know the other members of the group well enough to feel that they can rely on them, even in difficult situations. Meetings build self-confidence. People who have never talked to an audience before can use small group meetings to practice public speaking. As they learn that their opinions make sense, that what they think is of value, that their ideas are respected and listened to, they build up the confidence that allows them to play a more outgoing role in public.

Finally, meetings build solidarity. They help people change from a collection of individuals to an organization where they share certain common histories, culture, ideas, values, spirit, and goals, where people rely on each other as well as on themselves, where they gain in skill and self-confidence. Good meetings help people learn to work more effectively as individuals and together.

8. Strategy

STRATEGY is like a road map. It's a plan for getting from where we are to where we want to go. Planning strategy is like planning a trip. The same decisions need to be made when an organization develops its strategy as when a family takes a vacation.

We need to decide whether we want to travel by car, bus, plane, or train. Which one we choose will depend on how much money we have. It will also depend on how quickly we want to get where we're going and how much time we want to spend enjoying ourselves and building up spirits along the way. It will depend on whether we want to go straight to our end point or whether we want to leave open the possibility of side trips to other points of interest. Finally there is the question of dependability. If it looks as if it might snow, we might be more inclined to take a train than the family car. On the other hand, if the traffic on the roads looks heavy, we might decide to fly and not take the chance of arriving late at our destination.

We need to choose the route. The fastest route may not necessarily be the best. If we drive for fourteen hours straight on the expressway to get to our destination, by the time we get there the people in the car may be tired, cranky, and unable to enjoy themselves.

We need to consider the difficulty of the route. If it's one that we and others have traveled a number of times and the roads are in good repair, we can be fairly confident of an easy trip. If, however, there is a likelihood of bad weather, traffic jams, or road construction and detours, we need to consider alternate routes in case our original route becomes impossible to continue on.

Like planning a trip, planning a strategy begins with the knowledge of where we are and where we want to go. We need to know what our starting point is: what our membership's strength is, what its skills and abilities are, what our financial position is, who our allies are. We need to do some research to find out these things. If we don't do our research carefully, we may choose a way of getting where we want to go that we can't afford organizationally.

An organization's strategy needs to include activities that build up spirit, that keep people interested and involved along the way. Otherwise, by the time the goal is reached, the stresses within the organization may build up to the point where they cause problems.

An organization may run into roadblocks while trying to carry out its original strategy. It needs to have alternative strategies ready, just in case. If the organization in its strategic planning has already considered the possibility of roadblocks, it's much easier to change direction and still continue with the original momentum.

Planning a trip or a strategy doesn't guarantee that it will be successful. There may still be unexpected delays that we haven't thought about in advance. And no matter how careful we are, some things can happen to upset the best plan. But overall it's much better to have thought things through carefully before you start out.

Still, many of us at vacation time want to throw everything in the car and take off. Organizations often act the same way. There is the excitement of getting started, of wanting to move quickly, of hurrying to get where we're going. Too often the organization simply throws everything in the car and takes off. As a result many trips end in disaster at worst, and at best with less of a good time for their members than could have been had with good strategic planning.

What's the difference between strategy and tactics?

Strategy and tactics are often talked about at the same time, and sometimes as if they were the same thing. But they're really very different. Strategy is the overall plan for how we're going to get to where we're going. Tactics are the specific things that we do to help us get there: petitions, picket lines, marches, demonstrations, hearings, publicity and pressure campaigns. Tactics are important because they move the issue along and also build the organization. Because of their importance to people's organizations and because they are very different from strategy, tactics are discussed separately in another chapter.

What makes good strategy?

Making good strategy is mostly done by asking questions. It's an excellent process to use in a people's organization. Good strategy is best made through wide-open thinking—when people follow their instincts, their hunches, their crazy ideas. Good strategists are always asking, "What if we do something really different this time?" They're always looking for new ways to do something, for different approaches, for taking something that worked in one situation and using it in a completely different situation.

There are a number of qualities that good strategies have in common. They include the following:

(1) *Good strategy is thought out well in advance.* It takes into account what's likely to happen. It also considers what's not likely to happen but could happen anyway.

(2) *Good strategy builds on the experience of people.* It uses their skills to the best advantage. It stays within their experience so that their values fit in with what they need to do as part of the strategy.

(3) *Good strategy involves people.* It emphasizes not just where we are going but how we get there. Good strategy takes into account that people learn as much from the process as from the product. *How* we win an issue or achieve a goal can sometimes be as important to an organization and its members as *what* we win.

(4) *Good strategy is flexible.* It includes what we will do if the probable happens—and what we will do if the impossible happens.

(5) *Good strategy has depth.* It includes not just good ideas but the steps to carry out those ideas.

(6) *Good strategy is rooted in reality.* It starts with a realistic sense of what an organization's members can do and what they can't do.

(7) *Good strategy is based in people's culture.* It creates a sense of togetherness rather than of alienation or isolation.

(8) *Good strategy is educational.* Through the process of planning and carrying out a strategy, people learn more about themselves, about the organization, about politics, and about power.

Who should make strategy in an organization?

For all of the above reasons, it's essential that the members and leaders of an organization be involved in developing strategy. Because people's organizations exist mainly to win things that are necessary to the membership, the strategies that an organization carries out help define what that organization is and does. Few activities are as well suited to involvement by leaders and members as making strategy. Because the process involves identifying and defining issues, it helps people learn to think in long-range terms. They see the broad picture and how the individual parts fit into it. Because creativity is so important, strategy discussions can be particularly useful with people who do not have experience in organizing. Too often experienced organizers, who know the strategies and tactics that have been successful in the past, rely only on those strategies and tactics. They go back to what is familiar, to what worked in a similar situation. The leaders and members of an organization, who may have less knowledge of what has worked in the past, may be far more creative in thinking up ways of approaching different problems. They are less tied to the particular traditions of organizing which say, "In this situation, picket lines seem to work best" or "In this situation, a petition would be the right thing." The wrong thing, the unexpected, the new, the different may be the best.

Membership involvement also helps to ensure that the type of strategy selected will be within the experience of the members of the organization, that it will not violate their own limits and values. Often strategies that we use come from situations that are different in time, place, or culture from the people we're working with. When we try to transplant strategies and tactics, we often find that they don't take root very effectively. When the membership of a group is involved as a group in making strategy, they're more likely to develop strategies that fit with their own patterns of behavior and that honor their own values.

Finally, leadership and membership involvement in strategy development helps build the sense of ownership that is so necessary in motivating people. If the leaders and members of an organization are involved in making strategy, they will feel that it is *their* strategy. They will feel a sense of ownership, an investment in its success. People who are involved in planning and developing a strategy are also far more likely to be involved in helping to carry it out.

Good strategy is a team effort. As the members of an organization build strategy together they also learn how to work together. They become a strategy team. Like any other team effort, making strategy involves a division of labor. There are different jobs. There's the more hard-nosed part: figuring out what our own strengths and weaknesses are, looking at our organization, counting heads and dollars, deciding what is realistic and what is not. The same analysis also needs to be applied to the opposition: looking at what their resources are, going back through other campaigns they've been involved in to try to predict what they're likely to do in a given situation, as well as what they're not likely to do but could do anyway. These kinds of jobs require people with good, hard-nosed, hardheaded thinking ability who are not going to exaggerate what our membership is capable of or likely to do, who are not going to overlook the fact that the organization is broke and has not yet developed a good fund-raising plan.

Strategy also requires people who are dreamers, who are visionaries, who are always willing to say, "What would happen if we took it on? How could we build up to this?" Strategy making requires people who understand how strategy not only wins concrete goals but builds a sense of solidarity within the organization, how it can contribute to people's individual sense of vision, how it can broaden their base of experience.

Both dreamers and managers are important to an organization as it makes and carries out strategy. The different types of personalities working together, occasionally rubbing up against or conflicting with each other, can create the energy to produce really dynamic strategy.

How far in advance should strategy be made?

One of the important parts of strategy is time. In one sense a strategy is a series of steps. Some of these steps can be taken at the same time. Other steps follow each other naturally. Often a particular step needs to be taken before the next step can be taken. Because so many steps in strategy depend on previous steps, time and timing become very important.

Suppose that your organization is working to make property taxes fairer for working families who are home owners in your neighborhood. One of the tactics or steps in this long-range strategy is to have a public hearing attended by the board of tax assessors at which different home owners are going to testify about unfair taxes. Working backward from this particular step, you can begin to see all of the things that are necessary before this can happen.

The tax assessors need to agree to an actual time and place for the meeting and need to give a commitment that they will be there. This may be easier said than done. A completely different part of the strategy might involve how to get them to agree publicly to participate in such a hearing. Other steps would include making sure that there would be good attendance at the meeting, developing interest on the part of the media in giving good coverage, preparing members of the organization to testify, and developing plans for what would happen if things went differently than expected. What if the tax assessors agree to show up and then don't? What if the press doesn't come? What if a number of people who are not members of the organization come to the meeting and testify about the fairness of the tax system?

The long-range strategy of making taxes fairer for people in the neighborhood may involve a year or two of work. The actual amount of time necessary to win our goals can't be predicted at the beginning or even at the halfway point in trying to carry out the strategy. There are simply too many unknowns. So we have to make both short-term and long-term strategies. Long-term strategy is more difficult to make because the farther we get from where we are today in terms of time and resources, the less we know about the factors that determine our strategy needs.

This doesn't mean that it isn't important to make long-range strategy. An organization should have a sense of where it wants to be in five years, not just where it wants to be in two months.

But it's important to recognize that the longer term the strategy, the more likely that it will need to be changed in some ways as the campaign develops. An organization that has a solid group working to develop strategy can make fairly good predictions about where it will be in two months: what's likely to happen, what the reaction from the opposition is likely to be. But in a period of time as long as five years, there are simply too many things that we don't know to be able to say exactly what steps we'll be taking.

When should strategy be changed?

It's important that strategy be flexible. We need to make strategy in such a way that we are not locked into a particular series of tactics no matter what happens. We're always looking at what we would do "if." We're always trying to guess the changes that might affect what we do.

Some of these changes are predictable and others aren't. Sometimes we can set up alternative strategies depending on what is likely to happen. For instance, go back to the example of the community confronting the tax issue. One of the tactics or steps in the strategy is a meeting with the tax assessors. However, it's possible that no matter what the organization does, the tax assessors will not be willing to meet in an open setting. The organization's strategy plans would include two separate possible strategies depending on which happens. If the organization was able to get a commitment from the tax assessors to attend the public hearing, one strategy would be followed. If no matter what the organization did they were unable to get this hearing to happen, they would follow the second strategy. This might involve pressure on other branches of county government or personalized pressure against the tax assessors themselves. It might mean broadening the base of the organization to include other neighborhoods and communities as a way of increasing the pressure. What's important to recognize is that this strategy takes into account not only what the organization wants to happen. It also deals with what to do if the organization is not able to make the campaign develop in quite the way that it wants to.

In making strategy try to avoid the "Let's cross that bridge when we come to it" attitude. In a strategy meeting someone should ask, "What if the assessors won't meet with us?" Someone else may say, "Let's see whether they will or not, and then decide."

This would be a mistake. If an organization has only one strategy, then the members have a much higher emotional investment in its success. So if we have focused all our energy on getting a meeting with the tax assessors, some members will see that as a necessity rather than a possibility. It's better to say, "We're going to try to get a meeting with the tax assessors. If we get it, good. If we can't get that meeting, then here's another strategy we've developed and that we can move into. By developing alternative strategies and keeping strategy flexible, we are helping to protect the organization from focusing too heavily on a single step and from members becoming discouraged if that step is not successful.

The process of developing an alternative strategy sometimes results in strategy being changed altogether. It might turn out that as we talk about what to do if we don't get a meeting with the tax assessors, another strategy begins to look more promising than the one we were originally going to take. A strategy which in its early steps looks most attractive may in fact not be as good in the long run as one which at the beginning doesn't look as appealing. Sometimes as we think through all the strategy steps on an alternative route, we begin to realize that route is actually a better one than the one we were planning to take.

Through the process of evaluating alternative strategies, we also prepare the members of the organization for the possibility that strategy will need to be changed. If strategy is changed, they will be more likely to see it as a natural process than as a temporary defeat. We shouldn't pretend that we've won a battle when we've lost. But a long-range strategy view which provides alternatives in case of setbacks makes it easier to keep a sense of balance and enthusiasm around the issue and the strategy.

When it is necessary to make a change in strategy, even if this possibility has been carefully thought out beforehand, it's important to involve the members of the organization in the decision and to keep them informed of changes. Sometimes the alternative strategies will have been thought out well enough that they can be used as planned. At other times new information and developments make a total re-evaluation of strategy useful.

Sometimes we become too committed to our own planning processes. We put so much time and energy into coming up with strategies that we become reluctant to abandon them, even when it's clear that they're not working. But we should always be willing to evaluate and reevaluate how well our strategy is actually working out. Remember that strategy planning, no matter how carefully and how well it is done, is still based to a large extent on guessing. It's not any criticism of our strategy process that we didn't think of all the answers. It's not possible to think of all the answers, no matter how good we are.

When and how should strategy be evaluated?

The need to evaluate can come up in either the short or long term. A short-term evaluation might take place in the middle of a confrontation or negotiation. Let's say that we're members of a tenants' organization negotiating with the landlord over a rent increase. The landlord has announced a 20 percent increase. In our planning sessions prior to the negotiations, we agreed that we would demand no increase but that we would actually be willing to accept a $7\frac{1}{2}$ percent increase in the rent. In the negotiations, however, the landlord comes up with a totally different sort of suggestion. The landlord suggests that he will agree to no rent increase but that instead of a month-by-month rental, there should be year-long leases with a one-month security deposit for damage. This is a possibility that we had not thought of. Rather than trying to think this through in front of the landlord, the thing to do is to call for a "caucus." This means we take a break to discuss the new offer. We need to decide whether this is something the negotiating committee can agree to or whether it should be brought back to the membership for discussion. By caucusing in the middle of the negotiation we are also evaluating our strategy in the middle of carrying it out. It's usually better not to wait until it's clear that something is going wrong to evaluate the strategy and to decide whether changes are necessary. It's far better to have an ongoing process of strategy evaluation that continues even as we are carrying out the strategy.

There are several things that can be helpful in getting the evaluation process going. One is to have an ongoing strategy team which not only plans strategy but also evaluates it as it's carried out. It might be worthwhile to have a strategy committee which has the responsibility not only of planning the strategy but also of taking a look at it from time to time, of asking the hard questions, of testing assumptions, of evaluating how well the strategy is working. If the strategy is regularly reviewed, the chances are better that we'll see whether changes need to be made before we're dangerously close to a problem.

Something else that is helpful in evaluating strategy is to set up a series of checkpoints for the strategy. This is done as part of the planning process. In planning a strategy we work both backward and forward. We know where we want to end up and we figure out all the steps that need to occur to get us to that point. The more completely we're able to do this, the better we're able to monitor the strategy as it's carried out. If we have a checklist of eighty-two things that need to happen for the strategy to be successful, and if we're careful about checking things off as they either happen or don't happen, we can keep much better control over our sense of whether or not the strategy is working. It's too easy to go by instincts in a situation like this, to say, "Things *feel* right. We must be doing fine." We need to know more specifically whether the particular parts of a strategy are working. We can only do this by checking systematically against the original plan of action.

Of course, even this plan will be changed as the strategy proceeds. Our original checklist of eighty-two things will probably be increased by another thirty or forty items as we discover the small individual steps that we didn't think of in our original planning process. By checking ourselves against the strategy plan, we can tell whether our strategy is working or not, whether the assumptions we made are reasonable, and whether the steps that we decided on are realistic.

How do you set up a time line?

This checklist of steps also has to be placed in a time frame. Some things have to happen before other things can happen. Some things have to happen before a certain date if we're going to be able to meet other dates on the calendar. Developing a successful strategy involves not simply knowing the steps but setting up this "time line." A time line is a plan of action that ties the specific steps to when they need to happen. Here, for instance, is a fairly simple time line for the example of the meeting with the landlord. It shows the steps that are needed and when they must occur. Having time lines like this worked out in advance helps us to see whether we're making the kind of progress that we need to make or whether our strategy needs to be reevaluated and possibly changed.

TIME LINE

FIRST WEEK

Strategy committee meets to plan negotiation	Tuesday, May 5 7P.M.
Make sure school cafeteria is available for membership meeting on May 13	Wednesday, May 6
Run off special issue of newsletter to update members on issue, and to announce special membership meeting	

Mail newsletter so it arrives Friday	Thursday, May 7
Call high school students in members' families to come to poster party on Saturday	Friday, May 8
Gather at office to make up slogans and signs and posters for negotiations	Saturday, May 9 Afternoon

SECOND WEEK

Call members to remind them about meeting and check on transportation and day care	Tuesday, May 12
Membership meeting to revise/approve negotiating position	Wednesday, May 13 7P.M.
Type up and copy negotiating demands	After meeting
Negotiating team meets for final planning session	Thursday, May 14 8A.M.—Breakfast
Supporters gather at office	10A.M.
Leave in cars for downtown	10:30A.M.
Negotiating session with landlord	11A.M.

Another use for time lines is that they help us to compare the steps and the strategy to other organizational needs. We know from experience that if we're involved in work on a complicated issue which may take several years to solve, our leaders and members may become tired, drop out, or stop being involved. We know that this is more likely to happen if there are "dead spots" in the campaign.

Let's say that a community is fighting a high-voltage power line. The families whose land the line is going to cross decide to use court action as a way of stopping the power line construction and are able to obtain a temporary court order against the line. A court hearing is set for three months from the date. Often in situations where legal action is involved, nothing much will happen before the date of the court hearing. During that period of time, people will become restless, will wonder what's going on, and will have little involvement with the organization. When it comes time to bring them together again, it may be hard to do.

When we construct a time line, we can look at it and say, "Are there enough events in this period of time that involve people, that give people a sense of motion and accomplishment, that continue to link people to the issue?" If the time line shows that there are long gaps, we need to go back and create other activities as part of our overall strategy to continue to involve the membership. The need to continue building the organization is as much a part of strategy as the tactics which are used to accomplish the end goal. Remember that the strength of our organization is its members. If the strategy we use to fight an issue either alienates people or fails to involve them, we'll find ourselves without the members that are necessary to win at all.

What's the relation between strategy and issues?

The process of making strategy is critical not only to successfully winning on issues but even to deciding what issues we should work on as an organization. Too often in our organizing we do it the other way around. We start by choosing an issue and then work to develop the best strategy to deal with that issue. When possible, however, it makes more sense to start with a number of issues, to develop a strategy for each one, and then, by comparing those strategies, to decide which issue to focus on. It's not enough to know that an issue is important, that the people care about it, and that there is a strategy with a possibility of winning. We also need to know what other issues and strategies there are. This is particularly important because the long-range strategy for an organization cannot focus on only one issue. We need to build into the organization an overlapping of issues so that when we win a major victory, people don't simply say, "Well, that's it," and go home.

Developing strategies around a number of issues allows us to evaluate not just whether or not these issues are winnable but how they relate to some of the other organizational questions that are important to us. How will the strategy be successful in enlarging the membership base of our organization? How will it broaden the experience of our members and leaders? What new skills will it give us that we didn't have before? What old skills can we polish? Where will it build credibility for the organization? What things will it make possible that were not possible before? What allies can this strategy successfully involve? What other groups in the community can be brought in as a part of this strategy?

These are important questions. Let's say that as part of its long-range strategy our organization wants to be able to take on a major statewide campaign two years from now. In order to be able to carry out that campaign we know that we will need to develop good working relations with a number of organizations with whom so far we only have had limited contact: labor unions, church groups, other community organizations. In planning a strategy for the next two years it would make sense to focus on activities which begin to build relationships with these other organizations and groups. It would also clearly be important to avoid a strategy which might in some way alienate any of these groups.

A strategy has to take into account the long-range and the short-range goals of an organization. It also needs to define goals very broadly. We are talking not only about specific goals like tax reforms, rent control, and cleaner streets. We're also talking about the ability and strength of the organization to deal with larger and larger issues: the extent of our membership, the skills that members have, the quality of our leaders, the nature of our allies, the extent of our base of support, the coalitions that we're able to build, the credibility that we have. All of these are critical to the health of the organization and can only really be evaluated when strategy has been planned.

How do we plan for the opposition's strategy?

It's also important to recognize that strategy is not made in a vacuum. We are not the only ones who make strategy. The opposition—whether a corporation, an agency of government, a landlord, a public official, or a person in administration—also makes strategy. At the same time that we figure out how to most effectively oppose *them,* they work to figure out how to most effectively oppose *us.* We try to undermine their base of support. They try to undermine ours. We try to split them off from their allies. They try to split us off from our members and leaders as well as from our friends and allies.

Sometimes we approach strategy as if it were a game of checkers with only one player. If that was the case we would win every time. But for every move in strategy there is a countermove— sometimes two or three. Unlike in checkers, in organizing we don't need to wait until our opponent has taken a turn. We can take as many turns as we want. That may seem fine when we're the ones who are taking the turns. But when we get hit unexpectedly two or three times in a row before we get a chance to move again, it can be disastrous.

So good strategy also depends on a knowledge of the opposition. We want to anticipate the moves the other side is likely to make. Before we can decide on our strategy we need to know what their counterstrategy is likely to be, what possibilities are open to them, what things they might be able to do.

One of the most effective ways of doing this, and also one of the most enjoyable, is for the strategy team to reverse roles. For a few hours the leaders of our organization become the board of realtors of our city. Instead of talking about how to build people's power, we talk about how to destroy the community organizations that are opposing us and how to get our platform adopted by the city council. Working with this group, we go through the process of making strategy as best we can—for the other side. (Of course, we don't tell them the good ideas we come up with.) We do it just as carefully and systematically as we would make strategy for our own organization.

This approach is useful in a number of ways. For some reason it seems easiest to anticipate what the other side would do when we actually begin to think like them. We can be confident that *they* are actually doing this: sitting down in meetings talking about us, figuring out what they can do to put pressure on us, deciding on the best strategy and tactics. By pretending to be them, we can to some extent start thinking the way they think, looking at it from their perspective, and therefore seeing us as they see us. We begin to recognize from their perspective what their and our strengths and weaknesses are.

Once the opposition strategy has been constructed, we can then return to being who we really are, take a look at it critically, and compare it with the strategy that we were planning. We begin to have a sense of what the other side is likely to do, of what their timetable might be. As we begin to understand what the possible approaches are that they would take to the issue, we can also begin to evaluate our own strategy more effectively. In many cases we can see where our following a particular strategy would play into the hands of the opposition. In such a case we might decide that a different strategy would make more sense.

We can also make a number of moves to head off the opposition's strategy. One of the simplest moves is to tell people what to expect. This technique is used often in union organizing. In building a union inside a plant, one of the things that has been learned from years of experience is what management is most likely to do: the suddenly friendly talks from the supervisor, the threats, the intimidation, painting the canteen, improving the food, small wage increases. Often in a union organizing drive the organizing committee will put out a leaflet early in the campaign telling other workers what to expect from the company. That way when the company makes its moves, the committee can say, "We told you so."

Having a sense in advance of the opposition's strategy allows us to develop our own best strategy to deal with it. When we know what their approaches are likely to be, we know what information we will need and what research needs to be done. We can also see what new alliances need to be sought out. If we can see with their eyes our weaknesses and strengths, we may have a clearer sense of which weaknesses we most need to compensate for. We see where we are most likely to be attacked and therefore where we most need to strengthen our own situation.

Trying to think like the other side is one of the best ways of figuring out what their strategy is likely to be. But it also helps to keep our eyes and ears open. Sometimes people in the community who are close to the opposition may have a notion of what they're trying to do. It's worth asking around to get a sense of what tactics are likely to be used against us. Take a look at previous campaigns. Talk to other people's organizations in the area that have dealt with this particular opposition over the years. Ask them what the opposition is likely to do. Find out what they've done in past campaigns. Find out their patterns of behavior, their favorite tactics, their resources. Practice looking at situations from both sides. Look at the opposition and try to figure out how they think, what they're likely to do, what their resources are, who their friends are, where their weak spots and their strengths are. But also learn to look at yourself and your own organization with objectivity, neither exaggerating nor underestimating your weak points and strong points. The better we are able to do this, the better our strategy can be.

How secret should strategies be?

One of the questions that often comes up in discussions of strategy is how open we should be about the strategies we adopt. This is a difficult question. Obviously if the other side knows what we're going to do it will be easier for them to fight us. On the other hand, when we build organizations which are dedicated to democratic principles and where membership involvement is absolutely essential to success, secrecy hurts us. We may surprise not only the other side but our own members as well. If we are successful in carrying out a strategy based on a high degree of secrecy, what often happens is that many of our members also don't know about it. Therefore they don't understand it and don't feel the same sense of accomplishment about it. In addition, in a people's organization with a large membership base and many leaders, it's extremely difficult to keep a secret. Often the opposition has informers inside our organization anyway and knows what we're going to do. Although there is no absolute rule, it makes sense to develop strategies whenever possible which do not depend on secrecy for success. This isn't to say that an organization should send the opposition a copy of its strategy memo. But if our success depends on their not finding out at all, we're running a risk in most situations.

Sometimes the exact opposite is true and we actually want to let the other side know publicly what our strategy is. This is an important principle in negotiation. In negotiations we're often saying, "If you're willing to agree with us, fine. But if you don't, here are the next steps that we plan to take." This carrot-and-stick approach often works because the threat of a tactic is frequently more effective than the tactic itself.

What should be done when a strategy is finished?

No matter how carefully strategy is made, there is no guarantee that it will result in a victory. Sometimes no matter how hard we work, no matter how carefully we plan, we lose. A good strategy takes into account the possibility of defeat as well as victory. A carefully planned strategy in a people's organization spells out not only what we do after we win, but what we do if we lose. Too often we assume that we'll win, or at least fail to take into account the possibility of not winning. As a result, if we do lose after all, the organization has a hard time recovering. It's never easy to have a major loss, especially when months and even years of work have gone into a campaign. But the possibility of recovering and continuing to move in good directions is much better if we are realistic about our expectations and if we also plan for the possibility of not winning.

The best of all worlds is a successful strategy that ends in a major victory for the people. Victories are worth celebrating. An organization should take the time to whoop and holler, to give credit where it's due, to honor the members and leaders who played important roles, to have a good time. While each campaign should lead into the next, it doesn't hurt to give people a little bit of a break to celebrate.

Finally, after a campaign is completed, strategy should be evaluated in light of what actually happened. There are always lessons to be learned from the comparison between the early strategy of a campaign and the way in which it actually turned out. We learn from our successes and we learn from our failures. As we develop our leadership skills and our organizational strength, the process of building strategy becomes more and more effective.

9. Research

IN ORGANIZING, we do research in order to get the information necessary to make good decisions about strategy and tactics. When we do research in organizing, we usually know what kinds of information we are looking for before we start looking. We know what kind of information we need to make good decisions. The purpose of our research is to find that information.

What kinds of research do people's organizations need?

Almost all strategy decisions in organizing are based on some type of research. Sometimes we do research to find out what our members or people who could be our members think and feel about particular problems. When we do a door-to-door survey, whether we use a survey form or just talk to people, we're trying to find out what they think and feel: what issues are of concern to them, what they want the organization to work on, what kinds of work they would be willing to do.

We may also be trying to find out information on their attitudes toward our organization, their neighbors, other forces in the community, and the idea of organizing. So we take a poll. Candidates for public office take polls to find out what their stands on the issues should be. The difference is that we already know our stands on the issues. What we need to know is how people react to those stands. Surveys provide us with this type of information.

A second type of research that people's organizations often do involves resources. In developing a local fund-raising campaign, we might want to find out what kinds of events and activities have been successful in the past. We might also want to find out which individuals and organizations have supported organizing efforts through loans of equipment, use of facilities, or donations. Developing this kind of information helps us make better decisions about the kind of fund-raising events we might want to put on.

A third type of research has to do with building alliances and coalitions. We want to know about other organizations in the area: what their histories are, how they became organized, what issues they've worked on, what their successes and failures have been, what their leadership is like, how they operate, how open they are to working with other organizations. This helps us make both long- and short-range plans to broaden our base, not only through direct membership but through alliances and coalitions. It helps us think through how we can take on larger and more difficult issues through the use of greater resources.

A fourth type of research that people's organizations do targets the opposition. Whether we are fighting a landlord, a welfare department official, the management of a plant or corporation, a branch of city government, or a politician, we need to know as much as possible about that person or institution. If we are making demands we want to know whether the person or institution can meet them. We want to know their history as an opponent: how willing they've been to make concessions, what tactics they themselves have used, under what conditions they give in, under what conditions they confront, how willing they are to counterattack, what we should expect from them.

How does an organization decide what it needs to know?

Sometimes we describe the research that we do in people's organizations as "action research" because we expect it to lead to action. In this type of research we start by trying to list the specific pieces of information that will help us make our decision. We want to be able to state these needs as simply as possible as a way of making clear what it is we need our research to do.

One way of doing this is by coming up with a list of the questions that we want research to answer. For example, let's say we're trying to decide which of two landlords to go after in a tenants' rights campaign. We have already made the strategy decision not to take on both landlords at once, because this would only encourage them to join forces. Our hope is that if we attack one of the landlords the other one will stay out for the time being. After we win over the first, we can concentrate our efforts on the second. But which one do we go after first?

We can start our research by sitting down and coming up with a list of the information that would be useful to know about this particular landlord. A sample checklist might include the following:

(1) What pieces of property does this person own?
(2) Who rents from this particular landlord?
(3) What are the tax rates on this landlord's property?
(4) Are they high or low?
(5) What property has the landlord bought?
(6) What property has the landlord sold?
(7) What other business interests does the landlord have?
(8) Where does he live?
(9) What is his spouse's name?

(10) What are the names of other close relatives or friends who might be holding property in his name?

(11) What businesses does the landlord have an interest in?

(12) What politicians does this landlord have an alliance with?

(13) Which ones has the landlord supported through campaign contributions?

(14) Has the landlord ever been sued?

(15) Has he ever sued anyone?

(16) Has he ever been a target of action by a people's organization before?

(17) If so, what happened?

As this list shows, the process of designing research is not really very complicated. We tend to think of research as something very complex and difficult, involving all kinds of words and terms that most of us have never even heard of. But the information that is useful for people's organizations can almost always be described in simple sentences. A list like the one above can usually be put together by ordinary people using their own common sense.

Where can the organization find the information it needs?

The other fascinating thing to know about research is that most of this information is not very difficult to find. Most of the information listed above is contained in public records. For example, the county courthouse will have most of the property records you need to compile information. Courthouse records will include the property owned in the landlord's name, the property owned in the names of other people the landlord has relationships with, the assessed value of the property (which may be very different from the real value), the amounts of taxes paid on it, amounts of taxes that are delinquent against it, mortgages against the property, other liens against the property (such as liens placed by the government for back taxes), and records of property bought or sold in this person's name. Some courthouse officials will be more cooperative than others about making this information available, but legally it is public information and open to anybody who wants to see it.

Courthouses also have other information. If you go to the clerk of courts you can go back through the dockets and find out whether somebody was a plaintiff or defendant at any time—that is, whether they sued anyone or were sued. You can then go back and find out the details of the case, some of which may be very useful to you.

At the courthouse you can also find records of campaign contributions. These are now also public information. They are usually found in the Court Bureau of Elections, sometimes called the Board of Elections. Records and contributions at the state level are usually found with the secretary of state at the state capital. Campaign contributions for representatives to the United States Congress can be found with the clerk of the House of Representatives. Knowing how much a particular individual has given to candidates is a way of finding out how much those candidates owe that individual. You can then begin to figure out the links between the things that politicians do while in office and who they're doing them for. All these records are public information open to anyone who wants to take the trouble to look and who is bullheaded enough to deal with some of the resistance likely at first.

Remember that just because something is legally public information doesn't necessarily prevent public officials from saying you can't see it. They're most likely to do this if they think it would be better for them if you didn't have the information. Officials may hedge, hem and haw, or outright lie to you about your right to have the information. There may be unreasonable requirements for getting it. But if you keep after them, it's almost always possible to get the information you're looking for.

There are many other places to find information. Newspapers and other community publications have all kinds of detailed information. In some larger cities it may be filed in what's known as "the morgue" under the subject. You might be able to look up the name that you're researching in the morgue and find past news clippings about the person there. Many newspapers today do not allow outside people into the morgues and may even give you a hard time when you ask them to bring the information out to you. Here it helps to start cultivating some inside sources: friendly reporters or other people who work at the paper who would be willing to go back and check on the information for you. Radio and television stations have public files that anyone is allowed to look at.

How useful are personal contacts in research?

Much of the best information you get comes from person-to-person research. The kind of information you can find at the courthouse, at city hall, in the newspapers, in the public records of radio and television stations, and in other publications and documents can be tremendously useful. But in most communities, there are people who know the secrets you want to find out. A good research operation inside a people's organization relies very heavily on person-to-person contacts to find information.

Remember that not all people who work for an organization that is part of the opposition are necessarily themselves a part of the opposition. The friend of your enemy is not necessarily your enemy. Just because the politicians who control the courthouse are corrupt or in the pocket of the corporations, doesn't mean that everyone who works for them is, too. Many of them may live in neighborhoods where your organization has a base. They have the same problems and concerns as the organization's members. They may be able to find out information which is tremendously useful. Remember that these kinds of contacts sometimes go both ways and that information within your organization can be passed in the other direction. But, in general, inside contacts at the newspaper, city hall, the courthouse, the radio and television stations, and the different government agencies can often be a valuable source of information.

Contacts that are less direct are often just as useful. Sometimes we spend hours and hours going through records at the courthouse or going back through old newspapers when, if we had simply asked the question at a meeting of our members, somebody would have known the answer.

Who should do research?

It's important to involve leaders and members of the organization in research. This is often the easiest way of finding out information. Sometimes it seems that we've put so much emphasis on detailed research of printed information that we forget how much people learn about the opposition that they come in contact with every day.

The more members of an organization participate in the decision-making process, the more they'll feel a part of it and understand it. They'll feel the same sense of ownership over strategy and tactics, and will be more likely to play an active role in carrying them out.

Involving members and leaders in research also builds confidence. How many times have we been told by the politicians and the government officials, "Well, the decision is based on information that we have which we can't release. But if you knew what we know, it would change your mind."

People are intimidated by information. The public relations people for the opposition try to make us believe that the information on which political decisions are made is simply too complicated for ordinary people to understand. Union members in negotiations are always told, "We had to make this decision because of corporate financial considerations that go beyond the range of this particular plant." These kinds of statements are just smoke screens used to intimidate people, to prevent them from being able to push for their demands. When people have the information themselves, they're more likely to keep fighting back.

Being involved in research also helps educate people politically. Most of us know that we're getting the short end of the stick. We know that the corporations, politicians, and businesspeople are getting rich off us. But most of us don't know how bad it really is. Sometimes you have to see it to believe it, to get a real sense of how closely all of them are tied together, of how much they back each other up, how much money changes hands in political campaigns and over issues.

There are good examples of this sort of thing in a recent film called *People's Firehouse*, about a fight by community people in part of New York City. The city government wants to close the firehouses in their neighborhood. Through research, the community discovers that city government is responding to pressure from real estate interests who want to change that area from residential to commercial. By closing the fire department, the city is guaranteeing that houses will burn, that arson for insurance purposes will become more profitable. As houses burn down, gutted buildings and empty lots are created. These attract other undesirable elements which make the community less of a good place to live. This in turn drives people out and lowers real estate values to the point where speculators can pick up land and property at bargain prices. This is a good film to help people understand the ways in which research can be used to develop strategy.

It's surprising how often there are these kinds of links between money interests and government actions. Reserch uncovers these links. Knowing what's really going on behind the scenes helps people better understand the political and economic realities we face in our organizing.

What are other sources of information?

There are other good sources of information. Because power in this country is so concentrated, the individuals and corporations that our organization comes up against have very likely been a target of another organization as well. As a result, much of the information that we're looking for may already be in friendly hands. For example, let's say that your organization is fighting a rate increase by a local power company. You want certain information on the company's profits to use in the campaign. The chances are that the union which represents the power company's employees already has the information to use in developing its negotiating strategy. They probably have all kinds of other information which can be useful to you. Of course, the interests of your organization and that union may not be exactly the same. The union may feel that the rate increase is necessary to provide higher wages for its members.

It's not enough to find other organizations which have information you need. You have to begin building a relationship with them *before* you need the information. That way, when it's time to ask for help, there will be some trust already there, and a mutual self-interest in sharing information.

There are also a number of groups locally and nationally which specialize in providing backup research and information to people's organizations. These include public-interest research groups, single-issue organizations and coalitions, research and resource operations, research departments in other organizations such as unions, legal services, sympathetic individuals in agencies and universities. Some of these resources are very specialized, and can provide specific information such as how to get equal time on radio and television or what your rights are under a particular federal program.

Make sure your organization stays in control of both the information and the people who help provide it. For example, it's always good to find out what your legal rights are. But don't let a lawyer talk you into going to court if there are other ways of winning the issue that would involve more members of the organization. While there are some excellent people and organizations doing this kind of backup work, sometimes specialists can become impatient with the amount of time it takes a people's organization to make decisions or mobilize for action.

Use your imagination in trying to think of other sources of information. If you're researching an individual, try to think of anyone who might have any kind of relationship with that individual. What about members of the church that she attends? What about the people who work at her country club? How about some of her neighbors? What about the neighborhoods she used to live in? What about the places she used to work?

In some ways doing research is like being in a detective movie. You're always asking wild questions, taking crazy guesses, following your nose to where you think information might be. But remember that in all this we're concerned with the usefulness of the information. Facts are only good if we can put them to work. We're not trying to satisfy our curiosity, but to develop a framework for our decision making.

This is one of the dangers in research, especially when an organization has a professional research staff. If members of the research staff are not given specific directions, they sometimes try to find out everything about everybody. A typical example is when a research staff attempts to analyze completely the power structure in a community. Even in a small-sized town a project like this can go on forever. Some of the information will be directly useful and much of it will be fascinating. But unless it can be directly related to strategy and tactics, to the development of resources, or to attacking a target, it won't be very useful to the organization.

Who should control research in a people's organization?

Research in people's organizations needs to be carefully controlled. If we don't set our priorities before we begin doing the research, then the research begins to control the decision making rather than helping it.

We know that in many situations control of information leads to control of action. Within a people's organization the people who do the research and control that information can be tremendously influential in determining what decisions are made by the organization. It's important that the members and leaders of the organization control the ways in which research is done so that their decisions are not shaded by unbalanced information.

This can be a problem, particularly when an organization uses professionals to do part of their research. In general, the more the leadership and membership of the organization can do the research themselves, the better. In practice, however, there are some restraints which don't always make this possible. For one thing, there are the usual demands of time on the leaders of an organization—the number of things that they need to do and the limits on what they're able to do. Sometimes when certain of the sources are only open during business hours and an organization has a number of working people in the leadership, it may be hard for them to get to the courthouse or other places to do the necessary work. There are also some issues which are very technical. Utility rate increases, for example, are very difficult to do research on unless you have previous experience. In cases like this most organizations are forced to hire outside help to do the research for them.

The danger in this kind of situation is that then the people who are doing the research are in a position to influence decision making far more than those who are directly affected by the issue. Unfortunately, it's fairly easy for most of us to become intimidated by professionals even when they are on our side and we're paying them to do the work. In a situation like this it becomes more important than ever that the leaders of the organization set the terms of the research that they want done, so that they themselves control the use of strategy and tactics.

10. Tactics

TACTICS ARE THE SPECIFIC activities carried out by an organization as part of its strategy. Tactics are designed to create the pressures necessary to win on a particular issue. They also help to build the organization through the participation of members in the tactics.

There is a long list of tactics which have been used successfully by people's organizations. Common tactics include: strikes, boycotts, picket lines, sit-ins, public hearings, confrontations, press conferences, paid advertising, visits to public officials, actions, mass demonstrations, marches, petitions, letters, exposés, lobbying, leaflets, prayer services, silent vigils, civil disobedience, rallies, and legal action. In a long or drawn-out campaign several of these tactics may be used. Some tactics may be used twice or even several times.

The choice of tactics is difficult partly because on the surface it appears simple. Sometimes we treat the list of common tactics as a kind of shopping list. We select one or more tactics from the list to carry out regardless of the situation. For example, if we're confronting a public official, some organizers would almost automatically call for a sit-in or picket line in front of his or her office. Others would call for a march down the main street of town. Still others might decide to file a suit against the official. Often an organization will rely again and again on the same tactics, even when they haven't proven particularly successful in the past. Or it may rely on the tactic which is most available. Organizations with access to free attorneys, for example, tend to rely much more on legal tactics.

The problem is that tactics are not simply blocks to be stacked up until their weight breaks the resistance of the opposition. They have a far more complicated effect. They can change the ways in which our members see themselves and the ways in which they are willing to participate in the organization. They affect how our opposition sees us: our strength, our ability to sustain long campaigns, the depth of experience of our members and leaders. They also influence public opinion, which in turn helps determine what coalitions and alliances we are able to build.

What makes a tactic effective?

For all of these reasons, the choice of tactics is a critical part of planning strategy. The tactics that are chosen must have a real effect on the opposition. They must also involve the members and build the organization.

One tactic must also lead naturally to the next. It's rare that any issue can be resolved through the use of only one tactic. There may be some simple issues that an organization chooses which can be solved by one confrontation, one petition, one public hearing. But these are going to be few and far between. Generally we are looking not at a single tactic but at a series of tactics. This is the reason that tactics can't simply be chosen individually. The process of developing a strategy must include consideration of the whole series of tactics that could be used as part of a campaign.

Ordinarily in selecting tactics we start with those which require fewer resources and, as a result, apply less pressure. We go on to tactics which include major involvement of our membership and create a great deal of pressure. Tactics should include room for escalation. Say we begin by choosing the tactic that is the most difficult one the organization can pull off. What do we do if that one fails to get the results we're looking for? We want to have an "ace in the hole." If the opposition feels that we've done our best and they've still been able to resist our demands, our organization has painted itself into a corner.

For this reason we ordinarily start out with the easier tactics and reserve others in case they become necessary. There is also another reason for doing this. Tactics which create greater pressure on the opposition also create a greater counterpressure on own own organization and members. They are more difficult to put together. They demand more in terms of time and money. They also demand more in terms of the risks that people have to take, the extent to which they need to step out of themselves, the possibility of opening themselves to retaliation. A landlord may be willing to read over a petition and accept or reject its demands. But when a rent strike is called or when pickets appear in front of the landlord's house, there is a much greater possibility that the landlord will take action against the people involved in the rent strike.

The tactics used in a campaign affect our members. Tactics can provide a living education. They can build the self-confidence of our members. They can sharpen the skills that our members have: public speaking, thinking on their feet, learning to work together, thinking strategically. Tactics can build a sense of solidarity within the organization.

Because tactics are so important, it's absolutely necessary that they be decided on by the members of the organization. These are the people who will actually have to carry out the tactics. If a small group within the organization makes the decisions on tactics, that small group is likely to include the people with the most experience and the most self-confidence. They will probably have been involved in organizing for some time and will be more comfortable and familiar with different tactics, including those which involve confrontation and risk. As a result they will be comfortable using tactics which other members may not be as comfortable with. It's very important that in choosing tactics we stay within people's experience, that we not ask them to do things which they are extremely uncomfortable doing. Over a period of time, and after achieving some success, we can build up to the more difficult and confrontational tactics. If people are involved in deciding on their own tactics, they are more likely to feel a sense of ownership. This makes them more likely to help carry out the tactics. They're also more likely to recognize the bounds and limits of their own experience and to plan tactics that fit with their values.

In many communities and organizations it's common to find that people believe in the ability of "the system" to solve their problems. In the early stages of organizing, people may feel that it's important to do "the right thing": to ask politely, to talk nicely, to go through proper channels. As an experienced leader, you may feel sure they won't get anywhere. But this is something people need to learn for themselves. Most of us develop a distrust of the opposition over time as the polite discussions and promises continually prove to be empty. But our experience is not transferable to the other members of our organization. They need to experience for themselves the failure of the tactics which the opposition is always urging us to use. As they become disillusioned, they will then become more willing to accelerate the types of tactics to those which create more pressure on the opposition and which have less "politeness" in them.

For this reason, an early choice of tactics for a young organization might include petitions, writing letters, and negotiating sessions which are not too confrontational. When these fail to produce results, the same group will often become much more open to creating pressure on the opposition through direct action tactics such as sit-ins, picket lines, boycotts, mass demonstrations, marches, and strikes.

How do tactics work?

Successful tactics represent real power. In choosing a tactic we need to ask ourselves: How does this tactic convey to the opposition the real power that we have in this situation? What do we have that they need? What do we have that they *don't* need? What do we have that they don't want us to use? For example, a petition is effective with elected officials because the names on that petition represent potential voters who could go against that official or that party in the next election. The opposition will also ask itself in its strategy analysis what real power our organization has and how we are able to use it. Our power comes from our ability to withhold certain things that the opposition needs: our votes, our money, our labor, our cooperation.

Votes are a basic tool that people have. In this country a very small minority controls the lives of the vast majority. However, because the political process is extremely important to those in control, they still need our votes. When we use our votes together, we have tremendous power. Those tactics which demonstrate the numbers we have can be important where votes are important. Petitions, mass meetings, marches, and letter-writing campaigns can all demonstrate the numbers of people who might be influenced by the organization in a voting campaign.

Money is important. Because life can be hard economically for poor and working people, we forget that together we have a large amount of money. After all, we are the consumers on whom the corporations depend. When we refuse to buy into the policies of the corporations, we create real pressure. We change the real balance of power. So boycotts or rent strikes, which are difficult tactics to pull off, can be enormously effective because they cut away the economic underpinning of the opposition. Other tactics which are less difficult can still have the same kind of economic impact, because they threaten the opposition's ability to sell to us. Tactics which cloud the opposition's image, such as public hearings and exposés, are successful because they threaten the economic well-being of the opposition.

Our labor is also a critical factor. Production is necessary to profit. When workers refuse to make goods, the company loses money. The strike is so effective because it interferes with the company's production and therefore with its economic base.

Finally, people have the power to disrupt the orderly functioning of society. Corporate power depends on a number of important alliances with other members of society. These individuals and their institutions expect in return for their cooperation that society will function in a certain orderly way. Interrupting orderliness creates a back pressure on the opposition. For example, suppose that a people's organization has developed a campaign against a bank around the issue of red-lining. One tactic that has proved successful in this situation is for the members of the organization to tie up the bank physically by standing in long lines to open and close accounts. This makes it difficult for the regular customers of the bank to do the business that they need to do. In return they will create pressure on the bank to straighten out the situation. They don't necessarily care about the red-lining issue, but they do want to get their own banking done without aggravation.

How does an organization decide which tactics to use?

In looking at tactics, we need always to ask ourselves the question "How does this exercise real power?" What is there about what we are doing that will change the thinking of the people who can make the decision that we want made? In order to determine this we need to know who the tactic is aimed at and what is likely to influence them. This is part of our strategy planning. If our organization has targeted a company which discriminates against women in hiring and promotion, we need to know not only what we want from the company but who within the corporate structure can make the decision we want and make it stick.

By our tactics we're trying to change the attitude of an individual or group of individuals. We are trying to convince them that it's better to go along with our demands than to continue to oppose them. We need to keep clearly in mind who the target is for our tactics. Too often we judge the success of our tactics by the general publicity that we get, by what the television news reports say about us or by what's written up in the newspaper. The key is not what people in the general public think, but how what we do influences the decision-makers.

Part of making this determination is finding who within the structure we're dealing with can make the decision we need. Is it the manager? Is it the president of the company? Is it the chairperson of the board? Is it the board itself? Is it the people who have investments in the company? Is it major shareholders? Is it the friends and allies of the people in power? Is it the mayor? Is it the city council? Is it a combination of these forces?

Once we've decided to the best of our ability where the decision we want is likely to be made, we can begin to fix the target for our tactics. If we are targeting an individual, we want to know how that individual is likely to respond to different types of pressures. Here we need to be open-minded and flexible. Sometimes people's organizations feel that every encounter with the opposition needs to be a confrontation. But sometimes our goals can be accomplished without a confrontation. It is more important to accomplish our goals than to develop a confrontation. Sometimes a confrontation can make a goal more difficult to meet. After all, we are attempting to convince the opposition that because of the power of our organization it's easier to go along with us than to oppose us. Part of training them to accept this point of view is showing them that when they are willing to back down on an issue without confrontation, life is easier for them. If we automatically confront them no matter what, we lose the carrot-and-stick effect.

It's also true that individuals react differently to pressure. Some public officials and corporate managers can be pressured or threatened and are likely to give in to an organization's demands. Others do their best under pressure or attack. Sometimes it can be a mistake to pressure an individual who is clearly very comfortable or even happy in that situation. In choosing the tactic to use against an individual or institution, try to look into past performance. Knowing how an individual or institution has reacted to different types of tactics and pressure in the past will help us predict possible reactions in the future.

One interesting variation of the usual pressure campaign is to pressure an individual or institution other than the one we actually want to target. Most people do not like to be attacked for something that someone else did. It's sometimes more effective to aim a tactic at an ally of the individual or institution from whom we're demanding the change than at the actual individual or institution. Because they're not directly involved in benefiting from the practice that we want changed, they're more likely to react to the pressure and in turn put pressure on the individual or institution we are trying to target.

For example, in the J. P. Stevens campaign, much of the union's "corporate campaign" focused not directly on the J. P. Stevens Company but on those corporations which had directors on the board of the J. P. Stevens Company: Manufacturers Hanover Trust Company, Seamans Bank for Savings, Avon Corporation. When pressure was put on these corporations, and on the individuals within them, they reacted by putting pressure on the J. P. Stevens Company. Stevens was making a high profit from its own anti-worker policies. The other institutions which had representatives on the board of directors were benefiting only indirectly. When their own profits were threatened, they turned around and put pressure on Stevens to settle with the union.

This is an important principle to remember in choosing tactics. We need to define what the decision is that we want, who is in a position to make the decision, and who is in a position to influence the decision maker or makers. In this way we can expand the number of targets we have and the tactics we have to choose from.

What makes a good tactic?

We've talked about many things that go into making a good tactic. Here's a checklist to think about when choosing tactics:

(1) *A good tactic is winnable.* We have to be able to carry it off. The best idea in the world is useless if people won't do it. We might think it would be wonderful to dramatize the need for a hot lunch program by having senior citizens appear at city hall dressed as hot dogs. But they're not going to do it. It's a good thing, too. We might get good coverage on television, but we might also offend a lot of people whose support we need.

(2) *A good tactic affects a lot of people.* On the one hand, it has to affect the decision-makers whose minds we're trying to help make up. On the other hand, it needs to affect the members of the people's organization favorably. They need to feel good about the tactic.

(3) *A good tactic unites people.* It should bring the members of the organization together. It should help them feel closer to each other. Remember, we don't just think in choosing a tactic about how it's going to affect the decision-makers. We need to look at how it's going to affect us and our friends as well.

(4) *A good tactic involves people.* The best tactics involve a good number of the members of the organization. This doesn't mean that a good tactic needs to involve large numbers of people. There are many tactics that a small group can carry out very effectively. But it does need to be something that people want to do and in fact will do. This is most likely to happen if the tactic is fun, exciting, original, or something people have always wanted to do anyway.

(5) *A good tactic is strongly felt.* People become involved in an organization out of strongly felt emotions. A good organization can meet a lot of the emotional needs of its members. The tactics the organization chooses should take this into account. People need to feel that, in carrying out the tactic, they're doing something they really believe in.

(6) *A good tactic is simple.* It should have a direct and simple message, one that can be easily understood by the members of the organization, the decision-makers, their friends, our friends, and everyone in the middle, such as the newspeople.

(7) *A good tactic builds the organization.* When we carry out a tactic, we're in the public eye. Our activities are reported by the newspapers and on television and radio. Our members and people who could become members see and hear about us. What we do should say something to all these people about who we are and what our values are.

(8) *A good tactic is fun.* It's enjoyable. It provides people with a good time. It has humor and spirit. We try to use imaginative and creative tactics not only because they catch the attention of the media, but because they are enjoyable for our members. They give us something to talk about, something to remember, something to be proud of.

How can an organization tell if tactics are successful?

Choosing tactics also involves setting up the specific goals by which we evaluate them. The strategy for a long campaign may include possibilities for a number of tactics. As with so much long-range planning, what we plan for are options and alternatives. Step A doesn't necessarily lead to step B even if that's how we originally planned the strategy. After we complete step A we need to take another look and see whether it still leads to step B or whether we need to go in a different direction.

One of the ways we do this is to get together after carrying out a tactic and evaluate it. It's important that we collect our members and our thoughts and take a look at what happened. Did the tactic go according to plan? Did we get what we wanted out of it? How did people feel about it? Did they feel good about their role in it? Were they comfortable? Were they able to do what they wanted? Did they have a sense of success? How did the opposition react? Did they do what we expected them to? Did they come up with something completely unexpected? Were we able to think on our feet? If problems came up, did we remember to caucus and decide what to do?

The process of evaluating a tactic that has just been carried out should lead naturally into the next tactic. When a tactic is successful, the spirit that results will help move people into action. When a tactic is not successful, when the opposition has stonewalled or refused to deal fairly, the anger that people feel will also be a motivating force.

What are some of the tactics that organizations use?

There is a wide range of tactics available to people's organizations. We've talked briefly about some of them. Let's take a look in some more detail at some of the most common tactics and some of the ways in which they can be carried out.

(1) *Petitions* often come to mind first when people have a problem in common. A petition can be useful in involving members because a large number of people can circulate copies. Even the act of signing a petition is a step beyond sitting and listening in a meeting.

A petition should be clearly worded. It should be clear who the petition is aimed at and what the organization is asking for. It should be drafted in the name of the organization and not simply in the names of the individuals signing it. Sometimes an organization can use a petition to move beyond its membership, but the petition should still clearly state that it is the organization making the demand.

The power of a petition comes from the number of people who are showing that the issue is of importance to them. Because petitions represent the power of numbers, those numbers should be involved in presenting the petitions. As many of the people who signed the petition as possible should deliver the petition to the person or institution that has been targeted. That same group might also want to make a stop at the newspaper office or at the television or radio station with copies of the petition.

Signatures should be collected person-to-person, not by mail. The petition should also be presented in person. Be sure to keep the original and to make copies to present. Sometimes a people's organization has gone to a great deal of work to develop a petition and has sent the original in without keeping a copy, only to find that the original disappears and a large number of names are lost. Petitions are useful to save for future contacts. If an organization goes beyond its own members to get signatures on a petition, the response might show where there was interest in the issue. These might be good places to conduct a membership drive.

(2) *Letters* are similar to petitions. Letters are often used, particularly in legislative campaigns, as a way of letting elected officials know that there are numbers of people supporting a position.

Both letter-writing campaigns and petitions can be isolating because people take that step individually. But they can also be built into group activities. For example, if fifty people have come to a meeting to talk about an issue, you could tell everyone, "Go home and write a letter." But it would make more sense to have paper and envelopes there and have everyone take ten minutes to write the letters before leaving. Some people might even be persuaded to read theirs aloud to the group.

As in the case of petitions, it's useful to keep copies on hand of all the letters that have been written. This helps the organization keep an accurate count of what's happening. Sometimes an organization will decide to deliver the letters in person rather than simply sending them in the mail. A mail sack loaded with several hundred or several thousand letters dumped in front of someone's office or building can make a real impression. Again, it's important to involve the people who wrote the letters in delivering them.

(3) *Public hearings* are another way of focusing attention on the issue and people's support of it. Here we are moving from the written word to the spoken word. Hearings are an excellent chance for people to get up and tell their story. For many poor and working people, speaking is a much more familiar and comfortable act than writing. A hearing can draw on people's strengths in this area. Hearings can also be useful for attracting media attention.

Hearings are most effective when they're under the control of our own organization. In this situation, we set the timing and we control the agenda. We can make sure people are in a comfortable atmosphere. This kind of hearing can serve to reinforce people's feelings about the issue, about themselves, and about each other.

Other types of hearings are called by agencies and organizations that are part of the opposition. Often our organizations are called to testify at such hearings. These can be difficult. Our members can be put through hostile cross-examination. Such hearings are often held in courthouses or administrative buildings that are designed to intimidate people with the power of the institution rather than to make them feel comfortable and at home. These situations are usually far less successful in building the organization and the members' self-confidence than hearings we control ourselves.

(4) *Exposés* occur when our organization releases information that is damaging to the opposition. Some organizations will reveal the information in a news release or by giving it to sympathetic members of the press. However, when we've uncovered information which can be damaging—a conflict of interest, excessive profits on the part of a utility, something scandalous or

embarrassing to a public official—it's better to make an event out of presenting the information, to do something that dramatizes it. Such events can often be fun for our membership. For the moment we have the upper hand.

(5) *Confrontations,* also called *actions,* are one of the more commonly used tactics in people's organizations. In these a group of people confronts an individual or group of individuals with a specific set of demands. This can range from a group of workers going in to see the boss about unsafe conditions in their department to tenants confronting a landlord, taxpayers confronting a tax assessor, or any other group of citizens confronting a public official. In a confrontation the group has a certain specific demand, usually one which can be answered by "Yes" or "No." It's important to make demands reasonably simplified so that "Yes" or "No" responses can actually be made.

Confrontations work well because they give people a chance to vent their anger. As they confront the individual or individuals who have been responsible for so many of their problems, they recognize their own ability to stand up and fight back. This can be an enormously unifying experience when people do it together in a group. There is a certain feeling of the shoe being on the other foot, of watching the welfare director or rent collector who has given people such a hard time over the years recognize what it's like to be under that kind of pressure and attack.

Actions should be planned so that whatever happens is within the experience of the people involved. It's helpful to make them humorous and to center the confrontation around some event which symbolizes the issue: presenting the landlord with a jar full of roaches, giving a politician balloons filled with hot air, presenting a corporation with a papier-mâché loophole. These kinds of symbols help concentrate attention on the issue. They give people something to remember, something to be proud of. They also, not incidentally, give the media a hook to hang a story on.

(6) *Boycotts* are ordinarily fairly difficult to pull off. Because the average retail outlet depends on so many customers, it's often

very difficult for people's organizations to really cut off very much of their trade. Boycotts demand an enormous amount of energy. It's not necessary to cut off all of a store's or a bank's business in order to hurt it financially. Often the threat of a boycott is even more effective than a boycott itself. Sometimes an informational picket line in front of the store or bank in question is enough to create the pressure that the organization needs.

(7) *Strikes* continue to be one of the most important tools that people have. Other tactics depend on interrupting the functioning of an institution, an agency, even a city, much as a strike interrupts the flow of work in a factory. Sit-ins, lie-ins, and mass demonstrations can interrupt the ability of an institution to function efficiently. These tactics need to be chosen carefully because of the real risk of violent counterattack, arrest, or other retaliation. They should be used only when the people in the organization are clearly making a mutual decision to escalate to that level. This is particularly true of tactics which involve civil disobedience, where laws are deliberately broken and where there is a real risk of arrest.

What are negotiations?

All these tactics used individually and in combination are designed to move the opposition to a point where it is willing to grant our demands. However, it's unusual for any opposition to be willing to give in to our demands outright. Usually they are at first willing to give only something less than what we're asking for.

In these cases the organization needs to negotiate. Negotiations occur when the two sides (or the three or four sides) sit down together and try to come up with a resolution that is acceptable, if not completely satisfactory, to all parties concerned.

Much of the success that a people's organization will have in negotiations depends on its preparation. It's necessary to have a very clearly defined negotiating position. One of the easiest ways to come up with a negotiating position is to decide what it is that the organization is actually prepared to accept as a settlement for the issue. This decision, like so many others, needs to be made by a large number of people in the organization. Once we know what we really want, we build up our demands to construct a negotiating position. Negotiations are usually resolved by some type of compromise. As a result, if we go into a negotiation asking for exactly what we want, we may find ourselves unable to get that and forced to settle for less than we can really accept.

It's kind of like selling a used car. We know it's unlikely that anyone will offer us what we're asking for the car. So when we advertise the car in the newspaper, we ask for more than we expect to get. That way we have some negotiating room. We can come down on the price and still get what we want. When someone comes to buy the car, he offers less than what he is really willing to pay. He is hoping that we will accept his low offer. But if we're not willing to, then he can increase the offer somewhat without having to pay as much as we're asking.

The process of negotiating is the same. For example, in a wage negotiation as part of a union contract, the union might first ask for a 20 percent across-the-board wage increase. The company might begin its offer with 5 percent. The company would then increase its offer and the union would decrease its demand until a middle point could be reached.

The danger in this situation is that if all the members of the organization don't understand that the initial demand will be compromised in the negotiation, they may feel that the negotiating committee has sold out on the issue. It's important that all of the members of the organization have a sense of what can really be accepted as a settlement. Most organizations will use a negotiating committee to meet with the opposition to try to resolve an issue. Sometimes these negotiations can be held in front of a large number of the membership. Usually it makes sense for the negotiating committee to report back to the general membership with a final offer so that the membership has a chance to approve this offer. In some cases the membership might want to authorize a negotiating committee to agree to a certain minimum demand. However, in a number of other cases, the compromise proposed by the opposition will simply be different from whatever was set as the bottom limit. In this case it's necessary for the membership to make the decision on whether or not such an offer can be accepted.

There are also a number of issues which can't be compromised. When an expressway is being built through a neighborhood, when a community is about to be bulldozed for townhouses, when a shopping center is about to be built in someone's backyard, the only demand that an organization can make is "No!" There is no middle ground in a situation like this.

But in many other issues in which people's organizations involve themselves, the issue in the end will be resolved by compromise and therefore by negotiation. As in developing strategy, it's useful to prepare for negotiation by trying to think like the opposition. Role playing the process of negotiation is often useful as a way of figuring out what some of their offers and negotiating tactics might be. It also helps our negotiating team do a better job of representing our position.

What is the relationship between tactics and negotiations?

Ordinarily negotiations take place at a point in the campaign when the opposition is feeling the pressure and wants to settle the issue. How badly they want to settle the issue depends on how effective our tactics have been and on what they think our additional tactics might be. Sometimes as part of the process of negotiation we either hint at or say right out what some of these tactics are likely to be. A negotiation might include an agreement not to use certain tactics. For example, in the negotiations that settled the J. P. Stevens campaign, the union agreed that it would drop the boycott and would no longer use the tactics of the corporate campaign. The company was willing to sign a contract covering other issues in order to remove some of the pressure which the workers and their union had created.

Are there some tactics an organization should never use?

The question of tactics is often discussed in terms of whether the end justifies the means. This is an age-old debate and one to which there is no simple answer. But there are some rules that we should always keep in mind in determining tactics. The tactics should never be ones which are unacceptable to the members of the organization. They must be in keeping with our members' sense of values, with their sense of right and wrong. They must be the kinds of things that the members can be proud of and not feel uncomfortable with.

The only way that we can be sure that this is happening is to involve members in the process of determining tactics. If an organization lets a few leaders or staff persons determine the tactics and then tries to persuade the members to use them, there is a real risk that there will not be a comfortable fit between tactics and members. But if people are involved in thinking up, planning, and carrying out their own tactics, there is a much greater chance that the tactics will be ones that they are comfortable with. They will have much more of a sense of participation and ownership. When the tactics work, they will also have a much greater feeling that the success belongs to them and to their organization.

11. Training

ALMOST EVERYONE AGREES that training is an important part of an organization's work. But whom do we train? How do we train them? What do we want to train them in? What are the things that we expect them to learn? How long should it take? Who should do it?

As with so many of the other important parts of an organization's work, it's all too easy to become involved in a training program without thinking it through thoroughly. Often an organization which has just been through a crisis will say, "Well, it's obvious we need some training." They'll hire an outside trainer to come in and conduct a two- or three-day training session. Or the organization may decide to send several of its leaders or staff to a session in another city conducted by a regular training institution.

Both of these approaches are valuable. They're most valuable when they are part of a training program that is well thought out and carefully planned. Organizations should do training not just in response to a crisis but as a regular part of their work.

An organization's training program shouldn't be limited to formal training sessions. It should include all the different types of activities that can be planned to give the leaders, members, staff, committees, and boards more skill at what they do, more understanding of what they're involved in, better abilities at working together, and more spirit to carry on through long and difficult campaigns.

How does an organization set up a training program?

The starting point for setting up a training program is to identify the specific skills and knowledge that leaders, members, and staff of the organization need to have. There are four general areas that a training program will ordinarily cover:

(1) *Organizing skills:* This includes such basic techniques as choosing issues, working with individuals, planning strategy and choosing tactics, mapping out campaigns, developing a communications system, using the media, canvassing, developing grassroots fund-raising programs, conducting meetings, doing research and investigation, public speaking, and negotiation.

(2) *Leadership roles:* This includes understanding the roles of leadership at different levels within the organization, the responsibilities of elected officers and committee members, the ways in which leadership can relate to members, how to bring in new members and revitalize old ones, how to provide leadership, how to chair meetings, and how to develop other leaders.

(3) *Political education:* This means developing a sense of the framework in which our organizing takes place. It means becoming more aware of specific issues—such as tenants' rights, welfare rights, property taxes, insurance compensation, occupational health and safety—and of how these issues relate to the economic, political, and social situation in the community and country. It also means understanding the history of organizing in your local area, beginning to have a basic awareness of some of the

major movements for social change that have taken place in this and other countries, and developing a basic understanding of how politics and economics work in terms that can be easily explained to the other people in the organization.

(4) *Personal development:* People in the organization need not only skills and knowledge. They also need to develop the self-confidence to be able to work effectively. They need to begin to root the work they do in their own personalities, so that it's real and has the force of coming from who each one is as a person. They need to gain a sense of what is being done in other communities, in other states, in other areas of the country, and in other countries. They need to develop an understanding of the life-styles involved in leadership, including some of the conflicts and difficulties, as a way of being able to deal with them.

The list of skills, knowledge, and abilities that different people in an organization need to have will be different for each organization. It will reflect the organization's own priorities, how it is trying to build, and what it is trying to do. For this reason, decisions on training programs need to be made by each organization for itself. While it may take less time to borrow a ready-made training plan that another organization or training institution has developed, it's much more useful to go through a planning process to decide what training the organization wants to provide to its own members and leaders.

Training priorities are closely tied to the other priorities we set for our organization. Developing a plan for training is in many ways very similar to deciding on issues or tactics. We have to decide what our needs really are. We have to judge how easy or difficult it is to develop those particular skills or attitudes through a training program. We have to deal with the problem of how people feel about the different areas of training. Staff, for example, might want the leadership to become more sophisticated in its public speaking techniques so that they can represent the organization better at public hearings. Those leaders, however, might want to practice their skills at putting together and chairing neighborhood meetings as a way of building the organization locally. In the same way that an issue needs to be one that people feel strongly about, the people who are going to be trained need to feel good about what they're going to learn.

Who should set up a training program?

Because training is so closely tied to the overall strategy planning for the organization, a process should be developed to make training decisions within the organization. As much as possible this process needs to involve the people who are going to be trained. For example, if the board of an organization is going to be involved in the training, it would make sense to take part of a regular board meeting, or to hold a special board meeting, to talk about training needs and try to come up with a long-range plan for what the members of that board want to learn. The organization might want to set up a special training committee to work on developing the training program.

One reason it's often important to have a group within the organization responsible for seeing that the training program is planned and carried out is that training is one of the parts of organizing that is easiest to put off till tomorrow. Any organization has so many activities going on at one time and has to react to so many emergencies that those activities which don't stand up and shout for attention often get ignored. In a typical people's organization on any given day there are a dozen problems that need to be dealt with. One of the campaigns isn't going as well as it should be, a grass roots fund-raising event needs to be put together, there are problems with the budget, one of the staff people seems to be dominating the chapter she works with, someone is coming to visit from a funding agency, a couple of the leaders are angry at some of the staff. These issues need to be handled immediately. They tend to absorb the time and the thoughts of the leaders of the organization.

Training rarely stands up and demands to be dealt with. Leaders are rarely going to storm into the central office and demand to be trained or else. Members of a chapter are not going to put training on a list of non-negotiable demands. So it always becomes easier to put training off until next month or to spend the training money on something else.

This may work in the short run. In the long run, it hurts the organization. If an organization doesn't make and carry out decisions about how it wants its own leaders and members to be trained, then its leaders are less likely to grow to assume more responsibility within the organization. Training is a long-range solution to short-term problems. By developing skills among our leaders today we make it possible for them to play a more effective role in the organization tomorrow.

Who needs training?

One of the issues in developing a training program within an organization is who gets the training. Sometimes an organization decides to put most of its resources into training the staff. Staff training is obviously valuable. But there is also a need to train leaders. If staff is trained and leadership is not, or if the training given to staff is much more intensive than that given to leaders, a gap can develop between the skills of staff and those of leaders. In a situation like this it becomes much more difficult for the leaders to maintain control and decision-making power within the organization. When an organization has both leaders and staff, there is always a delicate balance of power: who makes decisions, who provides leadership, who sets priorities, and who does work. If one group is given skills that another group is not given, that makes the process of maintaining a balance or making a transition to a healthier balance more difficult.

An organization's training program should try, as far as possible, to have something for everyone. There should be training programs for beginning staff. There should be training for staff who have been with the organization for a while or who have other organizing experience. There needs to be training for the leaders of the organization. There also needs to be training for people who might like to become leaders. New members should, if possible, receive some type of training or orientation.

This does not mean that everyone within the organization receives the same type of training. A good organizational training program is flexible. It identifies different groups within the organization and puts together training programs to meet their needs.

When should training be done?

Training works best when the people being trained feel the need for that particular type of training. This is why it's so important to tie a training program to the specific needs and priorities of an organization. If the organization is about to undertake a campaign to enforce housing codes, it is probably not the time to try to recruit people for a training session on taxes.

As much as possible, training should be tied to what the organization is doing or about to do. This gives training a real usefulness. Too often we train people in the abstract. We give them skills that they don't see a use for right at the time. On the other hand, if training builds skills that people can go out and use, it means much more to them.

Training also needs to be tied to experience. We sometimes make the mistake of thinking that because someone has been through a training program that person is really trained in all the skills the program covered. One of our members comes back from a week at an organizer training session and we expect her or him to be able to do everything. But skills have to be practiced to be learned. The role playing that takes place in a training session is valuable practice. It can give people something very close to real-life experiences. But the real-life experience is also necessary.

A well-thought-out training program does all these things. For example, if an organization was preparing to testify at a utility rate hearing, it might schedule a training session with the leaders who would be involved in the hearing on how to act and react in a public hearing. This particular training session might include a discussion of ideas on what role leaders should take in a public hearing; practice in preparing and presenting testimony, possibly using videotapes so the people could see themselves in action; practice in responding to both friendly and hostile questions; and discussion of the organization's strategy for the hearing. After the hearing took place, another training session might be scheduled for people to talk about what they had done and to use their experiences as a base for more learning. They might be asked to go back through how they performed at the hearing and list what their strong points and weak points were as *they* saw it. Other people who were present might also add constructive criticism to help each other develop a sense of how they did. People could then work out some training exercises to practice the skills at which they felt weakest or about which they lacked self-confidence.

The best training is based on a cycle that combines training and experience. We train to prepare for experience. We then go through the experience, which provides specific benefit to the organization. We use that experience also as a base for more training to improve people's skills and build their self-confidence. By doing this we make sure that our training is not just theoretical but is closely tied to what the organization and its leaders are actually doing. We also take advantage of the experience by using it to tie our training to the reality that we have to deal with every day.

What kinds of training work best?

One of the exciting things about training is that there are so many different ways to do it. There is no single kind of training which is ideal for an organization. A good training program uses many different types of training. In this way training is kept fresher and people are more willing to be involved in the training program.

Some training can take place in formal sessions. There is an almost endless variety of ways to develop and present formal training sessions. In some cases (but not too many) you might want to use a straight lecture with questions and answers afterward. A discussion among the members of the group is one of the best ways of involving people and also getting a good range of ideas. Sometimes a group will break down into smaller groups for discussions. Some training can be done in teams of two or three persons, who then come back to the large group to share different ideas that have been talked about. Role plays in small groups and large groups are useful for practicing skills such as public speaking, door knocking, and planning.

How and when these types of training sessions are held is almost as important as what they do. A training schedule needs to be flexible so that it takes into account the needs of people's lives. Some training sessions might be scheduled just before an important event, with a follow-up session afterward to review and learn from what happened. If an organization was going to canvass a neighborhood for new membership, a training session might be scheduled right before the canvass began. If the leaders of the organization had planned to work on Saturday knocking on doors from one until five, a training session might be scheduled from ten to twelve that morning to review the skills that people need, with lunch afterward.

Often it takes more than one session to cover the necessary skills and information. Let's say new members of the organization's board of directors have just been elected. It might be useful for them to attend a special training session one night a week for four weeks to learn their new responsibilities and to develop additional skills.

Just as certain grass roots fund-raising events should be held annually, some of the organization's training programs—orientation for new members, basic leadership training, staff development, training for new board members—should be repeated regularly. If someone can't make the training this time around, he or she can do it the next.

Schedule training sessions the same way you do meetings,

with a careful eye to what people's patterns are in their work and other responsibilities. If people work during the day, it might be useful to have training sessions once a week after supper. On the other hand, sessions for retired seniors can be held in the morning or afternoon. Training can be spread over a long period of time, or it can be concentrated in a two- or three-day session. Sometimes it's harder to get people to an all-day or two-day session. On the other hand, it's possible to cover so much more ground and to build such intensity and feeling that it's often worthwhile to plan longer training retreats.

Be aware of some of the things that keep people from participating. Child care needs to be planned for in all of the organization's events. Remember the need for transportation. Schedule training sessions in places where people can feel comfortable: homes, housing projects, community centers, union halls, and churches or synagogues.

What about training through experience?

A lot of good training can be done through experience rather than direct teaching. Suppose that the organization is planning a strategy which involves pressure on the city council. One way of doing that training session would be to have a lecture on how city government operates. Another way would be to start by taking the training group down to city hall to actually sit through a council meeting. After the meeting, either that afternoon or evening or on a later day, the group can meet to discuss what happened and to review their strategy and tactics based on what they saw. Training that is based on real experience moves very easily into strategy planning. People are not only learning how a city council works. They're learning how *their* city council works and what they need to do to make it work better for them.

Many of the skills that an organization would want its members to be trained in can be learned through experience. The skill of working with people, for example, can be learned by doing it, especially if you work with somebody else who is more experienced than you are. If two people go door-to-door together they can take turns doing most of the talking and then help each other out with ideas about what was done well—and what could be done better. Experiences which teach particular skills can be scheduled into a training program. As much as possible, in trying to figure out how to train someone in a skill, ask what experiences this person could have that would make learning easier. Experience is one of the best ways to learn something, as well as one of the best ways to practice skills that are developing.

What are other training events and resources?

Other resources can be brought into a training program. Films are excellent for creating a sense of what it's really like to be involved in organizing. Follow films with a discussion. Ask people what they thought and how they felt.

Written and audiovisual materials can be useful. But don't just ask people to read something and let it go at that. If they read a fifteen-page handout on fund raising, it should be discussed the next time they get together as a group.

Films, books, and other prepared materials should be looked at in the same way as experience. They're valuable in themselves, but they're even more valuable if they're followed up by group discussion that ties the ideas to the specific needs of the organization.

One of the most valuable experiences for leaders and staff is to spend time working with other organizations. This is sometimes called "cross-training." Find another organization nearby or even in another part of the country with which a leadership or staff exchange could be worked out. Two of the leaders from your organization might go spend a week with the other organization and vice versa. Through cross-training, leaders get to compare notes. They get a sense of how another organization works from the inside. They might have a chance to do some door knocking or attend some meetings, strategy sessions, or fund-raising events. This gives them experience, skills, and new ideas that they can bring back to their own organization.

Conventions and conferences that bring people together from a broad range of organizations can be useful. It's often helpful when leaders from your organization are attending such an event to try to plan out in advance who they might want to see there and what things they might want to talk about. It's also helpful if they go with some specific assignments for what information, resources, and contacts they're expected to bring back to the organization.

Finally, it's often helpful for leaders to attend formal training sessions that are conducted away from the organization. Training needs to be conducted at different levels. It's important that people be trained with the people they work with. In this way we not only build skills, we also build interdependence and good working relations. But it's also useful for a leader to go to a training session in another city, where he or she will meet leaders from other organizations and can compare notes, exchange ideas, and build relationships. We need to see both what our organization is doing and what other organizations are doing.

Who should do the training?

As much as possible the training program we develop for our organization should rely on our own leaders, members, and staff. People learn from training as well as from being trained. We may feel we know how to conduct a good meeting. But if we're asked by our organization to train other people in those skills, we have to re-think what we do. We have to set our own thoughts in order. Doing this often makes us even better at conducting meetings. As we work with people—talking through our ideas, having our ideas challenged, and responding to those challenges—we learn from them as well.

If asked to conduct a training session, many leaders will respond the same way they probably did when they were first asked to conduct a meeting. They'll say, "I couldn't do that. Why don't we get somebody else? Let's get a professional consultant from the outside." But a good trainer has many of the same skills that a good leader does: ability to be sensitive to people, to listen, to plan, to create an atmosphere in which people are comfortable and can interact with each other. Thinking about the special skills that different leaders in the organization have can be a good first step in putting together a training team.

Of course, knowing something well, or being able to do it well, doesn't necessarily mean that you can train people in doing it. There are techniques for training that have been developed over the years by different organizations and individuals. It makes sense to know some of these. One good alternative in an organization would be to have a training director—someone who has training experience, possibly a person who has been trained as a trainer and who knows some of the different methods and techniques which are useful. The training director, however, should not necessarily be the person to do all the training. It should be his or her responsibility to involve other leaders in the organization in the training programs. So, for example, it might be that Ms. Brown, because of her success in raising money in her neighborhood, would be asked to work in a session on grass roots fund raising for other fund-raising committee members. The training director would work with Ms. Brown prior to the training session to figure out not only what she wanted to help people learn but some ways of setting up a training session in which people could learn these things.

How is a training session actually conducted?

Just as there's no one right way to do organizing, there's also no one right way to do training. Here's one way of presenting a training session on grassroots fund-raising. The same techniques can be used for almost any other topic.

(1) Welcome everyone to the training session. Have them introduce themselves. (5 minutes)

(2) Be sure everyone is comfortable. (Look back at the chapter on meetings for some ideas on how to do this.) Sit in a circle or around a table.

(3) Ask people for some ideas on why grassroots fund-raising is important. Write these down on a sheet of newsprint with a felt-tip marker. Be sure the following points are listed (if no one else mentions them, you should):

    (a) Funds pay for things the organization needs.

    (b) Fund-raising is something most people have some experience with.

    (c) Most members of the organization can take part.

    (d) It builds up participation in the organization.

    (e) It's a chance for members and leaders to learn new skills.

    (f) It helps make the organization independent.

    (g) People will be proud of what they do.

    (15 minutes)

(4) Ask everyone to write down or think of as many ideas for fund raising as he or she can. When everyone has finished his or her list, go around the circle. Ask each person to name *one* item from his or her list. Write each idea down on a piece of newsprint. Keep going around the circle until there aren't any ideas left unsaid. (20 minutes)

(5) Break up into two teams of three or four people each. Ask each team to come up with a plan for how their organization could actually carry out *one* of these fund-raising ideas. They should consider the resources needed, who would do the work, when and where the event would take place, whether volunteers would be available, whether other people would participate, and so on. (30 minutes)

(6) After a ten-minute break, get the whole group back together. Each team should present its idea, and the other team should comment on it. (20 minutes)

(7) Ask for volunteers to try to present one of the fund-raising ideas to the organization, and to actually try to carry it out. (10 minutes)

(8) Allow time at the end for refreshments and talking together. (20 minutes)

You'll notice that the training session is not theoretical but practical. People aren't being asked to design a fund-raising event for any organization, but for *their* organization. The event they design may even happen. The training session has a practical product that the organization can make use of. Remember, too, that people learn as much from experience as from anything else. If they actually get the chance to try out their fund-raising idea, they'll learn a lot about grassroots fund raising that they couldn't learn in a training session. To look at it another way, experience is also training, and it should be planned into a training and leadership development program.

One of the interesting things about this kind of training session is that you, the trainer, aren't really being asked to say very much. It's not like giving a speech or a lecture. Just as in organizing, you ask a lot of questions. It's up to the other participants to come up with ideas and do most of the work. But a lot of it will seem like fun. Everyone gets a chance to participate, to see his or her ideas written down, to be a part of a small team that actually plans a fund-raising event. They get to see how people react to their ideas.

What is the role of leaders in a training program?

Because training depends largely on two of the basic organizing skills that leaders have—listening and asking questions—it's not hard for a good leader to develop real skill at it. The principle of leaders training other leaders is very important to the organizations we build. The newer members and leaders being trained have a chance to learn from the experience of the leaders in their organization. They have the chance to see what the leaders of their organization look and talk like. They can ask questions about what it's really like to become a leader in a people's organization. By helping train other members of the organization, you can encourage and inspire them through your own history to become leaders, too.

Training which relies on the leaders of the organization is particularly effective because we are building people's confidence at the same time we are building their skills. We are recognizing in a very direct way the contributions that some of our leaders have made. We're saying, "You've done this well enough and know enough about it that it makes sense for you to be the person helping other people learn how to do it better."

In setting up this type of training program we're really stating a number of important principles. We're saying that training is a process of self-education and experience, in which leaders learn from each other as much as from trainers. In choosing issues and setting priorities we work from the principle that people know best what they want and what they can do. In setting up a training program, we're saying that the leaders of our organization as a group have most of the skills in which other people in the organization need to be trained. If we can figure out ways in which people can communicate these skills to each other, we can develop a really effective training program.

How does an organization get outside training help?

Another reason that it makes sense for an organization to develop its own training ability is cost. Bringing in trainers from the outside can be expensive. But there are times when hiring an outside trainer does make sense. If no one in the organization has much training experience, it's useful to have somebody who understands training techniques, who can help figure out a training program for the organization and instruct some of the leaders in training techniques. Often someone from the outside can see things a little differently, and can help an organization work through its problems a little more effectively.

There are two main ways to get this help. One is to bring in a trainer from the outside, on either a one-time or a continuing contract, to work with the organization. It's best to set up as a requirement of the contract that the trainer is expected to develop a training program which the leaders of the organization can continue to conduct on their own, rather than one in which the outside trainer continues to play that role indefinitely.

The other possibility, which many organizations find very effective, is to develop an ongoing relationship with a training institute, particularly one which can offer both a variety of training sessions and consulting by trainers with different skills and backgrounds. If an organization has this kind of relationship, individual leaders can be sent off for particular training sessions on subjects such as organizing, fund-raising, or administration. It might make sense to try to send two or three leaders from the organization at the same time to these training programs so that they have a chance to compare notes and reinforce each other both politically and personally.

How is training evaluated?

It's important that any training program be evaluated. Most organizations put too little emphasis on training, but it is possible to put too much emphasis on it. In developing a training program it's important to decide in advance how we will judge whether the training is successful.

One measure of success is participation. Training sessions are just like meetings. If people stop attending we must be doing something wrong. Let's say that we've scheduled a twelve-week training session in grassroots fund-raising techniques. The first two or three meetings are excellent, with good participation. By the fifth meeting, however, only two or three people are showing up. We need to back up and look at what's happening. We need to go back to the people who participated in the early sessions and ask them why they've dropped out. We need to try to figure out what it is that we're doing and see whether it's really useful or not.

We can also measure the training program against the goals we set when we originally designed it. For example, one of our organization's goals may be to get more leaders involved in the process of recruiting new members. So we set up a training session in working with individuals to try to give people more confidence and ability as they work on a membership recruitment drive. The training session may be going very well, with excellent participation. But if we schedule an evening for people to recruit new members and no one shows up to go out and work, we have a problem with our training. We may be giving people certain skills, but we're not motivating them enough to use those skills.

Training can't be a substitute for work. We don't want people so involved in role plays and discussion groups that training becomes more attractive than actually getting out in the streets and recruiting people into the organization.

How much training should an organization do?

Generally most organizations do far less training than they could. Training is one of the most useful things for the long run that an organization can do. The more people we train, the more leadership skills we develop, the more powerful our organization can become.

But there are limits to training. Generally we want to schedule as much training as people are willing to participate in, as long as this doesn't take away too much from the work that they need to do with the organization. There are a number of things we can do to try to strike this balance. One is to build training into the other events that take place in the organization. A part of every meeting can be given over to a brief training session, a discussion, a film, a planning exercise. An organization's events should be followed by a training session which tries to evaluate them and draw lessons from them. We not only do things, we learn from what we do.

An organization also needs to vary its training. It doesn't make sense to have only one training program and expect all the members of an organization to participate in it. Different people are at different levels of skill and confidence. They have different roles in the organization. They have different levels of interest in developing their own skills. An organization might need to have one very intensive training program for its most committed and dedicated leaders. There might be a very brief program for beginning leaders. If an organization has staff, they also need to be trained—sometimes separately, sometimes together with leadership. There should be specialized training for committees or for special events. The more variety there is in the training program, the greater the chances of keeping people involved in and committed to it.

What should be avoided in training?

Training is very useful in building an organization. But it's not a cure-all for organizational problems. There are a number of things that should be avoided in developing a training program.

One of these is a training program which suggests that there is only one way of doing things. Sometimes trainers seem to "lay down the law." They leave the impression that there's only one way to run a meeting or to pressure the city council. We want to be careful that our training emphasizes the need for flexibility and creativity, for new ideas and resourcefulness. We want to avoid any suggestion that we are training the leaders of our organization to do the same thing each time a certain set of circumstances comes up. In organizing, the same situation never comes up exactly the same way twice.

We want to avoid training in a way that goes against the other principles of our organization. If we are building organizations that stress democratic cooperation, then we contradict ourselves if our training stresses the value of outside experts. This is one of the reasons for developing a training program which relies on the skills and experiences of our own members. We're not only making the best use of our resources, we're also stating an important principle: People can learn from each other by working together cooperatively to figure out the things that they need to know.

We want to avoid becoming stale. Let's say we develop and conduct a successful training program. If we're still running exactly that same training program three years later, we're probably not flexible enough. The needs of an organization change. The resources of that organization change. The people who are capable of doing training change. We need to be open enough to continue to look at our training programs and be sure that they are still making the best use of our resources and responding as well as possible to our needs.

What makes good training?

Good training is just like good organizing. It makes people feel good about themselves. They not only learn skills, they learn attitudes.

Good training brings people together. A successful training session does not end with just a group of individuals, each of whom has learned. It becomes a group of people who in a real sense are being organized at the same time they are being trained. They develop increased respect for each other and for themselves. They develop more of a sense of how to work as a group, rely on each other's skills, and compensate for each other's weaknesses.

Good training communicates the values we try to build into our organizations: cooperativeness, democracy, self-reliance, the right of people to control their lives and make their own decisions. Who we train and how we train them are decisions that say a lot about who we are as an organization and where we're going.

What's the role of training in developing leaders?

An organization which provides training for its staff but not for its leaders is making a statement about who it thinks is most important. It's saying clearly who it really feels should lead and direct an organization. Good training in an organization should reinforce our belief in grassroots leadership, that people are their own best decision makers.

In training leaders we are making another statement as well. We are saying something very important about what we expect to happen in the long run. Over time, if we are to succeed in building real power for people, we need to develop many more leaders than we have today. These leaders need to have the skills and abilities that come not just from one training session, one organizing campaign, or even one organization. They need to develop a long history of experience, training, and discussion followed by more experience, more training, and more discussion. They need to be able to fight on an equal basis with the strategists for the opposition. They need to develop enough skills and experience so that as new organizations are put together and begin to look for staff, they look to the leaders of older organizations. The leaders, the organizers, the staffs of the organizations that we build over the next fifty years need to come more and more from the ranks of people who themselves have had the experience of being organized and organizing, or of being led and leading. The more leaders that our organizations can train and the better the training we can give them, the more skilled leadership all of us will have to rely on in the future.

12. Communication

COMMUNICATION is a long word for all the different ways in which people can relate to each other. Organizing and leadership depend heavily on communication. The ability of leaders to listen, to understand what people are saying, and to make sure they have the chance to say what's on their minds, builds grass roots democracy. Communication involves other members of the group in the organization. It gives them a stake in what happens. Communication is the glue that holds our organizations together.

Why should an organization have a communication strategy?

An organization needs to have its own communication strategy. The first question to ask in putting together such a strategy is "Who are we communicating with?" Within the organization the leaders need to be informed regularly of decisions that are being made and responsibilities that need to be carried out. Other members, who may be less involved day-to-day, still need to know what's going on and to feel a part of it.

We also want to reach those people we see as possible new members of the organization, and the people who are members of organizations that are allies or members of coalitions with us. There is also the opposition, the people we are fighting, whose decisions we want to influence. We need to impress them with our power.

In each case we need to communicate with a group, but we need to do it strategically. It's simply not true that the more people know about us and our issues the better off we are. We need to get away from the idea that information in itself is good. Instead, we should concentrate on getting the right information to the right people at the right time—through our communication strategy.

Who is responsible for the communication strategy?

Because communication does need to be strategic, it makes sense to have a communications committee that takes responsibility for it. Such a committee needs to make a number of decisions. It needs to target who it is that our communication is aimed at. Are we trying to reach our own supporters and members ("internal communication")? Are we trying to influence people outside the organization ("external communication"): the opposition, politicians, allies, members of coalitions, funding sources, legislators?

To create our strategy, our communications committee needs to ask some basic questions:

(1) Who is it that we're trying to reach with this particular system of communication?

(2) What is the most effective method of reaching this particular group?

(3) What is the cost of what we're proposing to do relative to what we are expecting from it?

(4) Exactly what is it we want out of this type of communication?

(5) What are we trying to motivate people to do?

(6) Who should work on what?

Meetings should be part of our communication strategy. Small meetings, house meetings, committee meetings, rallies, mass meetings all have a role to play within an organization's communications. We need to look carefully at the balance of methods we're using for trying to communicate both internally and externally and evaluate how effectively they're working.

Finally, we need to involve the members in our communication strategy as much as possible. Communication all too often becomes a staff specialty: One staff person writes the newsletter and makes most of the phone calls, and another writes all the leaflets. It is very important to spread these responsibilities out in our organizations. The more skills the leaders and members develop, the better—and the more likely it is that they will stay involved in the organization.

What is an organization's best form of communication?

Corporations, politicians, and others have long used a variety of communication devices to manipulate us and keep us unorganized. They have convinced "producers" to work harder, faster, and cheaper in order to get them to accept the decisions of management. They have told "consumers" which soap to buy, which car to choose, which candidate to vote for. They have carefully used communication techniques—including everything from behavior modification to video programming—to get their messages across.

But there's one major communication method where our organizations have the upper hand: person-to-person contact.

What is person-to-person contact?

Person-to-person contact is one of the great strengths of organizing. It is one of the things that offers the possibility of overcoming corporate power in the long run. The corporations only have billions of dollars. They do not have the number of people that are involved or could be involved in people's organizations.

For this reason, in developing a communication strategy for our organization, we want to rely as heavily as possible on person-to-person contact. Person-to-person communication carries the message that we see people as individuals, not simply as consumers or producers. When we communicate person-to-person we say that each person's ideas are valuable, that each person should have control of his or her life.

Suppose you're walking through your neighborhood shopping center on a Saturday afternoon. Someone walks up to you, looks you in the eye, and says, "Hi. I'm Si Kahn. I'm a member of the Eastside Community Organization. We're trying to do something about hiring policies in this shopping center that discriminate against women and minorities. We'd like you to read this petition and sign it if you agree with us." You may or may not decide to sign. But you're more likely to do something than if you just found a leaflet tucked under your windshield wiper when you came out of the supermarket.

The personal reinforces the impersonal. What is said to you is simple. It covers four basic points:

(1) I am.
(2) We are.
(3) We do.
(4) We want.

But because you hear these four key points from a real live person standing in a shopping center and not from a television announcer, they may move you into action.

We can extend this idea to many of the situations in our organizing. For example, let's say that the leaders of the organization have targeted a neighborhood as a place to build a chapter. As they go door-to-door, it's helpful to have along with them a piece of printed literature about the organization, telling how it got started, some of the things it's done, how to become a member, and what members do. Often when we talk to people face-to-face we give them a lot of information at one time. Sometimes this is more than they can think about at the time. If we have a printed piece to leave behind, they have the chance to reflect on and absorb the information. We are most effective when we consider people's needs just as we do our purposes.

How does an organization get and keep contact?

The realities of numbers may make continued face-to-face contact impossible. In an organization of thousands of members, it is difficult even with the best leadership to see everyone once a month. Most leaders cannot work full-time as organizers. One of the ways of adjusting our resources to the need is to rely most heavily on person-to-person contact to recruit people into the organization. Once contact has been established face-to-face, it can be more easily kept up in other ways: telephone calls, small group meetings, letters, and newsletters.

The telephone is excellent for keeping in touch. If the president of a people's organization calls his or her board members and committee chairpeople every week or so just to touch base with them, it will add to how much these people feel a part of the organization. It will also solidify the political position of that president.

The telephone can also be used to notify the members of the organization of an action that is coming up, a decision that was taken by the executive committee that people should know about, or a new move by the opposition that needs to be talked through and considered.

Sometimes the telephone is used simply to influence or persuade. For example, during an election campaign an organization might put together a phone bank. A phone bank is a group of people sitting together in a room with many telephones, calling voters and trying to persuade them to vote for a particular candidate. Because phone banks involve group activity, they build the organization better than if the same people made these calls from their homes.

The telephone in a way represents person-to-person communication. The other kinds of communication many grassroots organizations use—pamphlets, leaflets, bumper stickers, buttons, mailings—are less personal, but still useful.

How can an organization use literature most effectively?

The literature we pass out about our organization and its work is a very important part of bringing in new members. The people we have met person-to-person will want to know more about us, and leaflets give them some background on our efforts. Letters and newsletters keep members informed about upcoming events and recent developments. Though literature is generally less effective than person-to-person contact, it still plays an important part in our communication strategy.

Literature is often best produced by groups. Suppose some people sit down together as a group and say, "What is it that we want people to do as a result of this leaflet? What's the best way of catching their attention? What's a good line that would make them read this?" They're likely to come up with a much better leaflet or newsletter than if one person sits down and writes it.

Groups of people also tend to notice the faults that our leaflets so often have: too many words, not enough "white" or blank space, not enough graphics or photographs. As in so many areas of our organizing, the group process will work better than the individual process.

If an organization does rely on leaflets as part of its communication strategy, the following "tricks of the trade" can be helpful:

(1) Use different colors of paper for different leaflets.

(2) Use large print for the headlines—as large as will fit on the page.

(3) Use three or four headlines on the page. Write them so that if people only read the headlines they still get the main message of the leaflet.

(4) Use simple words. Write the way people talk.

(5) Don't crowd the leaflet too much. Leave big margins and lots of blank space.

(6) Use cartoons, photographs, and drawings to help catch people's attention.

(7) Keep everything short: headlines, sentences, words, paragraphs.

(8) Use local names when possible.

(9) Make sure the leaflet asks people to *do* something.

(10) Keep track of how many leaflets are printed each time. This helps you plan and saves money.

(11) Save the layout. The graphics and headlines can be reused.

(12) Ask the printer to return or save the negatives. This saves money if you have to reprint.

(13) Try to make sure there's a "union bug" on the leaflet, especially if you're working in coalition with unions.

(14) Make up a map of the community showing where leaflets can be posted without asking permission each time: bulletin boards, restaurants, schools, laundromats. You can give this map and a stack of leaflets to a member to distribute.

How can an organization evaluate its communication work?

Too often in an organization, we make decisions and carry them out without ever attempting to evaluate what has happened. As a result tremendous amounts of energy often go into forms of communication that may not be accomplishing what we want them to do. It makes sense for the communications committee to take on as part of its responsibility the evaluation of our communications.

It's not unusual for someone watching a television program about tax abuses to become very angry, then to feel on account of that anger that he has accomplished something, when he has really done nothing to change the situation. That is not what we want. We want people to think and feel, but we also want them to act. If we pass out a leaflet to a thousand people in our community telling them about the danger of having an expressway built through the neighborhood, but not asking them to do anything, we have no real way of judging how it affected their thinking unless people go around and see them afterward. If people are going to go around and see them anyway, there is no point in taking the time and energy necessary to leaflet that many people. But if the leaflet asks all of them to come to a meeting the next night at seven o'clock, we can count the number of people there. We can ask them at the door whether they came because of the leaflet. We can compare that with past attendance at meetings. In this way we can determine if the method of communicating that we have chosen to use is effective: Has it helped people to act?

As organizations develop we have a tendency to move more to the less personal types of communication. In the beginning most organizations put most of their time into door-to-door work, person-to-person contacts, house meetings, and small group meetings. As time goes on and organizations become larger they rely more on their newsletters, mailings, leaflets, posters, and stories in the press and on the public media as a way of informing their members. In order to evaluate the effectiveness of all these impersonal techniques, we need to go back to the person-to-person contacts. It may take sitting down with people individually or in small groups to ask the same questions about how our methods of communication affect them.

A communications committee might want to survey part of

the membership to determine what kinds of communication work best with them. Do they read the newsletter? Do they read the mailings? Do they come to the meetings? What does reading the newsletter do for them? Does it make them feel that they have carried out all of their membership responsibilities? Does it make them feel more like participating in activities that the organization sponsors? Only when we begin to understand which methods of communication are actually motivating our organization's members into action can we make good judgments about where to focus time and energy.

How does communication build the organization?

We want to be careful not to see communication in too narrow a sense. We want to look at the full range of ways in which people communicate with each other, at the full range of things that can be communicated: not just information but motivation, not just knowledge but spirit, not just strategy but solidarity. In many ways what we say we are and who we say we are, are a part of what we become. A broad communication strategy which takes into account all of the different ways in which people talk and listen to each other can tremendously strengthen our organizations.

Communication plays a critical role in shaping who we are and what we do. To some extent we become what we say we are. The way we describe our organization—its function, its history, its plans, its priorities—influences the kinds of members we attract, who in turn will reinforce the aspects of the organization which attracted them. As a result there is a real political decision made whenever we describe the organization and its functions to people. When we talk about members and what they do, we are also saying what we think members should be like. When we spotlight our leaders and talk about their lives and what role they play in the organization, we are also saying to other members that this is what an individual should do if he or she wants to be a leader.

For this reason we need to be conscious that our system of communication has a political role as well. It's not simply conveying information. It's creating expectations that the organization will have to live with. Whatever methods of communication we choose to use, one of the important rules is that they should build the collective process, that they should encourage people to work together, to do things together, to learn to rely on each other, to achieve interdependence.

Communication also builds more than just knowledge and action. It should build spirit and solidarity, a sense of belonging to the organization, of being a part of what the organization is and does. We need to broaden our sense of communication to know that it goes beyond meetings. It needs to dig roots in the culture within which we're working.

There are many ways of doing this kind of communication. Music is an important tool—people singing together, people writing their own songs and performing them. Theater, done both by others and by ourselves, builds a sense of spirit. Special events and celebrations are also forms of communication. All of the different types of art, of writing, of telling stories can contribute to the strength we need to build and keep organizations.

13. Media

MEDIA IS A WORD used to describe public forms of communication. Usually by *media* we mean newspapers, radio, and television. The word *media* is used mostly by people who don't work in the media, since people who work in newspapers, radio, and television often don't like to be lumped together and would rather have you talk about each of their specialties by name.

Using the media for external communication is a basic organizing skill. The key to learning this skill is understanding that, as with so many other aspects of organizing, media use has to be part of a well-thought-out strategy. It's not just a question of how you get the publicity for your organization, but of how this fits in with the other needs you have. It's important that we use the media and that the media not use us.

Why do we want to have the media involved?

There are a number of possible advantages to media coverage of an organization and its activities. Media coverage is a way of letting the opposition know how strong we are and what we're doing. When we have a demonstration attended by several hundred people, the politicians and officials who see it on the evening news are bound to be impressed. Regular coverage of an organization and its activities makes it harder for the decision makers to forget about us.

Media coverage can help spread the word about an organization to people who are not yet members. Sometimes people find out about what an organization is doing from television, radio, or the press and decide that they would also like to be involved.

The fact that an organization is regularly in the news makes it appear more legitimate. It says that we are alive and well, a force on the political scene to be reckoned with.

Good media coverage helps build spirit. Many members of our organizations have a lack of self-confidence. It helps them and all of us when our voices, our faces, our words are seen in black-and-white or living color. When, after a hard day demonstrating at the mayor's office, the people who went there can sit around a TV set and watch themselves on the evening news, it builds their self-confidence and spirit.

How does an organization develop a media strategy?

One of the first steps in developing a media strategy is to decide who in the organization will take responsibility for it. In a good-sized organization it might be useful to set up a media committee to deal with television (including cable networks), radio, and newspapers. This committee is ordinarily different from a communications or public relations committee, which deals with our own internal communication system: our newsletters, phone banks, door-to-door campaigns, leaflets, flyers, and other ways of getting the word around to our own members. A media committee would deal particularly with television, radio, and newspapers—*their* media, not *our* media.

One responsibility of a media committee is to avoid mix-ups. When we're recruiting members for an organization we don't want three or four people to knock on the same door in one afternoon. Likewise, we don't want three people calling the radio station in one day. We want to set up regular relationships for dealing with people in the media.

A good start for a media committee is to have a strategy discussion. Talk about why we want coverage in the media. Who do we want to aim it at? Do we want to aim it at the people we're fighting? Do we want to aim it at our own members? Do we want to aim it at the people we're trying to attract to the organization? Remember that whatever we say we are, people will also believe to a large extent what the media say about us. The more we rely on the media, the more risk we take that they will describe us in ways we don't like. This may drive people away from us rather than attracting them to us.

A media strategy will also be different depending on where we're working. In a small rural community, there may be only one weekly newspaper and two or three radio stations. It's fairly easy to deal with these people on a personal level. On the other hand, in a large city there may be dozens of radio and television stations and newspapers. In a small community local news will also seem relatively more important than it will in a city, where there may be hundreds of groups competing for attention. It's also true that a hostile editor in a small town can simply refuse to print anything about a particular organization. In a city which has several newspapers competing against each other and against television and radio, it may be possible to find one sympathetic contact to start and use that one to open up the others.

How does an organization build contacts with the media?

To make sure we get the best media coverage possible, we want to take an *organizing approach*. It's the same approach we take when we start organizing a new town. We could take the phone book and get a list of the names, addresses, and phone numbers of all of the people who live there. We could then call each of them on the phone or mail each of them a letter telling about our organization and what it does. But this approach would not be nearly as good as having the different leaders, members, and staff of our organization go to see people personally in their homes. The personal contact is what motivates people. It makes them feel wanted and a part of what's happening.

We want to take the same personalized approach to the media. We want to build good relations with people in the media. We want to know them and have them know us. In the long run the time taken to build these relationships will serve the organization well.

Try to look at it from the point of view of the people who work in media. Most of them put in long, hard hours at a job that, however glamorous it may seem from the outside, is often boring and demanding. Yet, except for the famous ones, they rarely have a chance to know what people think of their work (except when viewers or readers get mad enough to call up and cuss them out). Many people in the media suffer from a lack of personal contact with the public and are grateful when they get the chance to talk with some of us face-to-face.

How do you know whom to contact?

In a small community it's usually not too much of a problem to find out whom to contact in the media. The entire staff of the radio station or the newspaper may be only two or three persons (television stations are probably located out of town). Chances are that you already know who they are.

In larger areas, where the newspaper may have a staff of hundreds, you need to do some research to find out where to start. One way to do this is to carefully read or watch or listen to the news for several weeks. Which reporters and writers cover your neighborhood or community? Which ones cover the kinds of issues and activities you're concerned with? Which ones seem to have a real feeling for people?

You can also check with people in other organizations to find out whom they deal with. Go to some other neighborhood and community organizations, to unions and coalitions. Ask them which people in the media they've had good luck with. "Good luck" doesn't just mean getting a story printed. It's also fair treatment, careful attention to detail, quoting people correctly, a willingness to listen to what people are really saying. Often those reporters and writers who have been fair and careful over the years will have a reputation that is respected in the community. These are the people with whom you want to meet.

How do you go from contacts to relationships with the media?

Think about building a relationship with people in the media as you would any other organizing situation. You find out as much as you can about people beforehand so that you have some things to talk about with them. Be familiar with what they do. You don't want to say to a television reporter, "I really enjoy your show every morning," if the show is on in the evening. Go visit the people you want to meet. In many operations it's not difficult to walk in, ask for the person you want, and get to see him or her. Introduce yourself. Tell who you're with. Explain a little bit about the organization and what it's doing. If possible, discuss a newsworthy issue your organization is working on. Be friendly and open. Talk about the things you're doing, the things you hope to do. Tell the reporter some things that might be happening which she or he might want to cover.

If you're able to build a personal relationship like this with people in the media, it will make your future work much easier. Knowing to whom to go helps avoid one of the most common problems with the media: the news release that is mailed to the main address and gets lost in the shuffle. When people in the media know who you are and what you're doing, those same people are also in a position to argue inside their organization for the kind of media coverage that you need.

Try to offer your best contacts, tips, exclusives, and story ideas to your friends in the media. This will help you keep their friendship. *Always* be accurate about the information you offer. Your media friends will be just as embarrassed by mistakes as you will. They may begin to ignore you if you're sloppy or dead wrong too often.

Once an organization has identified good media contacts, the media committee should maintain a complete and regularly updated list of their names, addresses, and phone numbers. Many reporters change jobs often, so it's important to be on the lookout for these changes. The list should be available for all news releases and press contacts.

How does an organization plan events to attract the media?

By preparing a good media list for your area and by developing personal relationships with some of the people in the media, your organization is laying the groundwork for its own media strategy. The next step is action. We want to get media coverage for the organization.

Remember that the value of a tactic shouldn't be judged just by how it's covered in the media. Many excellent tactics can work just fine without any media coverage whatsoever. But if part of the purpose of an event is to get coverage, then you have to figure out how you're actually going to get the media there.

To make sure we get good coverage of our media events, we need to develop a sense of what is and isn't "newsworthy." Some of the things that make a story newsworthy are:

(1) If it involves a large number of people.

(2) If it's unusual. This is one reason that in planning tactics we often try to think up something that is new and creative.

(3) If it affects the people who will be finding out about it through the media.

(4) If it involves famous people, the kind who are often covered by the media anyway.

(5) If it's a "human interest" story.

(6) If it's happening at a time when news is slow. Try to plan news events on days when nothing much else predictable is happening.

(7) If it ties into other similar events that are being covered in the media.

The event itself has a lot to do with what kind of coverage you're able to get. Remember that different types of events are best suited to different types of media. For radio coverage you need something people can listen to. A silent candlelight vigil in front of the electric company may look terrific on television or in a photo on the front page of the newspaper, but it doesn't do much for radio listeners. In the same way, one person standing up and making a powerful statement is much more useful to newspapers and radio, which depend on words, than it is to television, which depends on pictures.

As a general rule, television wants motion, groups, and crowds. Try to have a colorful setting. For television and for photos, use large signs with three or four words on them so that they can be read at a distance. Keep people moving. On television it will look like a much larger crowd than you really have. Talking, singing, chanting, or shouting in the background also sounds good coming over the airwaves. Songwriters use the word *hook* for the repeated phrase in a song that gets your attention. Events should also have some kind of *hook,* an aspect that is either humorous or unusual, to catch the attention of the media.

A well-managed event will usually get better coverage. Someone should have the responsibility of dealing with the media at the event, whether it is a press conference or an action. But don't try to manage the media by telling them where to go and what to do. Just be friendly, available, and helpful. Have people on hand whom the reporters can interview if they want. Have brief prepared statements they can take with them and packets of background information for those who might want to go into more depth.

The person responsible for dealing with media at the event

should also try to get the names of all reporters present so that she or he can follow up later. This is also a good way of building the media list. Sometimes it's helpful to call people when they get back to their offices and ask if there is any additional information they need to put together their story. This may be the chance to get in one good last quote or, in some cases, to correct incorrect information.

It's important to remember that the media are usually most interested in something when it is new. The very word *news* suggests that something has to be new to be worth writing or talking about. So when an organization is beginning, when it has its first two or three public activities, the media are likely to be there and people will get to see or read about themselves afterward. Six months, a year, two years down the road it's far harder to get media coverage of events and activities.

Organizations can react to this trend in different ways. They can simply become discouraged, thinking that what they do is no longer important. This in itself can make organizing more difficult.

Organizations can also make the opposite mistake. They decide that what is most important is to keep their image alive in the media. They begin planning their strategy mostly to influence and attract the media. There are times when we want to do this. But we must first make sure that media tactics fit into the overall strategy for the organization.

How is a news release put together?

Once we determine what sort of events we want to plan, we need to ensure that the media pay attention to them. News releases are the basic tool used to get media coverage for an organization. A release serves several purposes. It lets reporters know that a particular event is going to be happening. It provides enough background information so that the media can make a decision on whether or not to send somebody to cover that event. If the media decide not to send anyone, there should be enough information in the news release to put together a story.

A news release is not difficult to prepare. It should be on one sheet of paper. Use letterhead stationery from the organization if you have it. Some organizations have special stationery printed up for news releases, but this isn't really necessary. In the top right-hand corner you should type *For Further Information;* under that give the name of the person or persons who will be responsible for maintaining contact. List both their office and home phone numbers. It's especially important that the media know where to contact you at all times. For example, suppose that you have a demonstration you'd like the press to cover. The demonstration takes place at four o'clock in the afternoon. The story for the morning paper will be written that evening after your office has closed. If the reporter needs additional information and isn't able to locate you, you may just miss out on the chance to make a good statement or get some additional coverage.

On the left-hand side of the page under the organization's name, put the release date. The most common date is *FOR IMMEDIATE RELEASE.* This means that reporters are free to use the information as soon as they receive it. If for some reason you don't want any of the information released, written about, or talked about until a certain time and date, put that time and date on the release. But it's better to have it marked for immediate release. If the date when you want the information released is so far off that you have to put a hold on the news release, it's better to wait a few days before sending it out.

Next, write a heading for the release. This should be informative, as simply stated as possible, and clearly aimed at the people you want to reach: SENIORS PLAN 2:00 P.M. DEMONSTRATION AT COURTHOUSE or EUCLID IMPROVEMENT ASSOCIATION WINS LOWER RENT.

The opening paragraph should include who, what, when, where, and why, preferably in the opening sentence. These are the five basics of a news release. For example, an opening sentence might read, "The Euclid Improvement Association has scheduled a public protest in front of the Utility Commission's office on Wednesday, October 23, at 2:00 P.M. to protest the proposed new 17 percent electric rate increase." Even if the person receiving this release only reads the first sentence, he or she still knows what it is about.

News releases are written in what is called "inverted pyramid style." Imagine a triangle turned upside down, with the big end at the top and the point at the bottom. When you're writing a news release, each paragraph should be a little less important than the one before it. One reason for this is that reporters often will put together a story directly from the release. In small-town and rural newspapers, releases are often printed exactly or almost exactly as they were written. If the news release is too long for the space, the editor starts cutting from the bottom. That's one of the reasons the who, what, when, where, and why should be in the first paragraph. If your release is printed as a story and you put the time and date of the demonstration in the last paragraph, it's likely to be cut out. If you make sure that information is in the first paragraph, it will be in any story that appears.

Paragraphs in a news release should be short. A sentence or two is enough. The release should be typed double-spaced with wide margins.

A news release should be factual. A news release isn't an editorial. If you want to say something that's a matter of opinion, you should put it in quotes as a statement by a spokesperson of the organization. For example, you shouldn't say in a news release, "The proposed rate increase is outrageous, especially for a utility company that has just reported a 32 percent increase in profits over last year." However, you *can* say, "Eula Smith, President of the Euclid Improvement Association, said, 'This increase is outrageous, especially since the utility company has just reported a 32 percent increase in profits over last year.' " Newspapers cannot quote a news release opinion; however, they *can* quote a member of the organization.

NEWS RELEASE

EUCLID IMPROVEMENT ASSOCIATION
300 West Fremont Avenue
Charlotte, South Carolina 29303
(604)344-3268

FOR IMMEDIATE RELEASE

FOR FURTHER INFORMATION CONTACT:

Eula Smith (704)376-9006 (day)
333-3420 (night)

July 14, 1981

EUCLID IMPROVEMENT ASSOCIATION SETS
ELECTRIC RATE PROTEST

The Euclid Improvement Association has scheduled a
public protest in front of the Utility Commission's office on
Wednesday, July 15, at 2 p.m. to protest the proposed new
17% electric rate increase.

Eula Smith, President of the Association, told a meeting
of the Association's Consumer Committee last night, "This
increase is outrageous, especially since the utility company
has just reported a 32% increase in profits over last year."

In 1980, the Euclid Improvement Association was one
of several groups in the city to successfully oppose a proposed 33% increase in natural gas prices.

"Our action last year saved citizens nearly $3 million,"
Ms. Smith stated. "We don't see why the companies need an
increase, with the profits they're making. Most of our members can barely afford their electric bills now."

The Association is expecting to present petitions with
over one thousand signatures opposing the proposed increase to the Utility Commission during the public protest.

At the end of the release you should put either *-30-* or #####. This means there's nothing else. If there is another page, put (*more*) in parentheses in the bottom right-hand corner of the sheet.

How should a news release be timed?

The best news release is only effective if it gets into the right hands at the right time. If your organization is having a press conference at noon on a particular day, you're not likely to get coverage if the news release is received by the radio and television stations and newspapers that morning. On the other hand, if you send the release out two weeks in advance, it's likely to be forgotten.

One of the ways you can make your timing most effective is to ask the people in the media themselves how much advance notice they prefer to have on events that they're going to cover in person. If you have to guess, forty-eight hours' notice is about right. This allows the television stations time to schedule their crews.

It often helps to make a follow-up telephone call the morning before an event to make sure that there will be someone there covering it. If you call and are told that no one is coming, don't argue too hard or make *too* much of a case for why a reporter should come. Follow-up calls are a gentle reminder, not an order to attend. If the station or paper says that they're not going to be able to assign someone to cover, you might ask if they'd like to have additional information sent over after the event to help them in putting together a story.

The timing of media events has a lot to do with whether you get coverage in person. For example, if you schedule an event at eight in the evening, you probably won't get very much coverage. There is not enough time to get film to the television stations for the eleven o'clock news. At most you may get a story in the morning newspaper. On the other hand, an event that's held at eleven in the morning can make the evening newspaper, if there is one, the morning newspaper, the six o'clock evening television and/or radio news, and the eleven o'clock television and/or radio news at night.

What other kinds of coverage besides news can an organization get in the media?

News is only one type of media coverage. In addition to news, almost all of the media do feature stories. You often see these in the Sunday paper or even on the evening news. On a "slow news day," when nothing exciting is happening, there may be a five- or ten-minute spot about an event, person, or organization. Sometimes these are called "human interest stories."

If you're going to try to get this kind of coverage for your organization, do some research. Take a look at what kind of feature stories are being done. Try to come up with some story ideas from the organization that fit in with that particular style. For example, if the local newspaper seems to like feature stories about colorful individuals, pick out two or three of the leaders in the organization who show those same kinds of qualities and try to interest the newspaper in writing a story about them.

News releases are not used to get feature coverage. This is usually done person-to-person, either by writing a letter to the feature editor or by seeing or calling him or her. If the ideas that you have for a feature story don't seem to interest the editor, ask him or her what *would* be appealing. It often takes more work over a longer period of time to get feature coverage than news coverage, so don't be discouraged if you don't get results at first.

There are many other ways of getting media coverage. Television and radio stations have talk shows. Although it's not easy for a grassroots organization to get its leaders interviewed on national television, in many cases local radio and television stations are very open to local organizations and their spokespersons. Listen to and watch talk shows in your area. Get a sense of what sorts of guests they're interested in. Try to develop an approach that makes sense to the organization. Find out who the producer of the show is. Call him or her and make an appointment to talk it over. Follow up. When someone is getting ready to go on a talk show, he or she should listen to it a couple of times to get a sense of the style the interviewer is likely to use. Then the person should do the same kind of practice and preparation as for any other kind of public appearance. The person should also take along his or her own list of questions that can be asked by the interviewer. Finally, other members should call during the show with questions designed to bring out the issues the organization is interested in.

Newspapers obviously don't have talk shows. They do have both guest editorials and letters to the editor. Letters to the editor should be short, less than two hundred words, and signed by at least one individual. If you make your letter to the editor longer, the newspaper will almost certainly cut it down to shorter length. They'll make the decisions about what gets cut out and what doesn't. It's much better to have it shorter but to say what you want it to say. If your newspaper has a guest editorial section from time to time or regularly, find out how someone gets to be a guest editor.

Public service announcements are sometimes useful in television and radio, depending on how your organization is seen in the community. Roughly one-third of the advertisements on radio and television are public service. If your organization wants to get public service time, it's helpful if you can prepare your own public service announcements. These need to be exactly fifteen, thirty, or sixty seconds long. If they're professionally produced and fit these time slots exactly, there is a much greater chance that they'll be used. On the other hand, the stations do not have any legal obligation to run your spots. If they don't do it, they don't do it.

A final way of getting word out through the media is to use paid advertising. Many forms of paid advertising are simply too expensive for the average people's organization. But others are surprisingly inexpensive. For example, in many rural communities a full-page ad in the county newspaper may cost less than $200. In many smaller towns a thirty-second spot on the radio may cost a dollar or less. Some organizations have even had good results by using the classified ads.

It makes sense to look at the cost of different types of advertising and to judge that against whom you're trying to reach—your own members, the opposition, potential new members in the community. Sometimes it's worthwhile to put out a little money in paid advertising in order to control exactly what we say, how it gets said, and when it appears. This may also occasionally be useful when a newspaper has been going back and forth about whether or not to give fair coverage. Occasionally if they see some advertising money coming in, they're more inclined to give us some of the coverage that we want.

What can go wrong?

There are problems in dealing with the media. Sometimes organizations become too dependent for their self-image on what the media say about them. They judge the success of an activity by what was written about it in the evening newspaper or what was said about it on the evening news. If an organization becomes too dependent on what the media say, it's vulnerable to shifts in media opinion. Sometimes these shifts are the result of the pressures that the opposition can put on the media through its paid advertising and political and social connections.

There are two main problems that we have with the media: bad coverage and no coverage. It's hard to say which is more difficult to deal with. Sometimes a newspaper or a television or radio station is so firmly in the hands of the opposition that it refuses to cover anything we do. At other times it covers our organization but distorts us, misquoting and misrepresenting us so badly that we might have been better off if there hadn't been any coverage at all.

Actually, it's fairly hard to tell which is worse—no coverage or bad coverage. The people who specialize in media for elections tend to feel, for example, that almost any coverage is good as long as your name is mentioned. This is called "name identification." They feel that what people remember is the name of the candidate, even if that candidate was being attacked.

It's not so clear that this applies in the case of people's organizations. But an unfavorable article is not always quite the disaster we think it is. In looking at the fairness of an article, don't be too concerned if every word we said isn't quoted exactly. It's hard for even the best reporters to get everything down word for word. What's important is whether the overall effect of the story is helpful to us.

What can be done about media problems?

When you're seriously misquoted in an article and when it clearly has a possible bad impact on the organization, it may make sense to get some kind of correction. But don't expect too much. Correction notices are usually an inch long and are buried someplace near the obituaries. People rarely pay too much attention to them.

If the media consistently refuse to give you coverage or keep giving you coverage that is really unfair or misleading, the organization needs to decide what to do about it. Look at the particular newspaper or radio or television station just like any other target and at the issue like any other issue. The issue is that the organization wants fair coverage for itself. The target is the newspaper or radio or television station which has not been doing the right thing.

The organization needs to go through a strategy planning process in which it treats the media just like any other target. Analyze structure, strengths, and weaknesses. Television stations, radio stations, and newspapers are just like other corporations. Somebody owns them. Somebody manages them. Somebody makes decisions. Some people have money invested in them. Some people are making a profit from them.

As the organization develops its strategy it can plan different tactics for dealing with the problems of coverage. For example, the organization may send a leadership group to negotiate with the management or owners of that station or paper. If negotiations fail, other tactics can be used. In the case of a newspaper, for example, people can be encouraged to cancel their subscriptions.

Be careful of using letters to the editor when you're involved in a complicated issue which divides the community. Remember that the other side can write letters to the editor as easily as you can. If the newspaper is taking sides on the issue, it's easy for the editor to publish more letters from the other side or to edit your letters so that they come out looking bad.

Someone once said that you never get the last word in a battle with a newspaper. That's true. Don't even try. Unlike television and radio, there are no legal restrictions on the fairness of a newspaper. A newspaper doesn't have to give anyone the right to reply. Newspapers have no obligation to be fair. There is no "fairness doctrine" and there is no "equal time" provision. If a newspaper publisher decides to treat your organization as badly as possible, he or she has a legal right to do so.

Radio and television stations, which are regulated by federal law, have to keep up with a number of complicated requirements in order to keep their licenses. These include maintaining public files which any member of the public can go and inspect. This gives people's organizations an opportunity to harass and pressure television and radio stations. In addition, their licenses have to be renewed every three years. People's organizations have the right to challenge those licenses. This creates a chance for leverage against the television or radio station which is giving us a hard time.

Remember, too, that the different types of media compete with each other. If you put a picket line in front of the newspaper office, you're fairly sure to be covered on the evening TV news.

The danger in targeting the media in this kind of pressure campaign is that it becomes too much of a target. We concentrate too much of our energies on what is only a means to an end. If we're involved in a campaign to stop an interstate highway and are getting unfair coverage from the newspaper, we can attack the newspaper to try to get fairer coverage. But we should always remember that our primary target is the highway, not the newspaper.

When should an organization exclude the media?

In all of the organization's dealings with the media, you need to keep asking questions: Why do we need the media at this point? Do we really want coverage? Is coverage useful? Is it necessary? Is it helpful to us?

Coverage needs to fit into our strategy. It needs to serve specific purposes. This is a hard lesson for most organizations to learn. It means that we have to be careful even with those media people who are most friendly and helpful to us. People in the media have organizational responsibilities just as we do. They're expected to come up with good news, with information, with ideas. It doesn't matter whether we told it to them at a formal press conference or over a beer at a party down the block. It's still information that they have a right to use.

A good rule is to never tell anything to a member of the media that you would not want to see made public. Be careful of trying to avoid this problem by saying, "This is off the record" or "confidential" or "background information." It's often difficult for a reporter to remember which things you said were confidential and which weren't, especially if you insist on going "off the record" a number of times during a conversation. It's far better to limit your remarks to the things that you wouldn't mind reading in the newspaper or hearing on the radio or television news.

An organization will sometimes want to exclude the media. It's often not a good idea to have people from the media sitting in on a membership meeting, a planning meeting, a committee meeting, a strategy meeting. If we permit a friendly reporter to sit in on a meeting where we're deciding strategy, the headline of the story may read CONFLICT IN NEIGHBORHOOD GROUP rather than what we want to see put out publicly.

Who should talk to the media?

One of the questions that often seems easy in an organization but which is really very difficult is deciding who should talk to the media and under what conditions. It's hard to resist the temptation to talk to the media when asked. Almost any of us are flattered when a television reporter comes up and asks our opinion. We find it hard when a reporter is particularly sympathetic not to talk about what the organization is doing. Sometimes we talk much more than we should.

Remember that just as we expect leaders to be loyal to their organizations, people in the media are loyal to the organizations that they work for: the newspapers, the radio stations, and the television stations. Their responsibility is to get as much news as they can. They are not responsible to *our* organizations. When they put a story together, they are not doing it from the point of view of what's good for our organization, but of what makes news. "What makes news," unfortunately, is often damaging rather than helpful to us. This includes leaders taking positions that the members of the organization don't know about, several leaders coming up with statements that conflict with each other, giving away strategy before time to take action, and talking about the internal problems of the organization.

Because it's so important that what gets said to the media be consistent and reflect the views of the organization, it's important that organizations decide who is going to speak to the media. This is often difficult. It's the same problem we talked about in the chapter on organizations. Individual board members need to learn that their power comes through the board and not through them as individuals. They should not, for example, make decisions on their own and ask staff members to carry them out without going through the formal decision-making structure of the organization.

In the same way, individual leaders should not talk to the media as representatives of their organization unless they've been asked to do so. They should not make statements that reflect the organization's policy unless that policy has been officially decided on. We need to train leaders in how to talk to the media. But we also need to train them in how *not* to talk to the media. We have to be comfortable saying to a reporter on the telephone, "Thanks very much for calling. I'm real glad you're interested in what we're doing. Could I ask you to call George Millay? He's the one who knows the most about this and can talk to you best. Here are his phone numbers at home and at work."

How can people prepare to talk to the media?

Talking with the media is one of the leadership skills that's easiest to practice. If you know that you're going to be one of those talking, ask some other leaders, members, or staff of the organization to help you practice. They can do it in a lot of ways. They can practice interviewing you on the telephone or face-to-face in person. Get different people to play different styles of interviewing: friendly, hostile, confidential.

You can also practice talking to the media in a small group, house, or committee meeting. You could, for example, pretend that it was a press conference. Make your press statement and then let other members of the group fire questions at you. Afterward you can discuss how well the questions were answered, how well your answers reflected the organization's policies, and what kind of effect you had.

In an interview, whether it's over the phone, in front of a television camera, or in someone's office, be yourself. Be friendly and open. Don't be afraid to say "No." If you don't want to answer, you can say, "The organization hasn't made a decision on that yet. But we'll be glad to let you know as soon as we do." It's far better to say that than to make up policy on the spot and then have to live with something that appears in the newspapers before the other members of the organization know about it.

In dealing with the media, go back to the rules on dealing with individuals. You shouldn't behave any differently with a reporter or interviewer than you do when you're knocking on doors in your neighborhood. You should not assume that they'll take the responsibility for the interview, so *you* should make an effort to put *them* at ease. Often you can prepare a list of questions for the interviewer to ask you. Make sure that the interview is comfortable. Create a natural setting.

Don't be afraid to say the things that you want to say. At the end of the interview you might want to say, "There are a couple of other things that I wanted to mention."

Sometimes, particularly if you're on a live interview on radio or television, you can answer a question that isn't quite what you want to talk about by quietly changing the subject. Only the most aggressive reporters are going to stop you and say, "That isn't what I asked about." Most of them will let you talk as long as it's interesting. You might practice in the practice sessions how to change the subject during the course of an interview. This is a useful way of getting information across the way we want it presented.

Media can be very important to a people's organization. They can be used to bring pressure on the opposition. They can create a sense of who we are which helps attract new members and allies. How our organization is portrayed by the media has a lot to do with our self-image. Our leaders' and members' self-confidence will to a certain extent depend on how they see themselves portrayed in the media.

What's most important is that our organization have an actual media strategy. We can't just take the position that more coverage is better. We need to try to figure out the ways in which media are most useful to us just as we would with any other possible tactic. As much as possible, we want to control our media rather than letting the media control us. We want to use media to build the organization rather than to undercut it. A well-planned media strategy increases our chances of being able to do this.

14. Money

ALMOST FROM THE BEGINNING in any organization we have to deal with two questions. One is "What are we going to do?" The other is "How are we going to pay for it?"

Even at the start an organization is going to run into some costs. There are refreshments for the meetings. There is the expense of mimeographing, photocopying, or printing leaflets. If the group decides to go downtown to a city council meeting, there is the cost of gasoline or of subway or bus tickets.

Sometimes we don't even notice these costs. Someone says, "I'll bring the Cokes and cookies." Someone else says, "I can use the mimeograph at my church to get the leaflets run off." Someone volunteers his or her car or truck. People pay their own way on the subway or bus. But these are still direct costs to the organization, even if people at the beginning are willing to assume them themselves.

As organizing goes on and the organization begins to grow, so do costs. There are long-distance phone calls to be paid for. A flyer now means not fifty copies but five hundred. The organization undertakes a legal battle and the lawyer needs to be paid. It opens an office, so now there are rent payments and utility bills. The organization decides to hire a full-time staff person and finds itself paying salary, Social Security, and travel expenses. It begins publishing a newsletter and so must pay for printing and postage. Next some of the leaders of the organization have to go to Washington to negotiate, so instead of subway tokens it's airplane tickets.

It's not hard for an organization which is active and growing to move very quickly from a Coke-and-cookies budget to one which requires thousands and thousands of dollars. As the needs for money grow, it becomes harder to run the organization on the kind of "I'll bring the ice" budget on which the group started out. Someone who works in an office downtown may be able to get fifty copies run free once or twice. If that person starts coming in week after week to run five hundred copies of a newsletter on the company copying machine, someone is going to start asking questions. People who didn't mind paying for gas when it was an occasional trip to the courthouse, may start feeling differently when it's an almost monthly 300-mile round trip to the state capital. An organization learns fairly quickly that it can't just depend on the individual members volunteering whatever is needed each time. The organization has to begin coming up with a financial plan for what its money needs are going to be and how it's going to get the funds to operate.

How does an organization do financial planning?

Too often people's organizations make only a halfhearted attempt, if any, at financial planning. Often what they do is to say, "Let's see how much money we can raise. Then we'll know how much we have to spend." Or an organization may decide what its needs are without looking realistically at how much money could be raised. Such an organization might say, "We have to have four organizers. We have $1,000 in the bank. So let's hire four people at $250 a month and we'll just raise money as hard as we can so that we'll be able to pay them next month."

Either way of doing things can lead to trouble. An organization may commit itself to a large monthly budget without realizing that it's almost always easier to raise money in the early days of an organizing campaign than farther down the road. When feelings are running high, people are willing to dig into their own pockets. Two years later, when things have slowed down, it becomes harder and harder to come up with the same amount that is needed to get by.

Too many people's organizations have had the experience of expanding rapidly to a large staff with many offices, frequent trips for the leaders of the organization, and many of the other things that money can buy: expensive photocopying equipment, computers, WATS lines. A year later the financial crisis hits. The organization can't raise the money it needs to pay its monthly bills and is faced with difficult decisions. Should the copying machine go back? Should staff be laid off? Should staff go unpaid? Should staff salaries be cut? Should expenses go unmet? Should travel be cut out?

It's not always possible to avoid these kinds of emergencies no matter how good your financial planning is. But a great many people's organizations have had the experience of becoming too large too quickly and then having to cut back suddenly when the money ran out. Knowing this, it makes sense to try to plan financially for the long run. This may mean building or expanding more slowly. But it can avoid the kinds of cutbacks that hurt an organization so badly. Money may not be the root of all evil, but it sure is the root of many organizational problems. We need to control the finances of our organizations and not allow money to control us.

Who makes financial decisions in a people's organization?

In a profit-making corporation, financial details are often secret. The shareholders, who in theory own the organization, are usually told only the smallest details about what is really going on financially inside the corporation.

In a people's organization, though, it's important for everyone to have a good sense of what's happening with the money. Nothing can break up an organization quite as fast as suspicion over money, because nothing raises suspicions quite as quickly as money does.

Part of the reason this is true is that the money people's organizations spend is money that really belongs to the members of that organization, It may be their dues money. It may be money that they contributed. It may be money that they have raised through grass roots fund-raising events. Even if it's money from outside the organization—from foundations, churches, or government grants—that money was still raised in their name and in the name of their communities, their hopes, and their dreams.

Since money is so hard to come by, people are going to be concerned about what happens to it. Most often the problems come not because the money is being spent badly but because people just don't know how it is being spent. So financial planning has to be done in a very open way, a way that involves members of the organization, gives them a chance to help make decisions, and reports to them regularly and very clearly on exactly what is being done with their money.

One of the first committees that an organization should have is a financial committee. A financial committee should be there not just to rubber-stamp the treasurer's report. Its' members should sit down and plan what money is going to mean to the organization, what they're going to try to spend and how they're going to spend it, what they're going to try to raise and how they're going to raise it. The financial committee also has the responsibility of trying to figure out the best ways of involving other members of the organization in this planning process and helping these members to really understand the decisions being made.

How is a budget prepared?

The world of finance is one of those worlds that highly paid professionals have made unnecessarily complicated. Doctors make a tremendous amount of money by giving complicated Latin names to things that everybody knows a short English word for. Some lawyers make a living translating simple English sentences into long, complicated paragraphs that only other lawyers can understand. In the same way, some financial planners have made the whole process of developing a budget and doing financial planning seem so complicated that no one but they could possibly do it.

The process of preparing a budget doesn't need to be complicated. The financial committee should schedule a meeting and set aside enough time to do some good thinking and hard work, away from phone calls and other distractions. A good starting point is to look at what the organization is already doing and spending. Make up a list of all the things that the organization has already spent money on. It would probably be helpful to go back through the books, the check stubs, and the receipts just to make sure nothing has been forgotten.

Some common things an organization spends money on are the following:

(1) *Staff,* including salaries, fringe benefits (such as Social Security, medical insurance, unemployment insurance, and workers' compensation), and expenses (such as telephone, travel, materials, and supplies).

(2) *Offices,* including rent, maintenance of equipment, lights, heat, water, sewage, and maintenance of the office itself.

(3) *Travel,* including travel for staff, leaders, and members. This may include mileage reimbursement, paying for gas for volunteers, in some cases repairing the cars of members if they break down while being used on organization business, rail tickets, bus tickets, air tickets, and rental of buses and vans for long-distance travel.

(4) *Telephone,* including telephones in the offices and reimbursement of staff and leadership for long-distance telephone calls.

(5) *Postage* for mailing newsletters and other letters.

(6) *Printing* of newsletters, leaflets, forms, reports, proposals, flyers, pamphlets.

(7) *Copying* or the rental of copying equipment.

(8) *Fees,* including legal fees, auditors' fees; and the cost of training for staff, members, and leaders, including fees to participate in outside training sessions and the costs of consulting trainers to come in and work with the organization.

(9) *Debt retirement* in cases where the organization has borrowed money and is paying it back, including interest on the debt.

Start with these categories and look at what your organization has paid out in each of them over the last year. That can be a good starting point for doing a realistic job of preparing a budget. In looking at what you want to spend over the next year, it's helpful to make both a minimum and a maximum budget. A minimum budget means the absolute least that the organization thinks it can get by with. A maximum includes the cost of doing all the things the organization would like to do and realistically thinks it can do in the next year. An organization might say, "Right now we have two staff people and they're doing the work of three. We really need a third staff person. That would take some of the burden off our first two. We could send the new staff person over to the other side of the city to work with two chapters that are organizing there. We don't want to add a fourth staff person because we don't have enough chapters for a fourth person to work with. At any cost we want to avoid laying off staff. So our minimum budget will have two staff positions and our maximum budget will have three."

It is not unusual for an organization's maximum budget to be twice the amount of the mimimum budget. If the maximum and minimum budgets are just about the same, you may not be thinking hard enough about what to do if there is really not enough money to go around. If the maximum budget is three or four times the minimum budget, it's possible that the organization is being unrealistic in its expansion plan and needs to take a harder look at it.

You should keep testing your minimum budget. Say to the group, "OK. Our budget for next year is $32,000. We're saying that's the least we can get by on. But suppose we can only raise $25,000. Where could we cut $7,000 more?" Looking at the budget this way may help you find other items that could be cut if necessary. People's organizations have such a hard time getting money that it's wise to make budgets as lean as possible.

Once a budget has been prepared, the financial committee usually recommends it to the board, which then either accepts it as is or changes it before accepting it. Once the final budget is approved by the board it should be presented to the members of the organization. A good way is to print the budget in the newsletter with some kind of explanation about what the money is really going for. Members of the financial committee might be able to help explain the budget by going to different chapter meetings and talking about it, including their description of how some of the decisions were reached.

Sometimes an organization will try to conceal some of the financial information because there is concern over what some of the members will think about it. Some leaders may feel that the salaries being paid to their staff will seem too high to some of the members. So they aren't open and direct about what the salaries are. The danger is what might happen later when someone finds out and makes an issue of the amount of the salaries. If there is going to be this kind of argument over any part of the budget, it should happen before the money is spent, not after. It should happen because people in the organization knew what was going to happen and decided to argue about it, not because they found out a secret that had been kept from them.

Making a budget serves several purposes in the organization. It sets program priorities as well as financial priorities. When an organization decides to spend $5,000 on lobbying trips to the state capital rather than hiring an additional staff person in a new neighborhood, the organization is also saying, "Focusing on an issue that requires lobbying as a way of solving it is a higher priority for us than expanding our membership in a new area."

Decisions about money reflect the priorities that an organization has set, whether those priorities are being set consciously or not.

Once the money decisions are made they begin to influence the way the organization works. This is one of the reasons why a financial decision-making process which involves both the members and the leaders of an organization is so important. When we say that money can control an organization instead of the organization controlling the money, we're talking about what happens when financial decisions are made without an understanding of the ways in which they can change an organization's priorities and programs. A conscious planning process to set the budget of the organization can prevent unwanted changes.

The financial planning process also serves to clarify goals for the organization that are shared by the members. When an organization goes through the planning process—with the financial committee setting priorities, presenting a budget to the board, discussing it, adopting it, explaining it to the members—it is also setting its own very important goals. If the members of the organization feel that the organization's goals are their goals as well, it makes it easier to involve them in different kinds of fund-raising activities.

Most of us have seen the thermometer poster that the United Way and United Fund use during their campaign drives, with the amount of money to be raised written along the side of the thermometer like degrees and the amount that has been raised so far painted in red. This kind of measurement of how far we have to go and how far we've gone so far in our fund raising is important. It gives the organization a goal to work toward and makes fund raising easier.

What kind of financial records should an organization keep?

Sometimes a people's organization gets the idea that it's not important to keep the kind of detailed financial records that a business keeps. Sometimes we think that because we're doing good work and fighting important issues, keeping good financial records isn't necessary. In fact, it is probably more important for a people's organization to keep good, solid, reliable, and understandable financial records than for other kinds of organizations. The reason is that an organization's financial records can be used to discredit or destroy it.

Sometimes the membership doesn't understand what is happening with the money and as a result loses its trust in the organization. Sometimes the opposition exposes financial and management problems as a way of attacking people's organizations. It's true, for example, that some unions have had conflicts of interest in the investment of their pension funds. But when has the federal government ever gone after a private corporation for its investment policies the same way that it goes after the trade unions? When the women of McCaysville Industries (who had started a cooperative sewing factory after a fourteen-month strike at the Levi-Strauss factory in Blue Ridge, Georgia) failed to pay certain taxes on time, the government padlocked their factory. When does the government ever padlock a factory owned by a corporation, no matter how serious the charges against it? People's organizations which receive funds from federal agencies, such as Volunteers in Service to America (VISTA), have been audited with a fine-tooth comb. Some of the people who work with these agencies and organizations have been hauled before congressional committees to testify. How often are business people forced to defend themselves before congressional committees?

A people's organization does not necessarily have to do anything wrong or be guilty of any financial mismanagement to be attacked. Such attacks should be seen as tactics that the opposition can use as a way of discrediting us, of forcing us to put energy into activities that are not as important as the issues we're working on, of dividing our membership, of making our membership trust us less.

No matter how carefully we keep our records, we cannot always prevent attacks on our financial management. Even if our books are perfect, if someone in Congress demands an audit for long enough and loud enough, that legislator will probably get that audit. But it's harder for one auditor to find any flaws if we observe the necessary procedures and regulations that apply to all organizations. It's absolutely critical that a people's organization comply with all local, state, and federal laws regarding payroll taxes, Social Security, workers' compensation, unemployment insurance, and payroll deductions. If an organization is receiving federal funds, reports have to be done correctly and submitted on time, or funds can be cut off.

Besides financial audits, an organization which gets federal funds to support its program can have its program audited. If the organization isn't doing what it said would be done with the federal money, the government can not only cut off the funds, but force the organization to pay back to the government the money that's already been spent.

The organization should also report regularly to its members on all money matters. If you have a monthly newsletter, it would be a good idea to print a monthly financial report showing what came in and what went out. It is also important to put together an annual summary that people can understand. Remember that even the most simple financial report can be difficult to comprehend. It's worth taking the time in meetings to go over the organization's finances and make sure that members really understand them.

Where can an organization get money?

There are two main ways in which a people's organization can get money. The funds can come from inside the organization: the contributions of members, the dues they pay, the money they raise through grass roots fundraising. The money can also come from outside the organization as grants from individuals and private foundations, from church organizations, and from the federal government.

Over the years many organizations have become very dependent on outside funds. Partly this came out of the experience of the mid-sixties when large grants were available to local community organizations through the Office of Economic Opportunity (OEO), which was part of what was then called the War on Poverty. In many cases a small community organization which had been getting by on a shoestring suddenly found itself with thousands of dollars in the bank, numerous staff people, and expensive equipment.

There is not necessarily anything wrong with an organization having this kind of money. The problem in this case was that the money depended on the continued goodwill of the federal government. So in many cases when an organization found itself beginning to step on local toes politically, it also found that there was a threat that its funds would be cut off. Having become dependent on these funds, such organizations found themselves in a difficult situation. Some changed their priorities in order to keep getting the funding. Others refused to change and had the funds cut off.

This is the real danger of outside funding for a people's organization. It encourages the organization to become dependent on a high budget level which that organization may not be able to keep up without the outside funds.

Suppose the organization you work with received a grant of $100,000 from a foundation, church, or federal agency to continue with organizing work. You would probably hire some additional staff people, rent a photocopier, put in a WATS line, schedule a number of trips for the leaders of the organization, contract for some training sessions, and undertake other improvements which would obviously be good for the organization. At the end of the year, however, the government announces that the grant will not be renewed. What do you do then? Do you lay off the staff? Do you send back the equipment? Do you discontinue the training and leadership development sessions?

This problem has arisen for a number of organizations because of rapid financial expansion through dependence on outside resources. This is not to say that an organization shouldn't use any outside funds. Outside funds are an important resource to people's organizations. But in planning to use them it's important to be conscious of the fact that they are not dependable resources and can be pulled out on fairly short notice.

Also, outside funding is rarely a long-range sustaining source of income to an organization. Most private foundations and church groups do not fund any one organization for more than three or four years. The Catholic Campaign for Human Development, for example, which is the largest single source of private money for people's organizations, will not give money to any group for more than three years.

Outside funding needs to be considered in the same way as any other resource or strategic decision of the organization. We need to ask, "How will this money, if it becomes available, fit into our long-range plans for organizational development and financial planning? Are we creating a one-time high that we will not be able to sustain? What are the chances that we will be able to build up our own internal fund raising over a period of time to make up for the loss of outside funding?"

Sometimes mutually satisfactory arrangements can be negotiated with the outside funders. In the case of private foundations, churches, and individuals, it's possible to request that a $30,000 grant be paid out over three years at a rate of $10,000 per year. This helps level out the organization's income, and gives a base to future financial planning.

It's also important that members of the organization understand and be involved in the decision to seek outside funding. Outside grants can create suspicion and division among the members of an organization. They want to know who these people and institutions are, and why they want to give money to the organization. They may be uncomfortable in the unfamiliar world of proposals, funding application forms, reviews and previews, site visits, outside evaluations, program audits, deferred expenses, and in-kind contributions. An organization which is going to look for outside funding needs to help its leaders and members become familiar with this mysterious world of institutions that give money away. Not just the organization's staff but also its leaders should be involved in preparing proposals, meeting with foundation and church executives, and planning for site visits and evaluations. Outside funding is an important resource for people's organizations. But it needs to be planned for carefully and integrated into the ongoing work of the organization.

How can an organization raise funds internally?

People's organizations have two main ways of raising funds internally. One is through dues systems. The other is through grassroots fund raising.

Dues systems have been used as a financial support by private organizations in this country for hundreds of years. Most churches receive a large portion of their income from variations of the dues system. Tithing, in which church members pledge 10 percent of their income to the church, is a type of dues system. Agreements to pay a certain amount each week or each month are also a type of dues system.

The union movement is perhaps one of the best examples of the strength of the dues system. We've all heard the expression "I've paid my dues." That expression is used not just to mean that someone has paid up but that he or she has certain rights that come as a result of having paid. This is one of the principles behind the dues system used in the American labor movement. When members of an organization do pay dues, it creates for them a sense of ownership. It is their organization because they paid for it.

Different unions have different systems for dues. Some require a fixed amount to be paid by a member each week or each month. Sometimes there is a certain amount that goes to the

international union and the local union can add on the amount
which it keeps. In other unions members are charged a certain
percentage of what they earn each week. For example, their
union dues might be two hours of work per month.

The political independence of the unions and their ability to
represent the self-interest of their members show the strength of
this type of dues system. Many of the larger unions have income
in the tens of millions annually. The United Auto Workers Union,
for example, had an annual income of over $250 million in 1980,
and in addition over $300 million in the bank in strike and other
emergency support funds.

This financial base gives the unions political independence.
Right-wingers are always complaining about the amount of
money that the unions put into political races. In fact, it is a very
small amount compared with what the corporations and their
friends put in. But it still is substantial. The unions long ago
learned a very important lesson: In order to be politically independent, an organization needs to be financially independent.

This is an important lesson for all types of people's organizations. If we want to have real freedom of action, we have to pay
our own way. In the short run, funds from wealthy individuals,
private foundations, church organizations, and government agencies may be useful. But often our organizations are going to be
fighting the government. They'll be opposing the private corporations that endow the foundations and in whose stocks the foundations invest. There is definitely a limit to how often you can bite
the hand that feeds you. As long as we're dependent on these
outside sources for our funds they will have a negative effect
when we set our priorities and develop our strategies.

A good dues system is one realistic alternative for people's
organizations. There are different ways of setting up a dues system. One fee can be charged for individual membership, another
fee for family membership, and a third for institutional or organizational membership. Dues can be paid weekly, monthly, or
yearly. There is no set amount that is right for a dues system. How-

ever, most people's organizations tend to set their dues too low. It is not unusual to find organizations which charge their members $2 or $5 a year in dues. If an organization is really doing a valuable job in defending the rights and increasing the benefits of its members, these amounts are far too low.

One reason dues in people's organizations are often so low stems from some of the thinking of the 1960s. The argument was made then that poor people simply don't have the money to belong to organizations. This just isn't true. Poor and working people are the main support of many important institutions in this country, including the unions and the churches. People individually may not have much money. But together they have a great deal. If an organization is important to a person or a family, several dollars a month is not too much to ask them to pay in dues.

Often our problems come about because we start an organization by offering people something for nothing. We don't charge membership fees or dues. We don't require people to play an active part in the organization or to work in place of paying dues. We don't ask them for contributions except occasionally. Then later, when the organization starts going broke, we come around and ask people if they'd be willing to put in $3 for dues. They're resentful, but they're right. We're changing what our expectations of them are. It's much easier to decide from the beginning on a fixed system of dues which treats each member of the organization equally, than to start out and hope to ease a dues system in slowly.

It does make sense to have some provisions for people who, for one reason or another, find it difficult to pay dues. One good option is to allow people to substitute work dues for cash dues, putting in a certain number of hours working with the organization in place of the cash payment.

One of the problems of a dues system in a people's organization is how the dues are collected. One of the key elements a union contract has is what is called the "dues checkoff." In this system the employer agrees to withhold the amount of the union dues from the employee's regular paycheck and to forward that money to the union. The employer acts as a collection agent for the union, and the union is guaranteed its dues money every month.

Because the members of people's organizations don't work at the same place and because we don't have those kinds of contract rights, the checkoff system isn't possible. Members either have to send in their dues voluntarily or the dues have to be collected. This is often a painstaking process and one that absorbs leadership and staff time. Some organizations are experimenting with having members check off monthly dues from their bank accounts or their Master Card and Visa accounts. This assumes, of course, that they have such accounts and cards, which many members of people's organizations do not.

The problem of how to maintain a dues system in a people's organization without totally absorbing leadership and staff time in the process is one that clearly needs attention in the coming years. The dues system itself is one of the best ways that an organization can build a solid financial base and at the same time give its members a sense of participation and control over the organization.

How does an organization develop a grass roots fund-raising program?

Raising money is an American tradition. One of the great strengths in the tradition of poor and working people in this country has been their ability to work together to accomplish what all of them wanted. Look at all of the churches and synagogues that were built by people's own hands with money that they raised together. Look at all the schools in rural communities that those communities built on their own. People are always putting on fund-raising drives to help co-workers who are hospitalized, to establish a park for the neighborhood, to build playground equipment for a local school, to support charitable organizations. Millions and millions of dollars are raised in this country each year. Each community has its own traditional ways of raising money. Here is a list of just some of the ways that community organizations have raised their own funds: benefits, canvasses, movies, potlucks, food feasts, raffles, auctions, lectures, cocktail parties, cookbooks, dances, house tours, bus tours, luncheons, theater parties, ad books, antique fairs, art fairs, dues systems, membership drives, carnivals, concerts, dinners, casino nights, marathons, movie premieres, telethons, tennis tournaments, bingo games, businesses, direct mail, rummage sales, yard sales, fish fries, punchboards, festivals, state fair booths, farmers' markets, gospel sings, calendars.

More and more people's organizations are beginning to rely again on grassroots fund-raising techniques to provide major portions of their budgets. A number of organizations are raising between 50 and 75 percent of their annual budget simply through such techniques. These approaches to the budget problems of people's organizations, however, have more advantages than the money that they raise. Grassroots fund raising works so well because the money is raised by the members of an organization *for* that organization. It not only raises money, it raises expectations by involving people in the process of building the organization. It not only stabilizes the budget, it stabilizes the organization by giving people a more concrete and specific sense of what that organization does. Grassroots fund raising is so effective because it's not simply a fund-raising technique. It is also an organizing technique which develops leadership within the organization.

Some organizations are experimenting with other ways of developing a financial base. Some own and operate small businesses and use the profits for the organization's operating budget. Others provide services to their members which also provide some income to the organization. Public Action in Illinois, for example, operates an insurance business which provides low-cost insurance to its members, with some funds left over to go into the organization's operating budget. The New Hampshire People's Alliance is considering establishing a cooperative which would provide low-cost eyeglasses to its members, with some funds left over for operations.

An organization should have a committee to oversee fund-raising activities. The fund-raising committee should be separate from the financial committee. The financial committee's role is to oversee the planning process that leads to adopting a budget. In other words, the financial committee is responsible for planning how the money is to be spent and seeing that it is spent in that way. The fund-raising committee is responsible for trying to meet the goals set by the financial committee: for figuring out how the organization is going to get the money and seeing that it does so.

What financial problems can an organization run into?

An organization can run into certain special problems with its money. Sometimes an organization raises more money than it needs in its budget. In a situation like this, it's often tempting to spend the money while you've got it. But it also can be important to develop the patience to put that money away for a rainy day and to provide a cushion in case next year's budget isn't raised. The fact that we're able to raise our budget this year doesn't mean that we'll be able to do it next year. There is real security in having money in the bank for emergencies.

Sometimes an organization runs out of money. There may not be enough money even to pay staff or the rent. In a situation like this there are several options. Sometimes it's possible for an organization to borrow money in the short term. But this has to be done extremely carefully. Say an organization borrows money for thirty days. The loan may help the organization get by the next month, but the crisis may be worse when the month is over. If money is to be borrowed at all, it must be borrowed with the full knowledge of the members and with a very clear and realistic plan for paying it back. At other times, it may simply be better to bite the bullet and make the necessary cuts in the organization's operating budget until more money can be raised. Again, these decisions need to be made as openly and with as much membership participation as possible.

Perhaps the most important point to understand about money and people's organizations is that they are inseparable. It's not simply how much money we have and what we do with that money. It's a question of *how* we set our financial priorities, which are our program priorities as well. It's a question of *how* we raise that money, not just how much we raise. In a people's organization finances and fund raising are part of organizing. Grassroots fund raising can do all of the things that good organizing does: build confidence, give members a sense of ownership, develop leadership, create in the community an image of what the organization is and what it does. The same skills that go into doing good financial planning can help people do effective strategy planning. If we keep in mind as we develop our finances the same principles that guide our organizing, we will strengthen both.

15. Coalitions

A COALITION is a group of organizations working together for a common purpose. Some coalitions work on a group of related issues. Sometimes a coalition is put together for the purpose of dealing with one issue only. When that issue is solved one way or the other, the coalition no longer exists.

Short-term coalitions are often easier to put together because they ordinarily only require that each participating organization be in favor of this particular issue. A single-issue coalition can bring together organizations which would otherwise have difficulty working together. In the long run, though, there is also a need to build coalitions which can fight on a number of issues, and which involve many different kinds of constituencies and organizations. These coalitions will need to be permanent and self-sufficient enough to build real power for people. Putting together these coalitions is one of the great challenges of organizing.

When does it make sense to form a coalition?

Let's say you're a leader working with a citywide organization. Your organization has been building its strength for two years. It's made up of thirty neighborhood groups throughout the city. So far you've fought mostly on local neighborhood issues: getting the city to fix some streets, clean out some sewers, tear down some abandoned buildings, build a few recreational areas.

This year at your organization's annual meeting, everyone decided something had to be done about the lack of decent public transportation. Neighborhoods felt isolated from each other and from other things that were happening in the city. People had a hard time getting to work or to school. Public services were unavailable to many poor people because of the lack of transportation. So your organization has decided to make a major fight to have the city put large amounts of money into public transportation. The city wants to use the money to build a civic center and attract conventions and trade shows to benefit the hotels and other business establishments. You recognize that your organization probably does not have the power to win on this issue. Then you begin to ask if it might be the right time to organize a citywide coalition to deal with public transportation and other issues.

You can start thinking about the strategy for organizing a coalition by remembering what you do when you first organize a small group among the people in your neighborhood or your plant. You try to find their common interests, the issues and values which bind them together. You try to figure out what each person's individual self-interest would be in becoming a member of an organization. You try to analyze the problems that might keep somebody from being a member of the organization, or even why it might be better for the organization if that person stayed out.

This is the same process that an organization needs to go through as part of the decision on whether or not it should work in a coalition with other organizations. This process often first takes place in the life of an organization when that organization is working on a difficult issue and finds itself at a point where it seems as if additional allies are going to be necessary in order to win.

What are first steps in organizing a coalition?

Start by looking at all of the possible constituencies that might join a coalition. Ask yourself: Does this issue affect the members of this constituency? What benefit would it be to them? What kind of organization, if any, does this constituency have to represent it? How are decisions made in that organization? What kind of power can the organization bring to this fight? What problems might it bring? Would its reputation be an asset or a problem to us? Does it have a past history that would create problems if it was one of the groups working on this issue?

One of the ways of approaching groups to get them to participate in an issue is defining the issue in a way that appeals to their organizational self-interests. Sometimes this is referred to in organizing talk as "cutting an issue." Take the issue of public transportation. Senior citizen groups could support it because most seniors either don't drive or don't have the income to own cars and they need access to services throughout the city. Unions might support it because it would mean additional jobs in construction and in operating an improved mass transit system. Women's organizations might support it if there were particular guarantees written into the program to assure safety at night for women using it. Minority community organizations might support a plan which assured service between their neighborhoods and places where jobs were available.

The process of putting allies together around an issue involves more than presenting the issue to each organization in a way that makes the members appreciate its value. It also requires dealing with each organization around what its members see as their self-interest and what they want as their price for supporting the issue. A seniors' organization, for example, might be especially willing to support public transportation if it involved reduced fares for seniors. An organization of the handicapped might be interested in special provisions for access. Minority groups might demand certain quotas on employment in the construction and operation of the system.

What are the advantages and disadvantages of joining or forming a coalition?

The probable demands of other groups need to be carefully considered by your organization in deciding whether or not these groups should be invited to take part in the overall campaign. Some groups might make demands that would conflict with the needs of your organization, so you must analyze your own organizational self-interests. Will the demands of the other groups be ones that will be unacceptable to some of the members of our organization? Will some of the groups be groups that our members will not be comfortable working with? Are some of the groups that would be brought in so large that our organization would lose its power to make decisions? Would the other groups get all of the credit? Do the other groups have the same kind of commitment to grass roots democracy that we have? Are they going to be open to involving the members and leaders of our organization in the decision-making process? Or are they simply going to want to sit down in a back room and have the top staff of the organizations make the decisions together?

There are rarely easy answers to these questions. An organization's decision to work with other organizations is a complicated and difficult one. It needs to be thought through carefully.

There are a number of advantages when an organization joins with other organizations around an issue. The organization can take on larger issues which require more power to win. It can establish its credibility in other areas of the community. It can develop alliances that can be useful later. It can broaden the experience of its own leaders.

There are also possible disadvantages. Members can lose the sense of participation that goes with making their own decisions. Some of the complicated negotiations and concessions that might result can undercut the feelings of solidarity within the organization. Other larger or more experienced organizations may end up getting credit for the victory. Your organization may be blamed if it's a loss. Some other organizations' values may alienate some of the members of your organization.

Many of these issues will be negotiated among the different organizations when they agree to work together. As a leader you need to be clear about what your own organization's self-interest is and what you see as the possible problems in working with the other organizations. Only if you do this kind of careful planning can you negotiate a position within the larger group that is as favorable to your own organization as possible.

What is the long-range strategy for coalitions?

One of the questions we have to deal with as leaders is what our long-range strategy for this country is. This means not just what do we do in our neighborhoods, in our constituency groups, and in our cities. It means also how do we make this country a real democracy, where decisions really are made by the broad majority of people, where poor and working people have a real voice and decision-making power, where there is democracy at all levels within society: in the home, in the neighborhood, in the community, in the workplace, in government at all levels.

In the past many organizing strategies have been based on the power of a well-organized minority. The civil rights movement was a minority movement. Black people are probably 12 to 15 percent of this nation's population. With support from other groups, they were able to put enough pressure and leverage on the national government so that certain laws affecting black people could be changed. In cities and counties where black people were in the majority, they were able to build important local power bases. However, the national movement quickly reached certain limits, which were a result of the limited power of organizing without a potential majority.

Blacks today do not have the power to change our national economic planning policies. These are based on having a 6 or 7 percent level of unemployment, rather than full employment. A national policy of 7 percent planned unemployment means that 50 percent of black teenagers will be unemployed. The policy of planned unemployment, along with so many other similar policies, can only be changed by a large number of people and organizations working together. We call this way of thinking a "majority strategy"—building a coalition that includes a majority of the people in the country to seek the changes we want.

The majority strategy starts from the idea that a very small group of people and institutions, mostly corporations, really run this country and benefit from the way it is run. The facts bear this out. One percent of the people in the United States own 25 percent of the wealth. According to the U.S. Chamber of Commerce, by the year 2001, two hundred corporations will own 54 percent of everything worth owning in the world. Even though many of these are American-based corporations, they are mostly multinationals that exploit all countries equally. So our country is being run by a very small minority for their own benefit.

The great majority of people in this country are neither well-off nor powerful. They share problems that affect all of them: poor housing, lack of income, poor health care that costs so much people can't even afford it, lack of transportation, poor education, inadequate public services, lack of power, lack of direct representation, bad health and safety on the job, discrimination. The people who share at least most of these problems make up between 60 and 80 percent of the people in this country.

Yet we are divided. Our neighborhood and constituency groups only deal with one or two of these issues at a time. The great challenge of organizing today is to find the common denominators that will bring together all of the organizations which could support a majority position: the neighborhood organizations, the constituency organizations, the statewide organizations, the trade unions, the women's organizations, the minority organizations, the senior citizen organizations, the churches and synagogues. A coalition based in these groups could have the power to make basic changes in our society.

What issues could help build a majority coalition?

So far the common denominators we've been able to find are very low ones. Each time an organization brings additional groups into a coalition it gives away something on its own issues. This is especially true as we begin to move from one-time to permanent coalitions put together not for just one issue but for the long haul. Such a coalition develops its own priorities and its own strategies. It has its own fund-raising program based, just as in smaller organizations, on a combination of outside funding, individual and organizational membership dues, and grassroots fund raising. It may have not only organizational membership but direct membership from individuals who are not in other organized constituencies. It may do its own organizing. For example, in putting together a coalition, your organization may decide that seniors would be an important force. However, seniors in your community may not yet be organized. Your organization might decide to undertake an organizing campaign aimed at developing a strong organization of seniors which would then become a part of the coalition.

Such a coalition can only be a powerful force for constructive change and progress in this country if we can define a program of common interest which does not give away issues that are of real concern to the members of the coalition, either organizationally or individually. All of these needs have to be balanced. Just as an organization cannot focus its energy on an issue that will divide the organization, a coalition cannot put major time or energy into an issue that will break it up. For example, some coalitions which include unions have found it difficult to take a stand on nuclear energy because the building trade unions want the construction of nuclear power plants to provide jobs for their members. Coalitions in which the Catholic Church plays a key role ordinarily cannot take a stand on the "right to choose" issue.

However, just as we deal with the problems of local priorities in grass roots organizations, we can also work toward solving these problems within coalitions. In a grass roots organization a chapter structure allows the local chapter to work on an issue which may not be of concern to the broad organization, or which in some cases the broad organization may even oppose. Chapters work together on issues that are of common interest. Similarly, in a coalition individual members need to be free to pursue their own priorities, even if they occasionally conflict with those of other members of the coalition.

Coalitions should work together on those issues which unite them. Just as an issue within a grassroots organization must build the organization, issues within the coalition must build the coalition. More and more we need to move in a direction which says, "We will work with you on this issue although we disagree with you on other issues," rather than, "Because we disagree with you on one issue, we cannot work together with you on others."

What is the relationship between a majority strategy and coalitions?

Few areas in organizing are as complicated or as difficult to think through as the whole question of coalitions. This is a key strategy decision. It involves defining individuals and their self-interests, which may be in conflict even within the same neighborhood. It means defining where our organizations put their organizing efforts. It means making decisions about what forces we line up with, which in turn may limit our ability to make other decisions. It means dealing with complicated patterns of conflicting self-interests among organizations and individuals.

The idea of democracy itself, the ideas set out in the Declaration of Independence and the Constitution, may be the common issue we need for a true majority strategy. Our histories, as well as our common needs and goals, may help provide the shared sense of vision and the positive statement of values we need to build a true majority coalition. The very idea of democracy involves as many minorities as possible getting together in such a way that the power of the majority is used to protect the rights of the minorities that together make it up.

The process of building these powerful coalitions is as necessary as the process of building organizations at all. The need is the same and the process is the same. Just as individuals need to move from their own comparative isolation to being members of organizations which give them strength and solidarity, so grass roots organizations need to join with other progressive organizations to achieve greater power at the city, state, and national level. Together we can go beyond our organizations and coalitions to a movement for real democracy in America. We will never agree on all of our objectives. But there are enough things that we do agree on to make this process necessary and possible.

16. Unions

UNIONS HAVE a long history in America. Even before the American Revolution, workers in the colonies organized into unions so they would have the strength to deal together with their employers. Over the years unions have been a powerful force for social change. Many of the working conditions we now take for granted, such as the eight-hour day, paid vacations and holidays, retirement programs, and medical benefits and insurance, were unknown until the unions forced employers to agree to them. Many other programs and benefits that today come through government agencies were first developed and worked for by the unions. In the early days of this country, for example, we didn't even have free public education. This was an early union demand. Social Security, workers' compensation, retirement benefits, Medicare, Medicaid, civil rights legislation, and disability insurance were all programs that the unions worked and fought for.

There are a number of reasons why it's important to understand unions, whether or not we ourselves are members. Some twenty million Americans belong to unions today. So when we talk about organizing and organizations, what people we are often thinking about is their own union experience.

Unions have a long history of organizing. In many cases their opposition is the same that we face when we organize other constituencies. The experiences of the unions, the lessons they have learned, can be important to all of us as we develop our own strategies and tactics.

In many communities the unions are a large and powerful force for progress. As a result, unions can be valuable allies. On issues of joint concern, unions can also be an important part of coalitions and political campaigns. Their membership base and financial independence make them a major cornerstone of any future progressive politics.

How are unions organized?

Many of the techniques used to organize unions are similar to those used in other organizing. But there are some special conditions. Up until the passage of the National Labor Relations act in 1935 the right of workers to organize into unions was not even recognized under federal law. The goal of workers in organizing was to force the employer to recognize the union as the bargaining representative for the workers in the plant. Because these workers had issues in common, they wanted to be able to negotiate with the company together. They had to put together enough power to force the company to negotiate and to agree to their demands.

This usually meant a strike. Although a strike is a specific tactic, it's also an example of a general area of tactics in which we withhold something that the opposition needs. In an election campaign we withhold our vote. In an economic pressure campaign such as a boycott we withhold our money. In a strike we withhold our labor. Because the company needs that labor to produce goods and make money, it is put under pressure to deal with the workers' demands through the union.

The idea of a union is sometimes called "industrial democracy." By industrial democracy we mean that workers inside the plants should have the same rights to representative self-government that they have outside the workplace as citizens of this country. These include the rights guaranteed by the Constitution and the Bill of Rights. The First Amendments of the Bill of Rights guarantees "the right of the people peaceably to assemble and to petition the government for a redress of grievances." Industrial democracy seeks to extend this right into the workplace. Industrial democracy means workers can join together to demand the improvements that all of them want.

Union members elect representatives to deal with management on their behalf. These representatives include shop stewards, who represent the workers in a particular department when they have a "grievance" or complaint against management, and who attempt to resolve that grievance on behalf of the workers. In many unions the stewards are organized into a stewards' committee which decides what further action to take when management refuses to deal with a grievance.

A local union also has its own elected officers, usually a president, vice-president, secretary, treasurer, and an elected or appointed negotiating committee. The negotiating committee is given the responsibility of meeting with management to negotiate for all the workers in the plant. The process of negotiation by a union is similar to that in any other type of organization. The local union, usually working through the negotiating committee, sets priorities based on what its members want and their sense of what they think they could get. They establish a series of demands that allows them enough flexibility to be able to compromise on some issues, but is not so far above what is realistically possible that the expectations of the members are raised too high. The danger in making a set of demands that is too far from what is possible is that the members of the union, just like the members of any other organization, feel sold out if those demands are not met.

As in any other negotiating situation, the process of union negotiation is one of give-and-take. Its effectiveness depends on the actual power of the union to put pressure on the company. Different tactics are used by unions to pressure a company. The most common tactic is the strike. However, unions also use other ways of pressuring a company during negotiations. These tactics might include increasing the number of grievances filed to put pressure on the company's administrative machinery; slowdowns in the workplace or other ways of interfering with production; publicity campaigns to force the company to defend itself on other fronts; rallies to build spirit and solidarity for a potential strike; harassment of management; agitation around issues in the workplace; informational picket lines and demonstrations; exposés of the company; and personal pressure against different members of management. Here the union is doing the same thing other organizations do: backing up its demands with a series of pressure tactics, leading up to the ultimate threat of a strike.

What are union contracts?

The goal of this process of negotiation and pressure is to come up with a *contract* between the union and the company. This contract is a legally binding agreement which sets out the rules under which both the company and the union must operate. Most employers do have rules and policies, including handbooks which they pass out to the employees. The difference between a set of management rules and a union contract is that management rules are only honored if management decides to do so. Management can break the rules it makes if it wants to. A union contract is legally binding on the company and can be enforced by the union if necessary.

What issues in the workplace are union contracts concerned with?

Union contracts cover a wide range of issues. The first is called "recognition," which means that management agrees to recognize the union as the legal bargaining agent for workers in the plant. Sometimes community organizations are able to reach these same kinds of agreements. For example, a council in a housing project might be able to get an agreement that the housing authority management would not make any changes in policies without first negotiating with the council.

Union contracts cover many different issues involving wages and benefits. These include policies on the length of the workday and the workweek; how overtime is assigned and compensated; when time and a half, double time, and double time and a half are paid; what people are paid for reporting when there is no work; and special payments when people are called in to do special work. Other wage-related benefits are vacation pay, bonus pay, holidays, pay for serving on juries, funeral leave, and emergency military leave. There are provisions to deal with pensions and the way in which they will be administered. There are agreements on how jobs will be given out, how jobs are posted when they are available, what procedures employees use to bid on those jobs, and how those jobs are given out. Contracts cover how transfers, promotions, demotions, and layoffs are to take place and how work loads are assigned. They deal with strikes, establishing when a strike can be called and what the company can and can't do in a strike.

One of the most important parts of the contract deals with seniority. The principle of seniority is simply that the better jobs go to those employees who have been there the longest. This creates a regular system by which workers can expect to move up in terms of position, responsibility, and income.

A second important part of the contract is called "checkoff." In a checkoff system, the company deducts union dues from each worker's pay and forwards that money to the union. In states which have so-called "closed shops," where everyone working in the plant after a certain trial period is required to join the union, the pay is deducted from the checks of all workers. In so-called "open shop" or "right to work" states, where an employee does not have to belong to the union to enjoy the benefits of the union contract, money is deducted from the pay of those workers who agree to it. This system provides a regular financial base and source of income to the union. This income is then divided between the local and the international union.

Prior to checkoff systems, unions had to go through the same procedures that community organizations do today in order to collect dues from members: going into the workplace with buckets, going to see workers at their homes. Trying to collect these dues on a regular basis took enormous amounts of time. It also meant that the union could not anticipate a steady and regular source of income. A checkoff system gives the union a regular, predictable source of income on which to base its internal financial planning.

A third key part of the contract is the grievance procedure. A grievance procedure is similar in some ways to a court system. When a worker has a grievance, he or she can go to the shop steward, who files a grievance on the worker's behalf. The shop steward is acting more or less as a lawyer, representing the worker to the company for the purpose of resolving the grievance.

Most grievance procedures include four or five steps. Usually in the first step the shop steward and the worker meet with the management person responsible for the worker's department. If the grievance is not solved to the satisfaction of all parties, it is carried to the next level of management, possibly to the shift supervisor. From there it goes to a third step, in which other representatives of the union—including, perhaps, a staff person, one of the union's attorneys, a chief steward, or other members of the grievance committee—meet with representatives of higher levels of management such as the personnel manager or the general manager.

The final step in a grievance procedure is called "arbitration." If the parties cannot resolve the dispute through the grievance procedure, it is referred to a third party called an "arbitrator." The arbitrator is like a judge. When a case goes to arbitration the company and the union are ordinarily given a list of five or seven professional arbitrators provided by a group like the American Arbitration Association. Each party in turn strikes off one person from the list until only one is left. This person becomes the arbitrator. In a strong union contract the decision of the arbitrator is final and binding and cannot be appealed to any court. If the union claims that a worker was unjustly fired and the arbitrator determines that the worker must be put back to work with back pay, interest, and full seniority, the company is bound under law to do it. A grievance system with binding arbitration gives the union the power to enforce the contract and the rights of its members in the workplace. Good grievance procedures include time limits so that the process cannot be drawn out over too long a period.

So there are two general areas in which the union provides for its membership. Through the process of negotiation the union seeks to improve wages and benefits for its members. Through the grievance and arbitration procedure it enforces the rules agreed to by the company and the union through the negotiation process, thus protecting the basic rights of workers in the workplace situation.

Many of the items which are now standard in contracts represent long years of bitter fighting between unions and employers to establish these provisions. Early union contracts, for example, covered mostly wages. Insurance plans, pension plans, health and safety committees, and educational benefits are recent advances in union negotiating. Unions often experiment with new contract items. For example, a number of unions are now trying to negotiate for the pension rights of their retired members.

What is the structure of an international union?

Ordinarily the workers in one workplace are represented by one local union. In some unions or when the workplace has few employees, a number of workplaces may be included in the same local. This local will have its own officers, stewards, grievance committee, and negotiating committee. Many local unions also have a permanent staff person. Sometimes this person is called a "business agent." In some cases a business agent is elected by the members of the local. In other cases the business agent may be an appointed staff person of the international union.

International unions are those which have membership in both the United States and Canada, as do most of the unions which are members of the American Federation of Labor and Congress of Industrial Organizations (AFL-CIO). Local unions can be thought of as chapters of the international. Different international unions have different structures relating the locals to the international. Some unions have regional bodies to which locals may send representatives.

An international union provides different services to its locals. Most international unions have a legal department that can provide attorneys to help in negotiations, in drawing up contracts, in complicated arbitration cases, and in strikes. The internationals ordinarily maintain occupational safety and health departments to assist workers on issues of workplace health and safety. Research departments develop information on the companies that is useful in preparing for negotiations and as ammunition to pressure the company during negotiations, organizing campaigns, and strikes. Education departments provide training to stewards, union officers, and other members of the union. Publication departments ordinarily produce a newsletter which goes to all members of the union, as well as other information for use in organizing drives and educational campaigns. Organizing departments provide professional staff persons who work on organizing new targets.

Unions differ in the amount of emphasis they give to organizing. In general, a union will seek to organize plants which strengthen its overall bargaining position. For example, if a company has twenty-three plants and the union represents ten of them, it would probably be more interested in organizing the remaining thirteen plants than in starting an organizing drive within a company where it had no representation. The different local unions could then work together and bargain in coordination for a master contract covering all the plants. The collective strength of all the different locals allows the union to put more pressure on the company than if it is only organized in half of the plants.

We see comparable situations in other organizing. If a city has nineteen different housing projects and the residents are only well organized in five, the organizing priority would be to develop local organizations within the remaining projects, as a way of being able to bring coordinated pressure on the housing authority.

How are unions organized?

One of the interesting things about union organizing is that there are actually federal regulations governing many of the ways in which it must be done. In the thirties, when this country was experiencing an enormous wave of union organizing, the government stepped in to try to regularize relationships between unions and management. They set up certain rules for unions which recognize the legal right of workers to organize.

These rules also set up a whole series of administrative procedures governing how unions can be organized and run. A company is only required to bargain collectively with a union if that union represents a majority of the company's employees. Under the law a union can go into the company with cards or petitions signed by a majority of the workers saying that they want the union to represent them. If the company agrees to recognize the union on this basis, negotiations can begin. Those negotiations will be legally binding.

In practice, companies almost never agree to recognize the union without a fight. So usually unions are recognized only after an election supervised by an agency of the federal government called the National Labor Relations Board. If a union is seeking to organize a workplace, it submits to the Labor Board cards or petitions signed by at least 30 percent of the workers in the plant.

The Board checks these petitions to make sure that they really represent 30 percent of the workers and then sets a date for an election to determine whether or not that union will legally represent the workers in the plant. Sometimes more than one union files for an election at the same time and both are on the ballot.

This procedure is usually complicated by a company counterattack. Companies will ordinarily do anything possible to delay an election, since statistics show that the longer an election can be postponed the less chance the union has of winning. One of the usual arguments is over which workers can legally be represented by the union. The unions represent those workers who are considered rank-and-file employees. However, this definition is often subject to argument. The company will argue that secretarial and clerical personnel should be included in the bargaining unit. The union will argue that because these people work closely with management they should be excluded.

Since this system was instituted by the federal government in the 1930s the techniques for organizing a union have become in many instances very similar to those used to win an election. In this respect organizing in many unions has become much closer to electoral politics than to neighborhood organizing.

A typical union organizing campaign would look something like this. The union would hear that in a particular plant there was interest in becoming organized. They might get a phone call from someone claiming to represent some of the workers in the plant. It might be a place that the union had been keeping an eye on for a while because of past activities. It could be someplace where they had previously had an organizing drive which had failed.

Many unions initiate an organizing campaign by going to the gate of the factory and passing out leaflets about the union. These leaflets may include a form or attached card to be mailed back to the union stating a worker's interest in organizing. The organizers will then begin contacting the people who signed and returned these cards. Those workers who have shown interest become the organizing committee. The organizing committee members are given representation cards and asked to get as many other workers as possible to sign them.

When the union has enough of these cards, it files with the Labor Board for an election. Legally the union can file when 30 percent of the workers have signed up for the union. In practice most unions will not file for an election until at least 50 percent of the workers have signed up.

The period between filing and the election itself looks in many ways like the campaigning for a traditional political election. The union uses small group meetings, rallies, speeches, direct mailings, telephone banks, visits to the homes of employees, bumper stickers, T-shirts, hats, leaflets at the gate, stickers, buttons, television ads, newspaper ads—all of the different methods of influencing opinion.

One of the differences between this style of organizing and an electoral campaign is the extent to which the company can counterattack. Ordinarily a company will mount an all-out attack on the union. The union will often be baited with whatever violence or corruption has ever occurred in connection with any union anywhere in the country at any time in the past. Companies will bring in high-paid consultants to direct their anti-union campaigns. They will spend massive amounts on different types of public relations. Employees will be brought into "captive audience meetings" where they will have to listen to company spokespeople talk about the dangers of unions, the high cost of union dues, and the violence involved in strikes, as well as what the company has done for the employees. Companies will make minor cosmetic improvements in the plant to try to convince workers that they don't really need the union representation. Workers will be alternately buttered up by the bosses and harassed and intimidated. Key leaders of the organizing campaign may be demoted, laid off, or fired. Many of these tactics are illegal. However, companies have discovered that it's effective to fire key members of the organizing campaign even if they have to reinstate them two years later with back pay, since examples of this kind will discourage other employees from working for the union.

Finally, the election is held. Representatives of the Labor Board count and tally the ballots. If the union wins, it is awarded the right to bargain with the company toward a contract. In reality, the company may or may not do this. If the union loses, it ordinarily leaves and moves on to another, more promising target.

One of the problems with this kind of organizing is that the union is only recognized if it can establish a majority. This is not the case everywhere. In some countries a company is required to deal with a union even if it represents a minority of the people in the plant. Even in the United States there is protection for workers' right to organize even when they're not able to establish a majority in a particular workplace. These laws are called the "concerted activities" provisions of the National Labor Relations Act. They derive from the right granted by the First Amendment to the Constitution to "peaceably assemble and to petition the government for a redress of grievances." These laws are basically designed to protect the rights of individuals to act in groups—to organize. In a workplace situation if one worker goes to the boss and complains, the boss can legally fire that worker. If two workers go to the boss and complain, they are acting in concert and cannot legally be fired. It's possible that the company will fire them anyway, but at least they do have the right to legal action if they are fired.

In other situations unions may organize in ways that are much more similar to the techniques used in building other types of people's organizations. Rather than moving quickly toward an election, they may work over a long period of time to build organization within the workplace. This approach emphasizes issues, and it involves developing an organizing committee that represents the different elements within the workplace: departments; shifts; types of jobs; women and men; different racial, ethnic, and age groups. It involves focusing on issues that can be won even before the union is recognized and a contract negotiated. In a situation like this, a union may use many of the same types of tactics that any other people's organization uses to win on issues: signing petitions, sending workers in a group to confront the boss, setting up informational picket lines, distributing leaflets, exposing the company in the press. In this type of organizing the union is attempting to show what it can do by actually winning victories for workers in the plant. It is building from the ground up before it attempts to seek formal recognition. Such an approach involves extensive training of workers themselves in organizing skills.

How can other organizations get help from unions?

Unions are like any other kind of organization. They have their own self-interests and their own internal politics. No two local unions are quite alike. International unions vary tremendously in their structure and politics.

When a community organization develops a plan for working together with unions, it needs to take all these things into account. The different locals will need to be approached differently. It's important to start by developing as much knowledge of the unions in your community as possible. What are the different unions? Who are the leaders of the unions? What is the history of unions in the community? How many workplaces have they organized? What are their contracts like? Have they been on strike? How are they seen generally?

Different unions have different names and internal structures. Most unions have locals. The International Association of Machinists, however, has lodges. Just as you wouldn't want to call a rabbi a priest, you don't want to call a lodge a local.

You won't necessarily contact the same person or committee in every union, since unions are very different in terms of their own internal structure. In some unions, even national officers are elected by popular vote. In others they're elected by representatives of regions and districts. Some locals elect their business agents. Others have appointed business agents.

Unions put different degrees of emphasis on different activities. Some put very large amounts of their resources into organizing. Others prefer to emphasize service to the locals. Sometimes a local union will have a great deal of participation by the rank and file. At other times it may not even attempt to involve its membership, and will simply let the officers and professional staff take care of any union business.

Unions also differ in terms of how militant they are; how willing they are to confront the company; what their political perspectives are in terms of the community; how they back up workers in their own individual grievances; how they view the questions of discrimination based on race, sex, and age; and how open they are to involvement with groups outside the trade union movement. Knowing where the unions in your community stand on these issues is critical to developing a working relationship with them.

In building relationships with unions, it's helpful to view them as you would any other neighborhood or constituency in your area, either organized or unorganized. You need to begin by developing relationships with the leaders of the union. You need to be clear that this is not just a one-way relationship, that you are not simply asking for help from the unions but are prepared to reciprocate. Too often other organizations view unions as large, wealthy institutions that are in a position to give help but do not need any kind of help.

How can other organizations help unions?

There are a number of things that other organizations can do to assist unions. Unions can often use help in organizing campaigns. It may be that members of your organization work in a place the union is attempting to organize. If so, it might be helpful to use the resources of your organization to help out in the organizing campaign. Most unions in a local organizing campaign are as overextended as other organizations in their campaigns. They can use the special skills that the leaders of our organizations have developed.

Sometimes they can use help in dealing with the press and publicizing the campaign. They may need people to help pass out leaflets or prepare mailings. The research that your organization has done could be helpful to the union in developing strategies.

In a strike situation unions are often even more open to outside help. Especially in a long strike, a union may begin to feel very isolated. It may need people to walk the picket line or to put out a strike newsletter. It could probably use researchers to do investigative work on the company and its management personnel. People can be helpful in trying to build broad support for the strike. Sometimes money is needed for food. Sometimes simply the presence on the picket of some people who are not themselves members of the union does a lot to decrease the sense of isolation that often develops in a long, bitter struggle.

In developing a strategy for working with unions, it may be helpful to start by analyzing the things that your organization does the best. As you begin to meet and know people within the unions, you then have a sense of what you can offer them. This is probably even more critical than what they can offer you. The question "What can we do for you?" is a very difficult one to answer, especially when the union doesn't know what you do well. If you can define the special skills that you have in your organization, you can be much clearer about what the terms of a working relationship can be.

Relationships with unions, like those with any other organization, need to be nurtured very carefully over a long period of time. Many unions are not used to relating to other institutions. They are, like many of us, occasionally suspicious of outside help. In the middle of a strike they may be fearful that other groups are trying to use the strike for their own self-interests. It makes much more sense to begin building relationships with the leadership of the union before a strike happens so that trust and some common understandings exist when it does.

As you develop working relationships with the unions, look for the kinds of issues that are of common interest. Unions will generally be most interested in those issues in which their members have a direct self-interest. Remember that the unions' responsibility is to their membership first, before broad social issues. In some cases these may coincide. But generally the leaders of a union local feel very strongly the pressure that members put on it. Members, after all, are paying every week to support the work of the union. When part of workers' paychecks goes into a union, they want to hold it accountable.

Look for the issues of common interest. For example, most unions are to some extent concerned with how a food stamp office operates, because in a strike situation they want to be sure that their members can get food stamps easily. Tax-reform issues have a direct effect on union membership. Energy issues are important.

On the other hand, there will be issues with which some people's organizations are concerned that may divide them from the self-interest of certain unions. The opposition will be quick to exploit these differences. For example, if an organization is undertaking a campaign to clean up pollution in its city, the opposition is going to be sure to point out that this is going to require expensive new controls at the industrial plants which will probably result in some of these plants closing and a loss of jobs. Members of your neighborhood organization may be opposed to the local interstate coming through the neighborhood, but the construction unions may be supporting it because it means more jobs for their members. The potential for this kind of division and for unions and other organizations being played off against each other shows the real importance of building good working relationships before these kinds of crises occur.

This work is worthwhile because of the tremendous resources that unions can bring to campaigns around issues and to broad-based coalitions. Unions have members that they can work to involve in these campaigns. Different unions will have different degrees of membership response and involvement and a different ability to influence the thinking and actions of their members. But in most cases they do have people who can be involved.

Unions have financial resources. In a campaign which is in their self-interest, they are in a position to put up substantial money, something which other organizations may be much harder pressed to come up with.

Unions have extensive internal resources. These will vary from union to union but may include research staff, attorneys, professional staff members, printing equipment, and access to computers. All of these can be useful.

The unions may have a great deal of visibility. In a medium-sized city, the leaders of the larger unions may be able to get press attention with relative ease. This can be used to highlight a particular issue.

Unions have a certain amount of political clout. Where unions are strong, numbers of elected officials will be to some extent indebted to the union. This means that there will be a willing ear at city council, in the mayor's office, and at the state legislature, as well as potential support for certain kinds of issues.

There may be differences in the way in which unions and other organizations organize. There may be disagreement on issues. But there is tremendous long-range mutual self-interest in a cooperative working relationship between the unions and other people's organizations. Both are interested in building long-range power for people. Both have the potential for broad-based membership involvement. And both in general have the same type of issue-oriented goals. The best of the unions are dedicated to real democracy, to leadership development, to building power for people. The unions are a basic part of any strategy for a real majority movement in this country.

17. Politics

IN ORGANIZING, few words come up as often as *politics*. We're always saying, "Well, that's politics." Or "What are the politics of this one?" Or "Where do they stand politically?"

The word *politics* can be used to mean different things, and is used differently by different people. But generally when we talk about politics, we're talking about the ways in which the different processes of government affect our lives. The list of ways in which government affects us is almost endless. The lives of poor people are almost always dependent on government programs: food stamps, Aid to Dependent Children, Aid to the Aged, Medicare, Medicaid, public housing, fuel assistance. The decisions that affect our neighborhoods are made by people in government: mayors, city council representatives, planners, community development directors, committee heads, bureaucrats from the Department of Housing and Urban Development (HUD). Workers are affected by the decisions at many levels concerning labor laws, occupational safety and health, retirement benefits, "right to work," and workers' compensation.

At the national level the laws that govern much of our work are made by elected officials in the Senate and House of Representatives. The interpretations of these laws are in turn made by the courts. But court appointments and how courts interpret the law are both influenced by politics. Liberal administrations have appointed judges to the federal courts who have tended to interpret the law to favor the rights of individuals. Conservative administrations generally appoint judges who favor the corporations and money interests.

At the state level we again confront a broad range of laws and agencies that affect our lives. State departments of labor, public assistance, utility regulation, occupational safety and health, all make decisions that can affect people for better or for worse. At the city and county level we find the same situation. Mayors, council members, and county commissioners daily make decisions that affect the fate not only of individuals but of neighborhoods and communities. Taxes, transportation, housing, redlining, police protection, fire protection, recreation, and delivery of services are all to some extent under the control of the different city and county political structures.

Not all power in this country is concentrated in the hands of government. But the political process reflects the needs and priorities of those who are in power. Corporations, banks, insurance companies, and wealthy individuals all work to establish "their" politicians in positions of power at the city, county, state, and federal levels. They then depend on these officials to make and carry out policies from which they can profit. When a city council makes a decision to withdraw fire protection from an area—leaving it open to red-lining, arson, land speculation and development by private interests—it is not doing so to benefit the city government. It's doing it to benefit the forces behind city government—the banks, insurance companies, corporations, and private developers—who stand to make money from the results of that decision. Power is being exercised *through* the political process rather than *by* the political process.

This is an important distinction. Sometimes it's easy to think that decisions made by government reflect only the opinions of the legislators. We always need to look behind the person or group making the decision to the institutions or individuals who will benefit from it. In analyzing a political decision we must ask ourselves, "Who stands to benefit from this? Who stands to make money? What ties do they have to the people making these decisions?"

One of the questions we end up asking ourselves is "If government in many ways is only fronting for the private corporations and money interests, why don't we go directly after the corporations and their allies? In going after government agencies and officials, aren't we really only picking on the little person? Why don't we go after those who are really responsible, who really stand to benefit, who are really making the decisions?"

The answer is that in many cases we do. But in many other cases, for reasons that become clear as we analyze the strategy involved, it's more effective to use the political process as a way of creating pressure on the power interests rather than going after them directly. Many of the major corporations are simply too large and powerful to be taken on all at one time in a direct assault. However, we often do have the power to take on and successfully pressure their allies at a lower level.

Let's say that Mola-Cola Company is developing a shopping center near a neighborhood. The neighborhood residents feel that the shopping center is going to destroy their neighborhood and the community life. They organize to fight back.

That neighborhood organization does not have the power to take on the entire Mola-Cola corporation and change all of its policy decisions. However, the members of the organization do have the power to fight Mola-Cola to the extent that it is involved in their own neighborhood. They also have the levers to do it. The president, the officers, and the major stockholders of a corporation like Mola-Cola are often, though not always, beyond our reach. They live protected lives far from where neighborhood people can pressure them. However, their allies are often living literally right next door: the local bankers, real estate investors, contractors, zoning board members, city council representatives, and other officials whose support is necessary if Mola-Cola is going to succeed in building a shopping center. They are within reach of our anger and tactics.

Here's another way of looking at it. The corporations use government and the political processes to control us. We in turn can also use government and the political processes to control them.

How do grassroots organizations become involved in politics?

Most people's organizations become involved in politics fairly early in their existence. Most of the problems we have in our communities don't just happen. They're caused by someone and they're caused for a reason, usually profit.

There is a theory that was popular in the 1960s that referred to poor people as "the forgotten Americans." It suggested that people were poor because no one knew they were there. According to this theory, once the rest of the country found out about poor people, something would be done to solve the problems of poverty.

But people are poor and powerless because there is profit in poverty. Poor people are not neglected. They are exploited. Change comes as a result of fighting back. Whatever the issue, there is usually a need for some type of political pressure to solve it. If an extra charge has been put on the residents in a housing project, we pressure the housing authority and its staff. In the example of the shopping center, we go after the developers and the investors who stand to profit, but also after the zoning board, the city council, and all the other agencies that have to license and approve the construction of any shopping center. If the issue is a tax increase, we go after the city council, the county commission, the board of assessors, the tax board, or whatever agency of government controls that situation.

Even where an issue is controlled by an appointed agency,

that agency is appointed by someone, usually by an elected official. These elected and appointed officials and the agencies they
work with become pressure points in a people's organization's
campaign.

What are the steps in a strategy to pressure government?

Let's look at a situation where a city is attempting to acquire and
bulldoze a poor community to make room for development. A
hundred or so families live in the area in both rented and owner-
occupied housing. They've decided that they don't want to
move to make way for condominiums and high-rise apartment
buildings.

There is a clear political pressure point in this situation. The
community development commission of city government is responsible for authorizing such changes; it made the initial decision to bulldoze the community. Obviously this decision must be
reversed. A reversal of the decision also has to be supported by
the city council, which can overturn a recommendation of the
community development commission.

A strategy to deal with the political factors involved in saving
the community must then include:

(1) How to reverse the decision of the community development commission.

(2) How to make sure that the city council in turn accepts and
reinforces this decision.

The organization could begin by making an analysis of the
community development commission and of the city council, including the elected and appointed officials and staff, to see where
there might be support for their position. It would be helpful to
also have an alternative position developed. Politicians are in the
habit of saying, "Well, it's fine to get in the way of progress. But
what sort of plan do *you* have?" In a situation like this, it's useful
for an organization to have a plan that makes good sense, that

serves the needs of the people, and that can be an alternative to be adopted by the agencies involved. If a community simply attempts to block a change without having an alternative plan, there is then the danger of having to face a second official plan which is no better than the first.

What tactics can be used?

There are a number of tactics that can be used to put pressure on the community development commission and the city council. These include the following:

(1) Meeting with the individuals on the commission to negotiate for the new position.

(2) Developing a petition signed by as many members of the neighborhood as possible to present to commission and council members.

(3) Packing a meeting of the community development commission or the city council with neighborhood residents.

(4) Putting direct personal pressure on the members of the community development commission or the city council.

(5) Developing alliances with other groups in the community to support the neighborhood's demands and tactics.

(6) Going to federal agencies which affect the operation of the city agencies and asking them to get involved.

(7) Developing a publicity campaign centered around the city council members' campaign contributions and other interests.

(8) Exposing both the city's plans to profit from bulldozing the homes of poor people and the individuals who stand to profit also.

How can an organization negotiate with government officials?

The key to success in a strategy of this nature is being able to negotiate with politicians around the issue of concern to the organization. In any set of negotiations it's important to have a very clear sense of exactly what it is that you need from this particular individual or group. These commitments should be made as clearly as possible. It's a good idea to get the commitment in writing. Prepare a memorandum of understanding after the meeting. Both the person with whom you met and the representatives of your organization put their names to what was agreed. This is one way of trying to make sure that a politician keeps his or her promise.

Having the statements of support made publicly is another way of trying to make sure that commitments will be honored. If a commitment is made in front of the press or in a letter to constituents, that's helpful. As much as possible, officials should be pushed to make their commitments in writing and publicly. This makes it more difficult for them to back out of the commitments.

If an official is not willing to make a commitment following a negotiating session, then the same kinds of tactics are used that would be used to pressure any individual or institution. As in all such situations, the organization's ability to finally get the commitments that are asked for will depend on that organization's power, both its real power and the perception of its power by the person or group in question. The creativity of your tactics, the nature of your allies, and your ability to pressure or disrupt will influence how the opposition will judge the organization's power.

Despite the best efforts of the organization, there is no guarantee of success. In many cases, a politician will simply refuse to go along with the organization's demands. The refusal may come in a long-winded statement of general support for the overall purpose of the organization and for the needs of the community. But the answer is still "No." Or the politician may make a commitment and then break it. Or the commitment may be made privately, with the politician saying, "I'm going to support you on this, but I can't afford to have too much pressure on me. So let's just keep this between ourselves."

Sometimes an organization can't do any better than such unsatisfactory commitments. They are much easier to get out from under than one that is written and public. But even in a case where a written public commitment has been made, an official may say, "Yes, it's true. I made this commitment. However, there are new circumstances which I think necessitate a reconsideration of the entire situation. I have considered this matter very carefully. I feel that in view of my responsibility to the people who voted for me the honorable choice at this point is to make a new commitment which I today feel is more realistic in view of the changed circumstances." Again, this is just a fancy way of saying "No."

So people's organizations have two problems in dealing with officials. The first is to get them to make commitments. The second is to make sure those commitments are kept. If a commitment is not made, or if one is made and not kept, the organization can only increase the pressure as much as possible in the hope of getting what it needs.

But in many cases pressure is simply not effective. The power of the opposition may be too much for us. The counterpressure on the officials who must make the decision may be too great. A large number of the people who are in public office today were put there by special interests: real estate developers, banks, big oil, corporations, the defense industry, private wealthy individuals, management. They owe allegiance to the people who paid for their campaigns. As a result, they are not going to be helpful to other people on issues where their financial backers have a strong conflicting self-interest.

Such situations exist at all levels. At the city council level the only real concern may be to make sure that the real estate developers are happy. At the state level the goal is to attract business at any cost. At the federal level legislation rarely favors working and poor people.

Should people's organizations get involved in electoral politics?

People's organizations, tired of going again and again to the same unresponsive politicians, often begin to consider electoral politics. They dream of voting out public officials who are unresponsive to their needs and putting into office those who are more responsive.

The question of whether or not to become involved in electoral politics is one which is difficult for many organizations to resolve. Many organizations—community and neighborhood organizations, in particular—have kept away from electoral politics. There has been the feeling that many of the goals of politics run counter to the goals of people's organizations. In electoral politics, attention is focused on the candidate as an individual rather than on the organization as a whole. In politics compromise is often the order of the day. Many organizations feel that the kind of compromising on issues often involved in electoral politics undercuts their base.

Political campaigns are either won or lost. In most organizing an issue can be defined in such a way that even if a total victory is not possible, a partial victory can be claimed. In politics you either win or you lose. Many people feel that it's more difficult to build an organization around an all-or-nothing situation.

There is a distrust among people's organizations of the corruption that often seems to go with electoral politics: the illegal campaign contributions, the bribes, the trading and stealing of votes, the wheeling and dealing. Sometimes there is also a sense that it's hopeless, that the corporations with their multimillion-dollar political action committees can buy elections no matter what is done.

There are other reasons why many people's organizations stay out of electoral politics. Many organizations have had good success in winning their issues without entering into electoral politics. Also, our organizations are used to working on one or two issues at a time, and to taking stands only on those issues. We often avoid taking stands on difficult issues, which might split our membership, in favor of working on those issues on which the members agree. The stands that an organization has to take because of its electoral work on the controversial issues, can cause splits and conflicts.

Much of the organizing we do does not depend on building a majority. A small but well-organized group of people, using good strategy and tactics, can make important changes in a neighborhood, community, or city. In electoral politics, at least a majority of those voting is required. This can be an unfamiliar change for our organizations. If a neighborhood organization plans to bring a hundred people to a public hearing and only fifty show up, the tactic can still be at least partly successful. If an organization needs to get a hundred additional voters to the polls to win a seat on the school board and only fifty vote, the election is lost.

As a result of these reservations, community and neighborhood organizations have traditionally not played a major role in electoral politics. On the other hand, other people's organizations, such as the labor unions, have a long history of political involvement. Labor unions have traditionally been major contributors to political campaigns. They are one of the largest sources of funds for political campaigns besides the corporations. Much of the progressive legislation that we have today which affects union members and other working and poor people exists because of the work done by candidates who would not have been in office without the support of organized labor.

Labor unions have contributed much more than money to the political process. In many areas they have been in a position to mobilize their members in order to support candidates. They may donate use of their mailing lists and publications; provide volunteers to go door-to-door in neighborhoods, work the polls, and give rides on election day; run voter registration campaigns among the membership; and pull together special events at which candidates may appear.

How does an organization decide to support a candidate?

Support for a candidate is usually decided by negotiation. The organization first defines what its own key issues are in a campaign. The organization also needs to decide what an official might be in a position to do during his or her term of office. This might be a complicated decision. The organization might feel that it does not have a realistic chance of winning any of the issues that are most important to it in the next session of the state legislature. Under these circumstances, do you pressure a state legislator who has been helpful to the organization in the past to take a stand on issues which cannot realistically be won, simply for the public relations value? If an organization makes this kind of demand, it's also asking that the legislator reduce his or her potential effectiveness in coming sessions.

These are decisions that an organization must make carefully. Once an organization has made the decision, the usual process is to negotiate with the candidates to see what their positions are on the issues of concern to the organization. This can be done in different ways. Sometimes the organization holds a "Candidates Night" at which candidates are asked to come and respond to questions from the organization. Sometimes this is done in written form. The organization presents candidates with a statement of the positions in which they're interested and asks them to respond on these issues. The organization considers the answers and then decides which candidate to support, if any.

The same process applies not only to individual candidates but to the national political parties as well. For example, the strategy used by Association of Community Organizations for Reform Now (ACORN) in the 1980 presidential election was to ask support for a people's platform dealing with a number of specific issues of concern to poor and working people. This question was also put to the two major national parties, asking them to incorporate the people's platform issues into their own party platforms. This same route is open to any organization. An organization also has the choice of endorsing or not endorsing candidates and parties. The organization says, "Here are the positions that each of the parties are taking. On the basis of these positions, we've decided to put our support behind this particular party."

The organization might also decide not to make a formal endorsement on its own, but to publicize the positions of the candidates on the issues of concern to its members and then allow people to make up their own minds. This is often necessary for organizations that operate with tax-exempt funds, because endorsement of a candidate in a partisan political race would be a violation of their tax-exempt status.

What can people's organizations contribute to electoral campaigns?

An organization's ability to deliver the vote is critical. Politicians today are highly sophisticated in their ability to analyze voting patterns. A great deal of the expense of politics today goes into modern techniques for polling, opinion taking, and computer analysis of voting records. One of the things that politicians and political parties do after an election is to look at the returns and analyze them to see which neighborhoods, communities, precincts, districts, cities, counties, states, groups, and constituencies voted for them and which did not. Let's say your neighborhood organization endorses a candidate for the city council on the basis of the commitments that candidate has made to the organization. If the election returns show that the people in your neighborhood split their vote evenly, then politicians will not take your group's endorsement seriously the next time.

This means that electoral politics in a people's organization must be handled carefully. If a decision to endorse a candidate is made by the leaders of the organization but the members do not share in that decision, then it's very likely that those members will not back the candidate the organization endorsed. Before becoming involved in this type of electoral politics an organization has to make a careful evaluation to see whether it can actually deliver votes to the candidates it endorses.

Votes are critical. But there are other kinds of help that a people's organization can give to electoral candidates. Money is always needed. The experience that a good people's organization develops in grass roots fund raising can also be used in a political campaign. As a general rule, the candidates that a people's organization endorses are the poorer ones in the race. They are unlikely to have support from corporations and wealthy individuals. Getting them elected is going to take money.

The organization can contribute volunteers. One of the reasons that electoral organizing is a good step for people's organizations is that its techniques are similar to those involved in neighborhood and community organizing. A good political organization follows the same lines that a community organization does. Just as a tenants' organization in a city would be organized block by block, with block clubs and block captains, political organizations like the old city ward organizations are organized block by block. Each block has a block captain. These block groups are then linked together in precinct organizations with precinct captains. A network is built that stretches out to each voter in the area.

There was a time when this was the most common form of political organizing. Many of the techniques that we use in community organizing today used to be part of political campaigns. Door knocking, petitions, membership drives, registration drives, rallies, fund-raising events, celebrations—all were used to build the party organization and to get out the vote. Today political campaigns rely more on expensive paid advertising such as television commercials and direct mail. This change has come partly because of the enormous amounts of money the corporations and their friends are putting into backing ''their'' candidates. It's also happened because ordinary people have not been very interested in getting out to work for candidates who were more interested in the corporations than in the average citizen.

These changes have helped create a situation where our organizations can make a real difference by participating in electoral politics. Many of the people in office today don't have an organized base. Instead of block and precinct captains, they have pollsters and advertising agencies. Their campaigns are impersonal. They treat people as averages. Ordinary citizens become profiles drawn from polls and computer analysis. Candidates are sold just like breakfast cereals. The average voter feels little sense of personal involvement and increasing frustration at the lack of a real choice. This is reflected in the small number of people who participate in electoral campaigns or even vote.

A grassroots campaign which goes door to door and involves people can win out over the corporate style of politics. A people's organization experienced in grassroots organizing can turn its resources, skills, and energy into a political campaign.

Should a people's organization concentrate on local, state, or national elections?

These approaches will work best on a scale that is close to the size and power of the people's organization. This may be different from the tradition of liberal politics in the United States. The labor unions, for example, have tended to concentrate on Senate and House of Representatives seats and on state legislative races, because so many of the decisions that affect their members involving labor laws, wage and hour legislation, health and safety standards, and retirement benefits are made at the state and federal level.

For community and neighborhood organizations, however, many of the most important decisions are made much closer to home. An enormous amount of money and people power is necessary to influence a congressional race. Many other races which are of great importance to neighborhoods and communities can be influenced or even decided with far less effort. Mayors, school board representatives, city council members, county commissioners, board of health members, tax assessors, and many other local officials are often elected by a relatively small number of votes. A well-organized grass roots campaign can make the difference between winning and losing an election. Local party structures are often fairly open and can be influenced in the same way as individual candidates. Local party organizations almost always have a hard time finding volunteers. If our organizations contribute some of those volunteers, they may find themselves with real influence in the campaign. It also makes sense to look at the possibility of our members running for elected offices within local Democratic and Republican committees at the district, county, and state level.

Partly because there is so much drama at the federal level, people's organizations are often drawn into national races for the presidency or for congressional seats. Obviously these are important. But people's organizations may fail to realize how much power is exercised by lower levels of government. Local government decides where the buses run; what the schools teach; where the police spend most of their time; where the new water or sewer lines run; what taxes are on homes, cars, and personal property; how tax money is spent. All these decisions are made close to home. These levers of power are within the reach of many people's organizations.

What problems can occur in electoral politics?

Involving people's organizations in electoral politics isn't easy. There are dangers. There can be a tendency to put too much value on politics, to put all the organization's resources into getting people elected and much less into building and maintaining the organization.

Many people's organizations find the coalition style of electoral politics difficult. In an electoral campaign there are usually two parties and two candidates. Other institutions and interest groups in the community split between these two camps. A people's organization may find itself in an electoral coalition with many groups which it finds difficult to deal with. The old saying "Politics makes strange bedfellows" is an accurate one.

Politics also makes for strange groupings of issues. An organization which has a single main issue may find itself backing a candidate who on most other issues does not support the positions that members of the organization hold. Should an organization fighting an expressway through its neighborhood support a politician who opposes that expressway, no matter what positions that politician takes on other issues? This is a complicated decision which can split an organization. In making this decision we need to consider how our members feel about the candidate's position on not just our issue but other issues as well. In thinking about how our organizations can influence electoral politics, we should remember how electoral politics can affect our organizations. Our participation should be in ways that help build the organization through increased membership participation, more public credibility, and new contacts and allies.

Sometimes this decision has a "lesser of two evils" feel to it. The two candidates in a race may be so unattractive that there seems to be little difference between them. Sometimes a people's organization has a hard time deciding whom to endorse—not because both candidates are so good on the issues, but because both of them are so bad. In a situation like this it is very difficult for the members of the organization to feel any real enthusiasm about participating in the campaign or using the organization's resources to participate in the election.

Should people's organizations run their own candidates?

In these situations we need to ask whether the organization should run its own candidates for office. Many people's organizations have not wanted to become involved in the apparent corruption of politics. They feel the organization could lose its own best leaders as they became candidates and possibly elected officials. They fear that the organization could be sold out by those people it helps elect, even when those candidates are leaders of the organization itself.

There is no point in being too idealistic about the benefits of people's organizations running their own candidates. Elected officials are subject to the same types of pressures regardless of whether they come from a law firm or a people's organization. But many officials do resist this pressure, especially when they're given backing by their constituency and the organizations that support them. We should not assume that candidates we elect, whether members of our organization or anyone else, will automatically do what's right. We need to keep the pressure on them and give them backing when necessary to allow them to continue doing the right thing.

We need to look seriously at the question of members and leaders of our organizations participating in electoral politics not only as voters and volunteer workers, but as candidates. There are many reasons why this type of electoral strategy makes sense in both the short run and the long run. As long as we take the "lesser of two evils" approach to politics we may get candidates who support us on one or two issues. But we are not likely to get elected officials who support the broad values of people's politics. How can a Congress which is three-quarters lawyers ever really represent the needs of ordinary people?

If we are really committed to the idea that people are their own best spokespersons, that they have the greatest sense of what their needs and rights are, that they are the most capable of building and leading their own organizations, then it's difficult to see how we can say, "But they should not seek public office." If we do this, we're saying that poor and working people are fit to lead their local organizations but not the larger institutions that really exercise power in this country.

What can an organization gain through electoral strategies?

If we don't take an active role in electoral politics, how can people ever exercise power in the United States? Government is not the root of power. It's a system through which power is exercised. Power comes from the money interests, the corporations, the banks, the holding companies, the real estate firms. But the institutions which have real power are not open to most people. They are not going to become bank directors or members of corporate boards of trustees, except as occasional tokens.

One of the few possible counterforces to corporate power is government. Government on all levels has the power to regulate or control the corporations. It has the power to distribute and redistribute wealth and income through the tax system, revenue sharing, and redistribution of funds at the federal, state, county, and city level. Clearly there are also ways of directly pressuring the sources of power. But government is an important indirect pressure, and one that is open to us. It makes sense to establish as much control over government through electoral politics as we can.

Electoral politics is not a solution to all the needs of poor and working people. There are many problems with an electoral strategy. We should not expect that simply because we elect the president of our organization to the city council he or she will vote with us on every issue, unless we do the continuing work to make sure it happens. If people's organizations decide to run candidates, they also will need to develop strategies to make sure that those candidates continue to be accountable to the organization. Elected officials who are our friends need to hear from us as much as those who are not. We need to hear from them. An organization which supports a candidate for office should expect that candidate if elected to come back and report to them in regular meetings, and to be part of making strategy and decisions.

No matter how careful we are, we will not always be successful. There will always be people we elect or help elect who go over to the other side. But to the extent that we're able to develop ways for continuing pressure and involvement, we can begin to establish power on our own through a direct role in government.

Even if we are not successful in electing a candidate, there are many reasons for running our own people for public office. Elections focus public attention on issues. Candidates for office are given tremendous legitimacy. An electoral campaign can be used by people's organizations as a tool for raising issues. If you go to a door as an organizer, you may or may not be listened to. But suppose you go to someone's door and say, "I'm a candidate for the school board in your district. I want to talk to you about the issues to find out how you feel." You're likely to be listened to. A campaign at a local level developed by a people's organization can be used as a way of focusing attention on issues as well as on candidates.

Electoral politics has its problems. But so do the other ways of trying to get power. And in this country electoral politics is a traditional way through which power is exercised. It's something that is within the experience of most of the members of our organizations. They're used to participating in the political process. They see it as a natural way for individuals and organizations to try to accomplish their goals. Many members of people's organizations don't understand an anti-electoral strategy which in effect says, "We're willing to try to influence power but not to take it." An electoral strategy which comes out of the experience of an organization's members, which focuses on issues, which is centered around not just elections but a continuing strategy to influence government, can make a real difference in all our lives.

18. Culture

CULTURE is the environment in which things grow. When we culture plants we try to provide the ideal conditions under which they can live and flourish: soil, water, air, light. In the same way, a person's ability to grow and flourish depends on her surroundings. A person's environment determines much of what she is able or not able to do, to feel, to think.

Many things go into the making of a person's culture. The different values he sees reflected in the society around him have a lot to do with determining his culture. There are different levels to these values. To some extent, people in this country are affected by a national set of values. But a person is going to be influenced the most by the values of those closest to him: his family, his friends, his neighborhood, his religious group, his ethnic, gender, and racial group.

How are cultural values expressed?

These values are expressed in many different ways. Sometimes they are expressed directly through the media or through the official pronouncements of people like ministers, priests, rabbis, and elected government and union officials. Values are also communicated by the behavior we see in the people around us. We not only listen to what our neighbors say, we watch what they do. If there is a contradiction between what they say and what they do, we're more likely to conclude that what they *do* is acceptable.

Values are different from community to community. Communities will share certain values and differ in others. There are both common and different values, for example, between Italian-American communities, Hispanic communities, and Appalachian communities.

Values don't only describe the way people behave. They also describe the way people *ought* to behave. For example, when you hear a man in a rural community say, "A woman's place is in the home," he is not just describing where he feels a woman's place has traditionally been. He is saying where in his opinion a woman's place ought to be. If you were organizing in a community where this was a common statement, you might find that it was difficult at first to get women to assume leadership roles, whether or not the men they related to were willing to assume these roles. Their doing so would go against the values of the community, as well as against direct pressure from their husbands.

Sometimes values are deliberately manipulated by an element in society to suit its own purposes. The "women in the home" example is a good one. At the beginning of World War II, because so many men were in the armed forces, there were not enough skilled workers to run the production machinery in factories of the country. The federal government started a major drive to recruit women into the industrial work force. This campaign was not simply an employment program. It also tried to change the value systems that might keep women from taking factory jobs. So the country was subjected to a massive propaganda campaign showing women at work in the factories. "Rosie the Riveter" became a national symbol. Women went to work, not simply because they needed the money or the job but because they felt they were doing the right thing, the thing that was expected of them.

At the end of World War II, the federal government had to deal with the reverse of this problem. Nearly twelve million veterans, most of them male, were returning to the United States and to civilian employment. There were clearly not enough jobs to go around. Many women were by that time working jobs in factories where they had established seniority and a right to the jobs. The federal planners were worried about what would happen if returning veterans came back to find no jobs for them. A similar situation at the end of World War I had resulted in tremendous unrest, organizing by veterans, armed seizures of courthouses, and a massive march on Washington that had to be broken up by federal troops. So the government launched a second propaganda campaign, aided by business and industry, to convince women once again that their place was in the home rather than in the factory. The "modern homemaker" was born and peddled to the American woman. By and large the drive was successful. The combination of economics and values drove women out of the factories and back into the home.

Why was such an outrageous and deliberate campaign to remove millions of women from productive work successful? It worked partly because all of us are tremendously affected by what we think is expected of us. What we do depends very much on our sense of who we are. We try to act within the values that we see in our families, among our friends, among our neighbors, in our religious group, in our community, in our ethnic, gender, and racial group. Even when we rebel, it is against these specific values. Even our rebelling has characteristics common to the members of the groups we belong to.

What are the culture and values of people in this country?

What complicates this situation is that few people in this country have a true sense of what the real values of their group are or have been. They accept instead the myths that are created for them. These myths are not accidental. They are deliberately created and reinforced by those in power. Those in power create stereotypes about different groups of people and work to have these stereotypes accepted by that group. Why do they do this? Because they know that individuals and groups tend to act within the limits set up by the way they see themselves, their own history, and their own values. If their sense of their own values can be changed to those that make life easier for those in power, then other people will be more willing to go along with the system.

You can see this operate very clearly in the way that minority groups are cut off from their own histories. Look at the ways in which black people have been shown in history books. The blacks who were held up as examples for other black people were men like Booker T. Washington and George Washington Carver. In one way it's important that they were noted at all, since for a long time individual blacks weren't even recognized. But it's also important to understand that these men believed that the only way for individual blacks to progress was to avoid any kind of organizing or collective action. They advised other blacks not to challenge the system in any way but instead to improve their level of education and skill. The message to black people was very clear: "If you want to get ahead you need to get along."

The problem with this idea was that thousands and thousands of black people who were educated, who worked through the system, were still being denied equal opportunity. The people in power were willing to tolerate a handful of Booker T. Washingtons, but not thousands.

The purpose of the myth was to cut black people off from their real history in the United States. In fact, from the time the first slaves were brought to this country, blacks resisted slavery. They organized, they established escape systems, they raised money and sent agitators into the South to help slaves go free, they fought in armed rebellions against the planters, they fought in the military against the Confederacy and the slave system. During Reconstruction, blacks served in high official positions and made important contributions to progressive legislation. Obviously it was not in the self-interest of the American power structure to have black people familiar with and proud of this history. What would happen if black people over the generations had all been brought up to believe that they had as a group resisted, fought back, stood up for themselves, tried to change the system, refused to cooperate? It would have been much harder for the power structure to keep black people in line.

Myths are not the only things that keep people from acting. The myths themselves are reinforced by official and unofficial power ranging from the ability to evict, arrest, jail, fire, deny benefits, intimidate, lynch, murder. By striking back at those blacks who attempted to fight against the system and by reinforcing those who were willing to cooperate, the establishment was able to make the myth of black cooperation more acceptable, even to many black people themselves.

This same process has happened to almost every immigrant group in this country. Native Americans fought for three centuries against the military power of the American government. Irish immigrants organized secret unions such as the Molly Maguires to fight for better working conditions in the coal mines of Pennsylvania. Finnish immigrants in the Midwest organized unions and cooperative associations. Jewish, Italian, and Slavic immigrants in the cities helped to organize many of the early trade unions.

Most of the groups that came to this country had been oppressed in their homeland and expected to find a greater degree of economic security in the United States. They rarely found it. Instead they organized and fought back against the system to try to get the rights and benefits to which they thought they were entitled. A majority of people in the United States today have parents, grandparents, great-grandparents, and great-great-grandparents who organized and fought back and resisted, who tried to change the system. What would happen if most of us believed that was what our families had always done, and that was what was expected of us today? So the people in power put on a continuing campaign to convince all of us that our people have always gotten along, never made waves, never stirred up trouble, always tried to work through the system, always used the right channels.

Women have also had their history hidden from them. History as it has been written and taught in our schools is the story of great men: presidents, generals, corporate leaders, inventors, politicians. The women in our history have been made invisible. Because the men in power have valued war, politics, and productivity, the history books reflect that. A different history of the United States, one which set progress in justice and the human spirit above battles and industrial development, would show women playing a far more important role. The invisible American woman, like the "happy homemaker" who replaced Rosie the Riveter, is a myth developed by people in power to help keep women in their place.

How can people in groups rediscover their culture and values?

Rediscovering our own true histories helps us restore the real values of our communities. It also helps rebuild the self-confidence and pride that both individuals and groups need—in themselves, their history, their culture. A priority in our organizing work is to help the different members of our organizations rediscover their own histories.

A starting point is to help people become aware of some of the deep-seated reasons that motivate them to organize and to become leaders in an organization. Most leaders are acting out of very strongly held and deeply felt beliefs. Start by trying to think of the things that motivate you to organize. Think about your answers to these questions:

(1) Why are you willing to put in the enormous time and trouble necessary to be a leader?

(2) Why is it important to you that people stand up and fight back?

(3) What is it about the things that you believe that makes you willing to take the risks that you take, to spend the time that you spend?

(4) What is it in how you feel about yourself that gives you the self-confidence and pride to be able to step forward?

(5) What is it in your beliefs about others that makes you work with them, over and over trying to develop their skills, their self-confidence, their beliefs in themselves?

For many of us these values come from our culture. We learn them from members of our family—from parents, grandparents, and great-grandparents—who taught us that it was our responsibility to stand up for what is right, to fight back against injustice. We learn from family members who told us about their own lives, about the ways in which they organized or stood up proudly and fought back. We learn from our religions, particularly when those religions stress the need for social justice and when the religious leaders with whom we identify also encourage people to work openly for change in the world. We learn these values from the heroes in our traditions, from the people we identify with, both those in history and those today: from Chief Joseph and Dr. Martin Luther King, from Cesar Chávez and Mother Jones, from Harriet Tubman and Sojourner Truth.

As leaders we need to hold these people up in our organizing as examples of how the values of our own culture can be honored. We need to become familiar with the history of these kinds of people so that we can talk about them as we work with other members of our organization. We want to be able to say things like "Let me tell you what Martin Luther King did in a situation just like this." When we present a tactic in this way, we're not just analyzing the tactic, we're also showing that it's acceptable in our culture.

People will be more willing to do what they think others have done, especially other people they see as being like them. People will see as possible that which is familiar, rather than that which seems strange and unaccustomed. It is useful to you as a leader to be familiar with as much of the history of organizing in this country as possible. But the starting point for your studies should be your own group, your own people: their history, their moments of pride and courage, their heroes, their victories, their defeats, their values.

In addition to helping the people you work with become more familiar with the known heroes within their culture, help them get to know the unknown heroes. People learn best by example. When we talk to people about options that come from another culture or another class, they often see these options as closed to them. They'll say, "Well, maybe *they* were able to do it, but they're not like *us*." One of the ways of breaking down this attitude is to let the people you work with meet other people who are just like them, who have organized and taken the steps that they are now thinking about taking. Take a woman from a housing project who has spent all her life on welfare. She feels the lack of confidence that keeps her from acting. If she can meet another woman who has lived the same kind of life but who has broken through to become a leader, it opens a sense of the possible to her. Through that meeting she begins to feel, "Here's someone no different from me, someone who has been through the experiences I've been through, someone who talks like I talk, someone who thinks like I think. She's been able to do it. I should be able to do it, too."

People learn best from their peers, from people who are like them, who share their values, who are a part of their culture. Part of our work as leaders is to begin building these bridges, to begin forming these links. By doing so we create living examples of what people can do and be.

How can culture be used as an organizing tool?

As people begin to organize together, they also begin to learn from each other's values. We are not simply building an organization, we are also reestablishing people's culture. We are creating a shared sense of history and democratic values, a common set of expectations within which to develop our strategies and tactics.

This can take place at the neighborhood or small group level. The techniques of consciousness raising developed by the women's movement are excellent for beginning to build a sense of solidarity among the people you work with. Try out these techniques. In one of the small group meetings, try encouraging people to talk about themselves, their histories, their hopes and dreams, their values, where they came from, where they're going. Choose a time when people's minds are free from other immediate concerns. Try to find a setting where people won't be interrupted and which is comfortable enough to put people at ease. You might start out by talking about yourself, how you got to be a leader, why you organize, what things you're fighting for, what things you care about. Talk about your heroes, the people from your group who influenced your thinking, the people you identify with, whose thinking you respect, whose visions meant something to you. Talk about your own family, the people you're close to, people you see as examples, other people you've met in your organizing.

Make room for other people to speak. You'll probably find that people will begin slowly at first. But with a little gentle pushing they'll warm up quickly.

The power that is unleashed in these sessions is often overwhelming. Most people don't know the strength of these feelings in other people. Most of us who really believe in democratic values grow up feeling isolated. We feel that we're the only people who think this way, who believe that strongly, who want to fight that hard. As we begin to discover that we are not alone, that there are other people who have thought the same things, felt the same feelings, and gone through the same emotional struggles, we begin to feel a sense of belonging, a sense of being part of something that is larger than ourselves. We're discovering the shared values and assumptions within our group, the ones that are rooted in our own personal realities. We are reacquainting ourselves with the history of our group. But we are also creating a new history based on what each of us is doing, what each of us feels, what each of us believes. Such a system of feelings, values, and beliefs is really a culture.

Part of the way in which we reestablish people's culture, in which we communicate this set of values to the people we work with so that they make them their own, is to build culture into our daily organizing. We want to relate what we are doing to the broad cultural experience of the people we work with. We want to make our strategies and tactics consistent with their experience and expectations. As these expectations expand, as they develop a deeper sense of themselves and their community, we can also develop a broader range of options which we can realistically carry out.

How can we build people's culture into our organizing?

We can build culture into our organizing in many ways. We can begin recommunicating to the members of the group the history that we're in the process of rediscovering. We can talk about it as we go door-to-door in our organizing. We can put in our newsletters and other printed literature historical examples of events and people that are important to know about. We can highlight some of our own members, talking about their roots and culture, their sense of values. We can put articles in our newsletters such as a member talking about how her grandmother helped organize a union in the sewing factory or how her grandparents helped fight the banks with the Farmers Alliance.

We begin reestablishing people's history in a personalized way that is open to other members of the group. It also opens the door for these people to begin talking about events which before they may have been reluctant to talk about. The people in power have been so successful in many areas in changing our values that many people who themselves were involved in political activity, in organizing, in resistance—or whose parents and grandparents were involved—have become ashamed to talk about these things. We need to honor what was done, to help people once again become proud of what they and their people have been able to accomplish.

We can build culture into our meetings. Music is an excellent way of building good feelings within a group. Singing together makes people feel strong and joined together. We can help people relearn the songs that come out of historical struggles, from organizing campaigns, about individual heroes, about strikes, about people's hard times, about people fighting back.

We can make our own songs, taking tunes that people know and writing new words that talk about our organizations, our targets, our special events, our tactics. It's surprising how many people are able to write and rewrite songs. Songs that talk about people by name, about the places they live, and the battles they've fought help keep a group's spirit together.

There are many other things that can be made part of our meetings. Films about other organizations and groups, about historical struggles in this country, often convey a sense of reality that's missing in printed material. Films such as *Salt of the Earth, Union Maids, People's Firehouse, Rosie the Riveter,* and *With Babies and Banners* not only bring across much of the feeling of those events, they also serve as an excellent starting point for discussions within the group.

We should also encourage the people we've met who have a personal or family history to come talk to the group about it. In almost every community there are older people and many younger people who have been part of women's struggles, union struggles, civil rights struggles, movements in other countries. These people are rarely ever asked to talk about their experiences. They need to share with us both the history itself and the feelings that brought them to be part of that history.

These events can also be the beginning of establishing a permanent record of our own history and culture as an organization. As we discover people who know parts of the history who can talk about it, we should record them on tape or on videotape. These tapes should then be transcribed as a part of beginning to develop the history of our group, based on people's own personal histories and recollections.

We should try to preserve the history of our organization and its events. When we hold an action, there should be photographs that people can look at later and remember the way things were. We should write songs to sing at these actions and to sing later. Some organizations have put together theater groups, both to recreate historical events and as an example of the way that things can be done. Other groups have done large paintings or street murals that show their own history as an organization or community.

How can we create and recreate cultural symbols?

In all this we should pay careful attention to the creation and use of symbols. Sometimes we will need to create and consciously promote symbols that people can identify with. But where possible we want to root these symbols in the historical symbols of our culture. For example, the Virgin of Guadalupe, a historical symbol taken from the Catholic Church of Mexico's struggle for independence, was used by the farm workers. The use of this particular symbol also contributed to setting the farm workers' tactics within a religious framework. By calling to mind the struggle for Mexican independence and the Catholic faith, the farm workers were able to root their strategies and tactics very firmly in the popular culture of their members.

We should also begin to retake the symbols of our country. We are the real Americans. The flag is our flag. It belongs to us, not to the corporations. The Declaration of Independence refers to our independence, not to making companies independent of any responsibility. The Bill of Rights is a statement of our rights, not the rights of politicians hired by campaign contributions. The Star of David and the cross are symbols of our concern for justice, not for a corporate misuse of religion.

By rooting our organizing firmly within the culture, the values, and the symbols of our society, we are doing several things at once. We are helping people to reestablish their history and rediscover their roots. We are helping people rethink their own system of values in a way that makes certain types of behavior more possible. We are beginning to preserve and remake a history not only of what was done before but what we are doing today. We are preserving this history in songs, in photographs, in films, in videotapes, in painting, in murals, in theater, in stories. We are taking the symbols of our country and our culture, and making them ours again.

As our organizations grow, people from different cultures and with roots in different historical struggles are brought together. We begin to expose them to a broader concept of struggle so that the members of our organization are aware not only of what has happened within their own particular group but also with what the history, tradition, and culture of struggle are in other areas of the United States, with other groups, and in other countries. We are creating in many ways a common language, a common culture that can help make more possible and powerful a real majority movement for change in our country.

Afterword

On the 25th day
of the month of September
in the year 1962
in Amite County
Mississippi
a man named Herbert Lee
was shot to death

Herbert Lee
was a cotton farmer
black
married
father of nine children

He had been working
in the Civil Rights Movement
in Amite County
where he had been born and raised

helping black Americans
finally gain the right to vote

On that September morning
so many years ago
Herbert Lee drove his truck
to the cotton gin

When he got to the gin
a white man named E. H. Hurst
was waiting for him

Hurst came around
to the side of the truck
stuck a pistol
in Lee's face
and ordered him to get out

Lee said,
"I'm not getting out of this truck
till you put that pistol down"

Hurst stuck the pistol
in his pocket
Lee got out of the truck
on the far side
and walked around
to where Hurst was standing
When he got there
Hurst pulled his pistol
and shot him

Herbert Lee
bled to death on the dirt
next to that cotton gin
in Amite County
his blood soaking into
the Mississippi earth

E. H. Hurst
white
male
member of the Mississippi State Legislature
was found not guilty
by reason of self-defense
by an all-white jury
of his peers

Bertha Gober
who was a member of the Freedom Singers
a group of young black musicians
who traveled the South
raising spirits and hopes
wrote a song
in memory of Herbert Lee

and in the small towns
of Alabama
Georgia
North Carolina
Arkansas
and Mississippi
they sang:

> We've been 'buked and we've been scorned
> We've been talked about sure's you're born
> But we'll never turn back
> No we'll never turn back
> Until we've all been freed
> And we have equality
> And we have equality
>
> We have spent our time in jail
> Had nobody to go our bail
> But we'll never turn back
> No we'll never turn back
> Until we've all been freed
> And we have equality
> And we have equality

We have walked through the Valley of Death
We had to walk all by ourselves
But we'll never turn back
No we'll never turn back
Until we've all been freed
And we have equality
And we have equality

We have hung our heads and cried
For those like Lee who died
Died for you and he died for me
Died for the cause of equality
Now we'll never turn back
No we'll never turn back
Until we've all been freed
And we have equality
And we have equality

In 1965
three years after Herbert Lee died
the Congress of the United States
in response to the rediscovery
of poverty in America
and to the organizing
by black Americans in the South
voted to eliminate
poverty in this country
permanently
once and for all
forever
indefinitely
and absolutely

Even in 1965 we recognized
that poverty is not just
being without money
It is being
cut off
cut out
cut down

It is being without power
and without the protection
people with power have

It is being without protection
from the powerful

It is being without choice
and suffering the indignity
of depending on being chosen

It is having no voice
and no one who *has* to listen
when you do speak

It is being shoved aside
when you aren't being used up

Not only those who have no money
suffer from poverty
but also those whose way of life
denies them the power
to control what happens to them

The poor are those
who have not yet taken back
what has been taken from them
who have not yet found
their own power

So many years after Congress
declared War on Poverty
the poor have not found
that power

So many years later
we have not eliminated poverty
in America

We have not eliminated poverty
when decent housing is often not available
even to those able to pay for it

and is almost never available
to those not able to pay

when the waiting lists
for public housing
are months and years long

when housing is bulldozed
in our central cities
to make way for shopping centers
and condominiums

when urban communities are destroyed
by red-lining
and rural communities are destroyed
by strip-mining

when the private homes
of poor and working people
are taxed at a much higher rate
than the profits of the oil companies

We have not eliminated poverty
when it takes a year of work
at the federal minimum wage
to meet the price
of a so-called "low-priced" car

but when poor public transportation
makes having a car
almost a necessity of life
in most cities
and almost all rural areas

when senior citizens cannot ride
the buses and subways
of our urban areas
in safety

when a woman cannot ride
in safety at night

when the handicapped
cannot find transportation anywhere
even to the few jobs
open to them

We have not eliminated poverty
when the cost of energy
is beyond the means
of most families

when the choice between
heating and eating
is a real one

when the choices we make
are not between luxuries and necessities
but between one necessity and another

when for millions of Americans
the necessities of life
have in fact become luxuries

when the supplies of heating oil
gasoline
and natural gas
which are necessary to people's health and welfare
are deliberately manipulated
by a handful of corporations
in a never-ending search
for higher profits

We have not eliminated poverty
when millions of people
who want to work
cannot find jobs
at any pay

When there is almost no protection
on the job
from sexual harassment

when racial discrimination
in hiring and promotion
is a fact of life

when pay scales
still favor white males
above any other group

when families working
40, 60, 80 hours a week
cannot make ends meet

when older workers
get pushed out when they reach 50 or 60
to make way for younger workers
who will work harder
and cheaper

when millions of older people
living on fixed incomes such as Social Security
that they worked a lifetime to earn
see their ability to live decently
eaten away by inflation

when your health and safety
on the job
are part of the price you pay
for having a job at all

when more Americans have died
from occupational diseases and accidents
than in all the wars
this country has fought

I did my part in World War II
Got wounded for the nation
Now my lungs are all shot down
There ain't no compensation

> *I'm gonna go to work on Monday one more time*
> *I'm gonna go to work on Monday one more time,*
>   *one more time*
> *I'm gonna go to work on Monday one more time*

The doctor says I smoke too much
He says that I'm not trying
He says he don't know what I've got
But we both know he's lying

The last time I went near my job
I thought my lungs were broken
Chest bound down like iron bands
I couldn't breathe for choking

The politicians in this state
Are nothing short of rotten
They buy us off with fancy words
And sell us out to cotton

The doctor says both lungs are gone
There ain't no need of trying
But living like some used-up thing
Is just this short of dying

They tell me I can't work at all
There ain't no way to shake it
But I can't live without a job
Somehow I've got to take it

Sitting on my front porch swing
I'm like a man forgotten
Head all filled with angry thoughts
And lungs filled up with cotton

Poverty
is still a problem in America
not only because
a large group of people
have too little

but because a small group
of people and corporations
have far too much

The gap
between those who have
and those who don't have
is being deliberately
and systematically widened

People who have worked hard
all their lives
who have put in their time
on the job
who have paid their taxes
and their dues
who have served their country
and their communities
are worse off today
in terms of what their money will buy
than they were in 1965
when the War on Poverty was declared

Today's economic realities
are creating
a new class of poor people
that is going to include
many people
who are not poor today
as inflation in the necessities of life
energy
food

housing
health care
eats away their standard of living

the poor are still with us
because there is profit in poverty

slum housing
is good for business

people who must work
for whatever they can get
are good for business

high profits
on medical care
are good for business

the ability to discriminate
in hiring and firing
is good for business

high taxes on homes
are good for business

Poverty will not be eliminated
by economic policies
that encourage unemployment
as a way
of controlling inflation

Poverty will not be wiped out
by political priorities
that limit health care
to those able to pay for it
but pay doctors more
than any other profession

Poverty will not be eliminated
by a system
that keeps women dependent on men
or on welfare
by closing some jobs to them
and paying them less
than other workers
on many jobs

If we are really serious
about eliminating poverty
in America
we need a national decision
that what's good for business
has to give way
to what's good for people

We must be clear
about who can make this decision

the corporations
are not going to make this decision

the politicians
whose fortunes and careers
are linked to those corporations
through campaign contributions
are not going to make this decision

the banks
will not make this decision

the real estate speculators
and insurance companies
will not make this decision

We are the only ones
who can make this decision

A change
to a society
that protects people first
before it protects profits
will not come
because we wish for it to happen
or because we wait for it to happen

It will come only
if we *make* it happen

Change will not come
because we are right
because we are good people
because we want it badly

Change will not come
because commissions are appointed
agencies established
books written
TV specials aired
movies produced
speeches made

Change will not come
because corporations
suddenly become concerned
or because politicians
suddenly become enlightened

One of the lessons
of the Civil Rights Movement
of the 1960s
is that no one
will *give* us
our freedom

no one
will grant us
the rights that we need

no one will donate
self-respect to us

no one
will make us a gift
of pride or confidence

no one
will award us
self-sufficiency

Freedom
must be fought for

pride
must be earned

community
must be built

power
must be taken

we can only count on
the things that we take
or take back

because whatever things
are given to us
will always be theirs
not ours

There is only one real way
to bring about change

and to eliminate poverty
in America

and that is to fight back
and organize

> *I have dreamed on this mountain*
> *Since first I was my mother's daughter*
> *And you can't just take my dreams away*
> *Not with me watching*
>
> *You may drive a big machine*
> *But I was born a great big woman*
> *And you can't just take my dreams away*
> *Without me fighting*
>
> *This old mountain raised my many daughters*
> *Some died young—some are still living*
> *But if you come here for to take our mountain*
> *Well I ain't come here to give it*
>
> *I have dreamed on this mountain*
> *Since first I was my mother's daughter*
> *And you can't just take my dreams away*
> *Not with me watching*
> *No you can't just take my dreams away*
> *Without me fighting*
> *No you can't just take my dreams away.*

Like the "Kentucky Woman"
in Holly Near's song
we need to build a movement
that not only
has enough soul and spirit
to sustain us all
and nurture us all

but that also has
the organized strength and power
to oppose those
who hold power now
whenever and wherever it is necessary
to challenge them:

on the block
in the home
in the barrio
on the reservation
in the holler
in the neighborhood
in the community
in the factory

There is no substitute
for this hard work of organizing

Even in this age
of electronic technology
and high-speed media
the most effective way of communicating
is still person to person

Organizing
is the process
by which we link individual people
together

This is the great strength
of organizing

Those who band together
become bonded together

Those who stand together
in silent opposition
or in angry protest
will grow together

Those who work together
march together
fight together
sing together

have the power
to eliminate poverty and powerlessness
together

But we cannot eliminate poverty
one person at a time

because the causes of poverty
are not only individual
but collective as well

People are poor
not only because they are unemployed
or undereducated
or in poor health
or badly housed
or depressed and discouraged
although poverty
and powerlessness
may cause all of these symptoms

People are also poor today
because the national commitment
made in 1965
to eliminate poverty
only asked the poor to change
and did not demand
that the institutions which cause poverty
change as well

The process of working for change
puts special responsibilities
on each of us

As organizers and leaders
we change the course of events
and are in turn changed
by those events

The way we build and rebuild our world
will determine
what that world looks like

We cannot build
a democratic society
by undemocratic methods

We cannot build a country
with equality for all
if we exclude some
from the process of building it

We cannot be narrow
in our definitions

None of us is affected
by just one issue

People who have poor-paying jobs
or no jobs at all
also tend to live
in poor housing

People who suffer
from bad health
caused by lack of medical care
also tend to lack education

People whose communities and neighborhoods
are ignored or exploited
also tend to be victims
of individual discrimination

In the same way
that none of us is affected
by just one issue
none of us is a member
of just one group

Poor people
are also women
working people
Hispanic
Native American
black
old
very young

Women
are also black
gay
straight
Asian-American
poor
unemployed

All of us
because we are members
of different groups
and are affected
by different issues
need to work together
and help each other

But any individual
any group
any issue
is only a starting point

Each skill we teach
increases
our mutual resources

each group we build
broadens the base
of the struggle

each leader we encourage
widens the possibilities
for all of us

each small victory we win
makes the larger victories possible

each connection we make
strengthens us all

each door we knock on
opens a door

It's always hard to know
what the work we do
has meant to other people
whose lives have been touched by ours

How many of us
would be here today
if at some time in the past
someone had not worked
to organize us

What would our vision be
if someone had not shared
their vision with us

How many communities
would be represented
here today
if someone had not started to work
in those communities
when they were unrepresented

In all of this
the single most valuable resource we have
is the individual person
who is committed to work

for basic economic and political change
in our society

The loss of any of these persons
is a blow to our struggle
to build a better world
for all of us

Bernice Johnson Reagon
who sang with the Freedom Singers
wrote this song:

> They are falling all around me
> They are falling all around me
> They are falling all around me
> The strongest leaves of my tree
>
> Every paper brings the news that
> Every paper brings the news that
> Every paper brings the news that
> The teachers of my sounds
> Are moving on
>
> Death comes and rests so heavy
> Death comes and rests so heavy
> Death comes and rests so heavy
> Your face I'll never see no more
>
> But you're not really going to leave me
> You're not really going to leave me
> You're not really going to leave me
> It is your path I walk
> It is your song I sing
> It is your load I take on
> It is your air I breathe
> It's the record you set that makes me go on
> It's your strength that helps me stand
> You're not really going to leave me
>
> I will try to sing my song right
> I will try to sing my song right
> I will try to sing my song right
> Be sure to let me hear from you

For each of us
there is a turning point

There is a moment in which we recognize
our own commitment
to the struggle for change

We can help others
reach that turning point

We can help them
achieve a sense
of what is possible

We can help them
rediscover
their own history
and herstory

We can help them
root themselves
in their own cultures

We can help them recognize
the strengths
in the cultures
of others

But we need to begin
to recognize the value
of our own work

Just as the work done
by women
by blacks
by Hispanics
by Native Americans
by young people

by old people
has never been properly valued
or fairly paid for

our own work
as organizers and leaders
is constantly downgraded
by a society that is impersonal
that places value on products and profits
ahead of human beings
that throws away
the old
the sick
the disabled
like empty pop bottles

We need to understand
that we too are workers
with skill
with experience
with insight
with dedication
with courage
with creativity

Look at the things
we know how to do

To create community
where there was none

To instill pride
where there was desperation

To build organizations
where there were only individuals

To turn powerlessness
into power

Look at what we have accomplished
over these years

We have built clinics
in our communities

rebuilt neighborhoods
in inner cities

challenged politicians
throughout the country

blocked the strip-miners
and the red-liners

won stop signs
and bus lines

we have even
stopped a war

We need to recognize
not only what we are doing wrong
and what we still need to do
but how very much
we are doing right

But if each of us
who have worked as organizers and leaders
were here today
we would still not have enough hands
for the job that needs to be done

For every community
that organizes successfully
there are many more
that try to organize
and fail

In many cases
we have the skills
as individuals and together
that can make the difference
between success and failure

We have the experience
that can keep a group
from making the mistakes
that other groups have made

As we move forward
what are our goals?

We want a fair distribution
of wealth, property, income, and power

We want jobs with good wages
and decent working conditions

We want a society
where people are respected
not only in spite of race
color
creed
national origin
sexual preference
age
and gender
but *because* of these things as well

We want an end to war
and an end to all violence against the powerless
at home
at work
and everywhere

We want an end
to unnecessary sickness and accidents
on the job

We want an end to discrimination
whatever it is based on

We want an end
to political favoritism

We want an end to government
of
by
and for
the corporations

We want an end
to the destruction
of our neighborhoods
and natural resources
for profit

As we move
forward
we need to begin to build
a national grass roots movement
which is strong enough
to accomplish these goals

These organizations
must be increasingly self-sufficient
in all areas:
fund raising
organization
leadership
culture
economics
politics

Our organizations
must continue their movement
toward financial self-sufficiency

We recognize the support
of outside funding sources
of government agencies
of foundations
of churches
of private individuals

Yet at the same time
we understand
the financial and political limits
of outside funding

If we want our organizations
to be politically independent
they also need to be
financially independent

We need to emphasize
grass roots fund raising
If we want to make
our own way
we must be prepared
to pay our own way

We must work toward
organizational self-sufficiency

The institutions and organizations
that we build
must belong to us

They need to have structures
that allow each member
a sense of belonging

and participation
and growth

They must have
membership bases
that reflect the makeup
of the community

They must have
leadership roles
that allow the people
who have not been heard from
to speak for themselves

We must continue to move
toward a self-sufficiency
of leadership

We must continue to insist
on the principle
that poor and working people
and all people who stand together
to get their rights
are their own best spokespersons

That no one has the right
to speak for anyone else
except the democratically chosen leadership
of the grass roots organizations
built by those groups themselves

We must create new chances
for grass roots leadership
to develop
through increased opportunities
for leadership training
through more cooperation
among the leadership

of different organizations
through leadership exchange programs
among different groups

We need to make it possible
for our own experienced
and skilled leadership
to work full-time
with their organizations

We need to move toward the principle
developed by the labor movement
that not only must the leadership
of an organization
come from the rank and file
but much of the staff as well

We need to make the improvements
in the wages and working conditions
of organizers
that will make it possible for leaders
to look toward organizing
as a full-time
life-time career

We must establish
cultural self-sufficiency

Because the future
is rooted in the past
we must understand that past
and weave it into
our present work

We need to encourage
every group
to rediscover
its traditions

and rely on those traditions
for strength
and unity

We need to understand
the strength of a movement
that sings its own songs

We need to take
the songs and stories
of struggle
and pass them on
to those we work with
and live among

We need to see self-sufficiency
in economic terms

As long as we depend
on the government
for our budgets
people will go hungry
when those budgets are cut

As long as we depend
on the corporations
for what we consume
we are in danger
of being consumed by them

We need to make sure
that people individually
have enough of an economic base
to survive

We need to abandon the concept
of fixed incomes
and insist instead

that people have certain fixed needs
and that these needs
have to be met
no matter what

We need to explore
not only alternative sources of energy
but alternative systems
for controlling and delivering
the energy we have now

We need to deepen our reliance ·
on cooperatives
to meet our basic needs
for food
energy
shelter
clothing
education
health care
child care

We need to look at cooperatives
as an alternative structure
within which producers and consumers
can relate to each other

We must continue establishing
political self-sufficiency
at all levels of government

At the local level
whether city, county, town, or district
we need to refuse the traditional choice
of the lesser evil
and begin to throw our votes
behind the leadership
of our own organizations
as they run for public office

At the same time
we must insist on accountability

Those whom we support
whether they come from our leadership
or from outside our organizations
must support us

We should never forget
that the squeaking wheel
gets the grease
and even our own leaders
when they are elected to public office
need to be pressured by us
if they are to carry out
our programs and priorities

How do we build
this national movement?

We build it
one step at a time

How do we build
a national constituency
for that movement?

We build it
one person at a time

So what can each of us do?

One of the rules of organizing
is that you start with people
where they are
and not where you wish they were

We should also
make it a rule of organizing

that *we* need to start
where *we* are

There is no part
of this country
that can be ignored
if we are one day to have
a real majority movement
for change

There is no constituency
however spread out in geography
that does not need
to consolidate itself
around its own issues

There is no problem
that does not need to be looked at
as a potential issue
for organizing

A national movement
for basic change
may not have the active participation
of a majority of the American people

But if it is to be successful
it must have
the active *support*
of that majority

Everything depends
on our building a base
that does involve
either the participation
or the support
of that majority

We must not only
be strong in our communities
but clear about the issues
that reach beyond these communities
to link us together

We cannot have
effective city-wide groups
if only two or three neighborhoods
are organized

We cannot have
effective organizations
at the state level
if we are spread so thin
that we are both everywhere and nowhere
at the same time

A strategy
to end poverty and powerlessness in America
must rely on more
than the already poor and powerless

It must include the millions of Americans
working with and without pay
in the workplace and at home
who share with the poor
a lack of power
and who increasingly
see their standards of living
eaten away

If all of us are not poor now
all of us share
in being powerless

If we are to have
national organizations to represent us

that have real power
if we are to have
national leaders
that are listened to
they must have a real base

Where does that base come from?

We build it
We organize it

One group at a time
one community at a time
one neighborhood at a time
one issue at a time

There are hundreds and thousands
of neighborhoods and communities
and constituencies in this country

Each of them needs to be organized
Each of them *can* be organized
if those of us here
and others like us
will see this as our focus
and accept it as our responsibility

We need to think big
and to think small
at the same time

We need to broaden our collective long-range goal
to the building of a majority movement
for basic change in America

And we need to narrow our focus
so that each of us individually
becomes an activist

in building that base
one place at a time

We know how far we have come
by how far we have to go

But we also know
how far we have come
by a single fact:

like the song about Herbert Lee says,
"Now we'll never turn back"
to the way things used to be

We have tasted the future

We have seen
if only for a moment
in the faces of people
feeling dignity
power
community
the vision
of a future just society

Old fighter, you sure took it on the chin
Where'd you ever get the strength to stand
Never giving up or giving in
You know I just want to shake your hand

Because people like you help people like me go on, go on
People like you help people like me go on, go on

Old battler, with a scar for every town
Thought you were no better than the rest
You wore your colors every way but down
All you ever gave us was your best
But you know that

People like you help people like me go on, go on
People like you help people like me go on, go on

Old dreamer, with a world in every thought
Where'd you get the vision to keep on
You sure gave back as good as what you got
I hope that when my time is almost gone
They'll say that

People like me helped people like you go on, go on
Because people like you help people like me go on, go on,
*   go on*

(Words and music by Si Kahn;
Copyright by Si Kahn;
All rights reserved.)

Index

Corruption, 313, 320
Courage, of leaders, 28
Court Bureau of Elections, 179
Courthouse records, 178–179
Cross-training, 214–215
Culture and values, 325–337
  built into people's organizations,
    334–336
  defined, 325
  expression of, 325–327
  manipulation of, 326–327
  myths vs., 328–330
  as organizing tool, 332–334
  people's organizations in rediscov-
    ery of, 76–77, 330–332, 333–
    337
  recording and preservation of, 335–
    336
  symbols in, 336–337
  understanding of, essential to lead-
    ers, 30
"Cutting an issue," 279

Day care, meeting attendance and,
  132, 153
Declaration of Independence, 285, 336
Defeats, recovery from, 173
Democracy, 24, 172, 303
  decision making and, 67, 68, 147–
    148
  industrial, 289
  leaders committed to, 32, 52
  majority strategy and, 281, 285
  training methods and, 223
Demonstrations, 187, 191, 201
Discipline, group, 35–36
Discussion groups:
  emergence of issues in, 94–95
  training in, 212
Doctors, organization of, 3
Dues systems, 266, 269–272
  charges too low in, 271
  collection methods in, 271–272, 291–
    292
  examples of, 269–270
  work as substitute for cash in, 271

Education, free public, 7, 88, 287
Elections, electoral politics, 30, 312–
  323

accountability and, 322
candidates endorsed in, 314–315,
  316, 320
candidates from people's organizations in, 320–321
coalition style of, 319
contributions of people's organizations to, 316–318
groupings of issues in, 319–320
influencing of, 4–5
issues raised in, 323
level of involvement in, 318–319
majority needed in, 314
political organizing and, 317–318
political parties endorsed in, 315
problems encountered in, 319–320
pros and cons of involvement in,
  312–314, 321–323
in union organizing, 295–296, 297–
  298
volunteers in, 317, 319
Employers, organization of, 5
Endorsements, 314–316
  of candidates, 314–315, 316, 320
  delivery of votes and, 316
  of political parties, 315
  tax-exempt status and, 316
Energy issues, 284, 302
Equal Rights Amendment (ERA), 86,
  88
Ethnic groups, as constituencies, 85,
  86
Exposés, 187, 192, 199–200, 310

Fannin County, Ga., protest against
  property taxes in, 17–18
Fear:
  meetings in overcoming of, 154
  in resistance to organizing, 12
Feature stories, 247
Federal funding, audits and, 266
Films:
  culture and, 335
  as training materials, 214
Finances (see Money; Money raising)
Financial committees, 129, 260, 261,
  263
First Amendment Rights, 289, 298
Flag, as symbol, 336
Flexibility, of leaders, 27